CONSERVATORY

AND INDOOR PLANTS

PLANTS FOR WARM GARDENS

Essex County Council

Many libraries in Essex have
facilities for exhibitions
and meetings —

enquire at your local library
for details

VOLUME I
CONSERVATORY
AND INDOOR PLANTS
PLANTS FOR WARM GARDENS

ROGER PHILLIPS & MARTYN RIX

Assisted by Alison Rix   Layout by Gill Stokoe

PAN BOOKS

Acknowledgements

Most of the specimens photographed in the studio came from the following gardens and we would like to acknowledge the help we had from them and their staff.

The Crown Estate Commissioners at the Savill Gardens, Windsor Great Park; The Royal Botanic Gardens, Edinburgh; The Royal Botanic Gardens, Kew; The Royal Horticultural Society's Garden, Wisley; The University Botanic Garden, Cambridge; The Chelsea Physic Garden, London; Tresco Abbey Gardens, Isles of Scilly; Eccleston Square Garden, London; Sandling Park, Kent; Knightshayes Gardens, Devon; Trewithen; Trebah; Mottisfont Abbey, Hampshire; The National Botanic Gardens, Kirstenbosch; Longwood Gardens, Pennsylvania; Huntington Gardens, San Merino, California; Santa Barbara Botanic Garden; The Vernon Geranium Nursery, for most of the pelargoniums; Oldbury Nurseries and Clay Lane Nursery for most of the fuchsias; Stanley Mossop for the achimenes; John Vanderplank for the passionflowers; Nuccio's Nursery; Reads' Nursery; Green Farm Plants; Special Plants; Trehane Camellia Nursery; Hollington Nurseries; the Plantsman Nursery; Marston Exotics; Barter's Farm Nurseries; Holly Gate Cactus Nursery; Westfield Cacti; Fibrex Nurseries; Burnham Nurseries.

Among others who have helped in one way or another we would like to thank: Harry and Yvonne Hay, Derry Watkins, François Goffinet, Andrew Paterson, Guy and Emma Sisson, Y. P. Tsang, Graham Quinn, Noel Kingsbury, James and Tania Compton, Alan and Carolyn Hardy, John Coke, Terrence Read, Charles Quest-Ritson, John d'Arcy, Diana Miller, Susyn Andrews, John Bond, Hans Fliegner, Jim Gardiner, Mikinori Ogisu, Mike Nelhams, Hazel Key, Peter Barnes, James Smart, Leigh Walker, Pamela Egremont, Ted Rix, Geoffrey and Katie Goatcher, Fred Boutine, Jennifer Trehane, Marilyn Inglis, Meg Baker, Anne Thatcher, Jill Bryan, Ray Waite, Mike Marsh, John Watkins, Lorna Mercer, Debby Curry, Peter Bradley, Rupert Bowlby, Jill Macphie, William Waterfield.

First published 1997 by Macmillan General Books
This edition published 1998 by Pan Books
an imprint of Macmillan Publishers Ltd
25 Eccleston Place, London, SW1W 9NF
and Basingstoke
Associated companies throughout the world
ISBN 0 330 37375 7
Copyright in the text and illustration
© Roger Phillips and Martyn Rix 1997
The right of Roger Phillips and Martyn Rix to be identified
as the authors of this work has been asserted by them in accordance
with the Copyright, Designs and Patents Act 1988.

9 8 7 6 5 4 3 2 1

A CIP catalogue record for this book is available
from the British Library.

Typeset by Parker Typesetting Service, Leicester
Printed by Toppan Printing Co. (Singapore) Pte. Ltd

Contents

Winter in the Serre de la Madonne above Menton

Introduction

In this book we illustrate over one thousand three hundred trees, shrubs, perennials and bulbs suitable for subtropical gardens and cool greenhouses. Most will tolerate a degree or two of frost overnight, and so will survive outdoors along the coast of the Mediterranean, in Florida and coastal and southern California, in Australia, northern New Zealand and in the hills in the tropics. Depending on the climate where they grow wild, some need wet winters and dry summers, some require dry winters and wet summers, and many are tolerant enough to grow well in both types of climate. A large number can be grown indoors in winter and planted out in summer when the danger of frost has passed. In general, we have not covered cacti, succulents or annuals in this book; they will be the subjects of later volumes in this series.

The Photographs

The majority of pictures in this book were taken by the authors using Ektachrome 64 professional film; the film used for the field shots was pushed one stop in development. Several different exposures were taken of each shot, one as indicated by the camera's exposure meter, the others a half or one stop above or below those indicated. On an automatic camera the same effect may be obtained by altering the film speed indicator.

The studio shots were taken on a Hasselblad 500 C/M with a normal lens and a studio flash as a light source. The field shots were taken with a Nikon FM and a variety of lenses, using natural light.

When shooting flowers in the garden or in the wild it is preferable to work with a tripod so that you can take advantage of the opportunity to use a slow shutter speed and therefore a smaller aperture, giving a greater depth of field. In practice the best speed to use is 1/15th sec., although if there is a wind you may have to go to 1/30th or even 1/60th. In bright light conditions the camera can be hand-held with the speed set at 1/60th sec.

The Order

The plants are arranged in families and the families are further arranged into traditional botanical order, beginning with the Magnolias and ending with the daisy family, monocotyledons (the lilies, orchids and grasses) and ferns. This is the same order that was used in *Perennials*, although in that case the plants were also divided by flowering time. The exact order follows a handy little book by Davis and Cullen called *The Identification of Flowering Plant Families* (1965).

THE NAMES The names generally follow those used in *The RHS Plant Finder*, and if they differ, the *Plant Finder's* name is included as a synonym. The *Plant Finder* has established itself as the most accurate and up-to-date list of names of cultivated plants readily available, and can now be bought on CD-ROM.

THE TEXT The text begins with a brief mention of the type of plant described and its most important characteristics, followed by its country of origin, habitat and flowering time in the wild. This is intended to help travellers who may want to see the flowers in the wild, and gardeners who can use the information to grow a relatively unknown plant more successfully in their own climate. Note that spring-flowering plants in the southern hemisphere flower in July–September. The text continues with brief measurements of the important parts of the plant and concludes with a sentence on cultivation and likely minimum temperatures for survival. Measurements are given in metres, centimetres and millimetres; as a guide 1m equals around 3 feet, and 2.5cm equals an inch.

The Victorian conservatory and kitchen garden at Glenbervie near Stonehaven

The Abbey ruins at Tresco, Isles of Scilly

TEMPERATURE The temperatures given are only intended as a rough guide to those that a particular plant might survive. Hardiness of plants is an inexact science, depending on many factors. Intrinsic in a species is the frost tolerance that it has evolved in its native habitat; a plant from a high altitude may be much hardier than one of the same species that originated at a low altitude. Therefore the high-altitude form may do better in a cold garden while the low-altitude form may be more tolerant of heat and grow better in a hot garden.

Growing conditions in the garden also affect hardiness; soft, sappy growth with a high water content is more easily damaged than hard, well-ripened growth. A dressing of potash in late summer also helps to increase hardiness of plant tissue.

The quotation of a frost figure, as we have provided here, does not take into account wind speed, air moisture or duration of cold. Thus a plant which may survive unharmed $-5°C$ overnight on a still night, may be killed when the $-5°C$ is accompanied by a drying wind and lasts for several days. For example, a shrub of *Clianthus puniceus* in my garden in north Devon, which in 1995 survived several still nights of $-6°C$ or so unharmed, was killed by east winds of $-5°C$ which lasted several days in early 1996. In this case simple protection by a sheet of bubble polythene or polypropylene fleece would probably have enabled the plant to survive, and it might even have survived had it been planted on the west rather than the east side of the house. Even different branches of the same plant may react to cold differently; as every gardener knows after a cold winter, a shrub may lose some branches completely, while others are undamaged.

Begonias and petunias in the conservatory at Glenbervie

Approximate conversion table of °F/°C.

USDA zone		°F	°C
		60	15
		50	10
Above	10	40	5
zone	10	32	0
zone	9	20	−5
zone	8	10	−10

Citrus wrapped for the winter at Les Cèdres, Cap Ferrat

Mist in the Blue Mountains above Sydney

Main Wild Localities of Subtropical Garden Plants

Wild plants are not evenly distributed across the globe; some areas and some climates have a much richer flora than average for a number of reasons – continental drift, lack of ice ages causing extinctions, by their varied topography or by the effects of climate. The six main areas of Mediterranean climate mentioned below have floras exceptionally rich in species and are the homes of some of the best tender garden plants. Summer-rainfall areas are also rich where they are adjacent to tropical areas, as in Mexico or southern China, but do not have the exceptional diversity of the Mediterranean areas.

WINTER-RAINFALL AREAS The Mediterranean climate enjoys cool, wet winters and hot, dry summers. Areas of Mediterranean climate usually lie between colder summer-wet areas and deserts, or sometimes between mountains and sea. Plants from Mediterranean areas therefore grow mainly through the winter, and become dormant or partially dormant to survive the heat and drought of summer.

1. California and Baja California The Californian landscape consists of dry rolling hills between the sea and the Sierra Nevada mountains, in places covered with evergreen scrub, here called chaparral, composed of *Ceanothus, Mimulus glutinosus, Ribes speciosum* and other shrubs; in other places it is covered with grassland and annuals, sometimes beneath widely spaced

Podalyria calyptrata flowering after a fire on the Cape peninsula

Cork oaks resprouting after a fire in Corsica

oak trees. In other areas, mainly in the north, there are high, rocky hills with mixed evergreen or coniferous trees, again interspersed with shrubs. The coastal hills are cooled in summer by fog from the sea. Inland of the Sierras are the deserts of Arizona and eastern California, around Palm Springs. Beautiful bulbs such as *Calochortus* are a feature of the ground flora throughout the area. Important garden plants originating in California include *Ceanothus* and its hybrids, *Carpenteria*, *Arctostaphylos* and *Calliandra* in the drier parts.

2. Chile The Mediterranean climate in Chile is confined to a small area between Santiago and the Atacama Desert, which, like California, is confined to a narrow coastal strip between the mountains and the sea. The Valparaiso area has chaparral-like scrub with the Chilean palm *Jubaea* as a distinctive feature. Some of the best sites are oases in the desert, which receive almost no real rainfall, but are fed by winter mists and fog from the sea. It has a restricted but fascinating flora, highlights of which include *Tropaeolum* species, *Mutisia*, *Puya*, *Oxalis*, *Alstroemeria*, *Hippeastrum*, *Leucocoryne* and other bulbs. It is also the home of familiar annuals such as *Petunia*, *Salpiglossis* and *Schizanthus*.

3. Mediterranean basin The whole coastline of the Mediterranean Sea has the typical summer-dry climate, mainly between the sea and the mountains, as in the south of France and Turkey, but in much of North Africa this climate occurs between the sea and the desert. Typical scenery consists of rolling hills covered in low scrub, here called *maquis* or *garrigue*, of *Cistus*, rosemary, lavender, oleander and evergreen oaks. Bulbs such as crocuses, tulips and anemones, and annuals like marigolds and *Convolvulus minor* are also features of this area.

4. The Canaries and Madeira The flora of the Canary Islands is peculiar: a little of it is like the Mediterranean, some of it is like the mountains of tropical Africa and much of it is unique. It is also very varied as you go up the mountains, and as you travel from an eastern to a western aspect; from dry, desert areas with cactus-like spurges to moist tree-heather and laurel forest bathed in wet fog even in summer. Many plants flower during the mild winters or in early spring on the shrub-covered hillsides. Familiar garden plants include the succulent *Aeonium*, the florists' cineraria and the shrubby daisy-flowered *Argyranthemum*. Among the specialities are the silvery-leaved *Lotus* species, now very rare in the wild, but commonly grown in hanging baskets. Some are found in the Cape Verde Islands too.

5. South Africa The winter-rainfall area of Cape Province is one of the richest areas for plants in the whole world. It stretches from the Orange River mouth in the northwest to the Cape Peninsula, and from there along the coast east to Port Elizabeth.

Terraced valleys in Madeira stretch up into the clouds

The hills and mountains are mostly of acid sandstone covered with scrub, here called *fynbos*; fire is a very important element in the ecology of the fynbos, as it is to a lesser extent in other Mediterranean areas. Most of the soils are rather peaty, improved every few years by ash. Inland of the Cape are the deserts of the Karroo, famous for their succulents, and to the east there is a sudden transition to the summer-rainfall area of Natal. The climate of the Cape Peninsula itself is moderated by the effects of summer fog.

The most familiar garden plants that originate in the Cape are undoubtedly the pelargoniums, which were first introduced in the 18th century, and have been grown and hybridized in Europe and North America ever since. The illustrations of Andrews' *Geraniums* (1805) and Sweet's *Geraniaceae* (1820–30) show the popularity of the genus in the early 19th century, when new species were much sought after and numerous new hybrids made. A few of these, for example, *Pelargonium × blandfordianum*, survive until today. Other familiar genera include *Erica*, *Protea*, *Watsonia*, *Lachenalia*, *Amaryllis belladonna*, *Nerine* and mesembryanthemum.

6. Southern and Western Australia The marvellous potential of the Australian flora is only now beginning to be appreciated, mainly in Australia itself. Some genera, such as *Acacia* and *Eucalyptus* have long been cultivated abroad, and indeed have become serious pests in many areas. There are few high mountains in Australia, and, like South Africa, the soils are usually poor, derived from ancient sandstones. Fire is again an important element, and it has long been known that many plants only germinate after bushfires. The richest flora is in Western Australia, but plants from the mountains of the southeast which have cooler summers with a little rain are often easier to grow. Other important genera include *Correa*, *Callistemon*, *Banksia* and *Alogyne*.

Garrigue in southern Spain near Ronda

A clear evening follows the afternoon thunderstorms near Himeville in the Natal Drakensberg

SUMMER-RAINFALL AREAS The second group of subtropical plant areas have mainly summer rainfall, or rainfall all year round. Plants from these areas therefore grow in summer and many are completely dormant in winter.

7. Florida and the Gulf Coast The natural flora of Florida is restricted by the flat, swampy nature of the land, and the occasional freezing air which penetrates from the north. Natives of Florida include some of the waterlilies, but of course the potential for gardening is great, and most of the plants shown here will grow outside without trouble, provided they have some protection from extreme summer heat, or in the case of Mediterranean species, from summer wet.

8. Mexico and Central America The great diversity of climate and topography in this area means that the flora is very rich; temperate genera such as *Aquilegia*, *Cornus* and *Pinus* have survived from periods of cooler climate; tropical genera such as *Fuchsia* and the *Bromeliaceae* have moved in from the south. Desert plants such as *Agave* coexist with wet-loving tropical families such as *Bomarea* and *Laelia*. Most of Mexico has a rather dry, cold winter and warm, dry spring, followed by a hot, wet summer. At the same time the limestone crags and screes in the northern mountains produce numerous species of genera such as *Salvia*, which are also tolerant of summer drought. Numerous familiar garden plants originated in Mexico, not least because the pre-Columbian inhabitants were great gardeners. Examples include *Dahlia*, *Achimenes*, *Cosmos* and Poinsettia as well as numerous vegetables such as maize, runner beans and pumpkins.

9. South America, subtropical areas and foothills of the Andes The plants of the great tropical forests of the Amazon are outside the scope of this book, but in the foothills of the Andes and other mountains cool-loving, summer-flowering genera abound. Eastern South America, outside the tropics, is another rich area. In general the climate in this area is similar to Mexico, with dry winters and hot, moist summers. In the mist forest of the mountains the summers are wet and cool, and many of the most exciting species of *Fuchsia* from this habitat are unhappy if kept too hot in summer. Other South American plants commonly cultivated include *Begonia* (the ancestors of the tuberous ones), *Bougainvillea*, *Jacaranda*, *Gloxinia*, *Sinningia*, *Hippeastrum* and *Passiflora*.

10. Southeastern and tropical Africa The summer-dry climate of the Cape changes abruptly east of Port Elizabeth to a subtropical summer-rainfall climate which is fully established at Durban. The area between holds some interesting plants such as the pale blue Plumbago, a most popular plant as it can tolerate drought or water in both winter and summer. Essentially the same summer-wet climate is found throughout East Africa in the mountains, though around the equator, such as in Kenya, there may be two rainy seasons. Familiar garden flowers from this area include the florists' gladioli as well as the scented Acidanthera (*Gladiolus callianthus*), *Saintpaulia*, *Streptocarpus*, *Clivia*, *Gloriosa* and *Impatiens*. The mountains of the Drakensberg in northern Natal produce nearly hardy (zones 7–8) summer-flowering species such as *Phygelius*, *Dierama* and *Diascia*, *Kniphofia* and *Schizostylis*.

11. South China and Himalayan foothills This huge area stretches from Taiwan, across southern China into northern India and Kashmir. Winters are dry and minimum temperature depends mainly on altitude. Zone 9 (−5°C) plants generally occur below 2000m in the southern Himalayas. Summers are wet, and in the mountains cool too, because of the cloud. In places there is almost continuous rain brought by the monsoon, though in some areas – the other side of a mountain range or

Subtropical forest at the foot of Omei Shan

the bottoms of the valleys – the summers may be hot and dry because of the rain-shadow. Numerous garden plants have originated in this area including *Citrus, Camellia, Cymbidium, Primula sinensis*, and, of course, China and Tea roses, which have been cultivated by the Chinese for over 2000 years. More recent introductions include *Gardenia, Mahonia, Jasminum polyanthum, Hedychium* and *Luculia*.

12. India The subcontinent of India moved from near the coast of Africa to collide with Asia and pushed up the Himalayas; as a result its plants have many African as well as Asian affinities. Not many plants from peninsular India or Sri Lanka are commonly cultivated, but there are many very beautiful ones which are rare such as the pink-flowered *Plumbago zeylanica*. *Impatiens* is a particularly rich genus in south India and the mainly African *Gloriosa* is also common.

13. Borneo, New Guinea and Pacific islands The mountains of Borneo and New Guinea are full of exciting plants, but few have become established in cultivation; the showy modern *Impatiens* is a recent import from New Guinea and most of the spectacular tender rhododendrons come from this area. *Begonia, Hoya* and *Gesneraceae* are others well represented in the cool mountain forests, and many grow well in a cool house at the Royal Botanic Garden, Edinburgh.

14. New Zealand This must be one of the most favoured areas of the whole world in which to make a garden, as both temperate and subtropical plants will thrive over most of North Island and in the warmer parts of South Island, where rainfall is distributed throughout the year, with more in winter. Wind also has an important modifying effect on the vegetation. The New Zealand flora itself is quite poor in genera, as are most island floras, but is especially well endowed with ferns. Important garden plants include *Clianthus puniceus, Metrosideros* and *Hebe*, of which there are 78 species in New Zealand.

Groundsel in mountain forest in Mexico

On the edge of Zomba mountain in Malawi, an ancient *Xerophyta* hangs over the cliffs

11

The garden of the Carnivore restaurant near Nairobi

The Subtropical Garden

Those fortunate enough to garden in frost-free or almost frost-free climates can grow most of the plants shown here in the open garden. In Europe subtropical climates are confined to the shores of the Mediterranean and the western coasts as far north as England and western Scotland in warm spots. In addition, the Atlantic islands are especially favoured, including the Isles of Scilly, the Azores, Canaries, Madeira and Bermuda. In North America these areas coincide roughly with zones 9 and 10, areas where *Citrus* can survive. These are in Florida, the Gulf Coast and the coastal parts of California. In the subtropical areas of Mexico and South America, Africa, Australia and New Zealand, all except the high mountains or deserts come into this category, and in the tropics proper, cool places in the hills or high plateaux such as are found in Kenya, are ideal places to make a garden. Many of the pictures here were taken by my brother Anthony Rix, who with his wife Anita made a very interesting garden near Blantyre, Malawi.

As far as gardening and plant growth are concerned, the two main types of climate mentioned in the previous pages – the winter-rainfall and dry-summer climate and the subtropical climate with relatively dry winters and rain in summer – have important influences on the type of garden to be made.

The Mediterranean climate proper is relatively restricted in the world, but is a popular place to live or spend a holiday. California, the Canaries, the Mediterranean coast, the Cape, central Chile and Western Australia are the main areas of this climate in the world. They are exceptionally rich in native plants, which will make a good basis for a naturalistic garden, and are good for growing many others plants with the aid of irrigation. Summer heat and dry atmosphere may restrict the growing of plants such as rhododendrons or orchids to a lath house or an area where they can be misted down frequently.

The subtropical climate with its summer rainfall is found in Florida and the states on the Gulf of Mexico, as well as in eastern Mexico and in the mountains of Central and South America, in northern New Zealand, in Natal and central Africa and in the east of Australia. Here plants from other summer-rainfall areas may be expected to do well, and many plants from summer-dry areas will survive provided they can tolerate wet in summer. Some, for example, the oncocyclus irises, are more sensitive than others in this respect, and it is especially important that these do not receive irrigation in summer. They may, however need extra water in spring, and bulbs, in particular, may be better grown in large pots or tubs which can be brought under cover in summer when the plants are dormant.

In both climates much can be done by making the most of whatever microhabitats are available. In a Mediterranean climate a ravine or an enclosed shaded area under a tree or near the house can be used for subtropical epiphytes or forest plants. In a wet-summer climate a sunny, rocky bank with very well-drained soil can grow Mediterranean shrubs or bulbs.

There are several good books on the techniques of gardening in Mediterranean areas: I am particularly impressed with *Mediterranean Gardening* by Yves Menzies, published by John Murray in 1991. It is designed for the Mediterranean in France, Italy and Spain. For California, the *Western Garden Book* is indispensable, both for its gardening instructions and detailed maps of the temperature zones for the West Coast. For South Africa the writings of Sima Eliovson, published by Howard Timmins in Cape Town are to be recommended, as is her book on bulbs for bulb-lovers anywhere. Other books on Cape bulbs can be found in the bibliography in vol. 2. For mountain climates in the tropics, A. J. Jex-Blake's, *Gardening in East Africa* (4th ed.) 1957, published by Longman, is a good book which can often be had from second-hand bookshops. There are now numerous fine books on Australian native plants for gardeners. For this book I have used both the one-volume *Australian Native Plants* by John W. Wrigley and Murray Fagg, (2nd ed.) published by HarperCollins, and the many volumed *Encyclopaedia of Australian Plants* by Elliott and Jones, published by Lothian.

Sir Joseph Paxton's conservatory wall at Chatsworth

The Conservatory or Greenhouse

HEATING Most of the plants shown in this book can be grown in a greenhouse or conservatory with only sufficient heat to keep out frost in winter. Even a degree or two below freezing on an exceptionally cold night will not harm most plants, provided that the temperature rises again in the daytime. Most plants are also hardier if dry at the roots. The type of heating used can vary; electric heating by a fan heater is the easiest to

Pelargoniums, *Sutherlandia* and *Iris tectorum* var. *alba* in a cold greenhouse

PESTS AND DISEASES Pests, and to a lesser extent diseases, always loom large in the minds of gardeners, and especially those with greenhouses. The closeness of the plants, the lack of wind and absence of bird predators mean that pests can breed and spread very quickly, and be difficult to control once they are established. The secret is eternal watchfulness, to spot and eradicate any pest the moment it is seen, and before it has had a chance to breed. Check any new plant, from however reliable the source, to avoid bringing in a new pest. As a child I bought a small cactus, I think a *Mamillaria*, with small plants clustered round it; between these a mealy bug was hiding, which spread into other plants, in particular an old vine, before I spotted it. It was not until moving house some forty years later that this pest was finally left behind.

All common garden pests can be serious indoors; slugs, snails and mice love to come in during the winter; greenfly and whitefly breed especially quickly in spring, red spider mites during hot spells in summer. One vine weevil grub, brought in deep in the roots of a potted plant, can hatch in May and start an infestation which will devastate begonias, fuchsias, roses and anything else with juicy roots.

The best strategy is to have a bug-gun of some sort at the ready and ruthlessly kill any bug the moment it is seen. If an infestation begins to build up it may be necessary to buy a biological control predator, but these must be used in the right conditions of humidity and temperature or they will prove a waste of money. Another strategy is to spray at regular intervals with soft soap, which kills all leaf pests, and use the vine weevil biocontrol twice a year on all potted plants, inside and out, irrespective of whether any vine weevils have been seen. Many nurserymen now use an insecticide called suscon green which comes in the form of a minute blue-green capsule, to control vine weevil which has become a really serious pest since the use of aldrin as an additive in potting composts was banned.

Encarsia for the control of whitefly

install, and is as reliable as the source of supply. For a very precious collection it can be supplemented by gas, and I have used without trouble butane gas heaters to keep out frost. They can be adjusted to come on only when needed and can either remain on a pilot light or, to save fuel, be relit if a freezing night is forecast.

LIGHT It is important that light intensities in winter be as high as possible for any plant that is trying to grow through the winter. In northern Europe especially, winter can be very cloudy, and plants from Chile or South Africa are used to much sunnier winters. Extra lighting can be very useful for plants such as pelargoniums and bulbs such as *Lachenalia* which grow through the winter. Either high-powered mercury vapour lamps, or growers' strip lights can be set up over the plants according to the maker's instructions, and set on a time clock to give a twelve-hour day, or be put on and off by hand in dull weather.

HUMIDITY Without special treatment a greenhouse or conservatory tends to become too hot, dry and sunny in summer, and too wet and dank in winter. In summer, especially if flowering plants like gloxinias are being grown, shading will be needed, and extra humidity should be provided by spraying water on the paths and gently misting the plants. High humidity with frequent spraying and syringing also keeps down the worst pests, the red spider mite.

Excess humidity in winter is more difficult to cure. A fan heater to raise the temperature a few degrees and to keep the air moving is a help. One great advantage of a conservatory attached to the house is that dry house air can be let in on cold days in winter, to keep a buoyant atmosphere. In a free-standing greenhouse the only available ventilation may be from foggy saturated outside air which encourages all sorts of mould and mildew.

Achimenes showing damage by Western Flower Thrips

Magnolia campbellii subsp. *mollicomata* at Nymans

Magnolia campbellii

Michelia figo

Magnolia championi in the New Territories in Hong Kong

Magnolia campbellii Hook. & Thoms.
(*Magnoliaceae*)   A large deciduous tree,
spectacular when flowering in early spring
before the leaves open, native of the E
Himalayas from Nepal (where it is always
white), to SW China in Yunnan, growing in
temperate rainforest at 2400–3600m. Tree to
35m; leaves 11–25cm long, elliptic to broadly
obovate. Flowers 20–25cm across, with 12–16
petals, white to pink or rich purple.
Subsp. **mollicomata** (W.W. Smith) Johnstone
from China and Burma, differs in its silky
hairy flower stalk, which is smooth in subsp.
campbellii from Nepal and NE India. Both
require deep, rich moist acid soil and are
intolerant of dry winds. The flowers are often
ruined by spring frosts but the buds are hardy
when tightly closed. Trees grow well and fast
in subtropical climates with wet summers.
Min. − 10°C.

Magnolia championi Benth.   A shrub or
small tree with closed white flowers, native of
SE China including Hong Kong, growing in
scrub in the hills, flowering in April–May.
Shrub to 3m; leaves 8–15cm long, elliptic,
evergreen or deciduous. Flowers 3cm long,
creamy-white and cup-shaped, with 3 sepals
and 6 petals. For any good soil in sun, with
ample water in summer. Min. 0°C.

Magnolia delavayi Franch.   A large
evergreen tree or shrub with dull leathery
leaves and scented flowers, native of SW China
in Yunnan and Sichuan, growing in the wild as
a shrub on limestone pavement or in open
scrub, at 1500–3300m, but forming a large
tree when protected, flowering in late spring
and summer. Tree to 15m; leaves 13–35cm
long, to 20cm wide, ovate to nearly round, dull
dark green, paler beneath. Flowers 15–20cm
across, creamy-white, cup-shaped, with about
9 petals. For any good soil in sun, with ample
water in summer. Not very tender but the
large leaves need shelter. Min. − 10°C.

Magnolia grandiflora L. Southern Magnolia
A large evergreen shrub or tree with shiny
leathery leaves and huge scented flowers,
native of SE North America, growing in forests
on the coastal plain, flowering in summer to
autumn. Tree to 30m; leaves 8–20cm long,
ovate to nearly round. Flowers 20–25cm
across, with 9–12 petals. For any good soil in
sun, with ample water in summer. Not tender,
but is best in warm climates and in sheltered
gardens; it needs the heat of a wall to flower in
cool areas. Min. − 10°C.
There are many named cultivars, including
'Goliath' and 'Little Gem', a dwarf with
flowers 15cm across. A few such as 'Maryland'
and possibly 'Exmouth' are hybrids with *M.
virginiana*. Named clones raised from cuttings
should begin to flower in 2–3 years, seedlings
take much longer. 'Edith Bogue', which
originated in New Jersey, is reputed to be one
of the hardiest cultivars.

Magnolia nitida W. W. Smith   An upright
shrub or small tree with brilliantly shiny dark
green leaves and pale yellow flowers, native of
SW China, especially NW Yunnan, SE Xizang
and NE Burma, growing in open forests from
2000–4000m, flowering in March–April. Tree
to 15m; leaves 5.6–10cm long, elliptic,
purplish when young. Flowers 8–10cm across,
with 9–12 petals, the outer purplish on the

back. Fruit short-stalked. Suits any good moist soil in partial shade and shelter, with water in summer. Grows outside in sheltered gardens in SW England but is rare, although cuttings have been rooted successfully by Roger Clark at Greenway. Min. −5°C.

Michelia doltsopa DC. (*Magnoliaceae*)
An evergreen tree with dull leathery leaves and scented magnolia-like flowers, native of the E Himalayas from C Nepal to SW China and Burma, growing in forests at up to 2500m, flowering in March–April. Tree to 15m or more; leaves 8–18cm long, ovate-oblong. Flowers 8–10cm across with 12–16 petals, produced in the axils of the previous year's leaves, not terminally as in *Magnolia*. Suits any good soil in sun or part shade, with water in summer. Grows outside in warm gardens in SW England. Min. −5°C.

Michelia figo (Lour.) Sprengel   A dense evergreen shrub with leathery leaves and cup-shaped, fruity-scented flowers, native of SE China and commonly cultivated, flowering in March–May. Shrub to 6m; leaves 3–8cm long, stalkless or with very short stalks, elliptic to oblanceolate. Buds covered with red-brown down. Flowers creamy-white to yellowish inside, usually purplish outside, about 3cm across. Suits any good soil in sun or part shade, with water in summer. Min. −5°C.

Michelia yunnanensis Franch.
An evergreen shrub with thick leathery leaves and starry flowers, native of SW China, especially Yunnan, growing in scrub on rocky hills at up to 2500m, flowering in April–May. Shrub to 4m or more; leaves 4–8cm long, narrowly obovate. Buds covered with red-brown fur. Flowers 7–9cm across. For any good soil in sun or part shade, with water in summer. Min. −10°C.

Pseudowintera colorata (Raoul) Dandy (*Winteraceae*)   An evergreen shrub with naturally brightly coloured leaves and small yellowish-green flowers, native of New Zealand where it is common in forests from sea level up into the mountains, often forming thickets after the forest has been destroyed, flowering in summer. Shrub to 2m; leaves 2–6cm long, elliptic. Flowers 8–10cm across, followed by small black berries. An attractive small colourful shrub for acid, peaty soils. Min. −5°C. *Pseudowintera* is close to the more familiar *Drimys* from South America.

Michelia yunnanensis in Lijiang

Michelia doltsopa in Madeira

Magnolia grandiflora

Magnolia nitida at Trewithen, Cornwall

Pseudowintera colorata in Cornwall

Magnolia delavayi

Tree Euphorbias in a dry valley near Oudtshoorn, South Africa

Cadaba aphylla (Thunb.) Wild
(*Capparidaceae*) A leafless shrub with green
succulent stems, native of South Africa in the
Karroo and north to tropical Africa, growing
in dry rocky places. Flowering in August–April
(spring–summer). Stems cylindrical, to 2m.
Flowers in umbel-like heads, about 10mm
long, red or rarely yellow. For dry, well-
drained soil. Min. 0°C.

Capparis acutifolia Sweet, subsp. ***bodinieri***
(Lév.) Jacobs syn. *C. acuminata* Lindl. non
Wild (*Capparidaceae*) A much-branched
shrub or small tree, native of India, Burma and
SW China in Yunnan, growing on rocky slopes
and banks at about 2000m, flowering in May–
July. Stems to 7m, but usually about 3m;
leaves ovate, usually 11cm long, 4cm wide.
Flowers about 2.5cm across, with white
stamens. For a hot position with rain in
summer, dry in winter. Min. −3°C or less for
short periods if dry. Subsp. *acutifolia* is found
in SE China, Vietnam and Taiwan.

Capparis spinosa L. var. ***aegyptia*** (Lam.)
Boiss. A straggling shrub with white flowers
and beautiful crimson stamens, native of E
Mediterranean area, growing on old walls or
cliffs near the coast, flowering in June–
September. Plant woody at the base with
annual stems to 2m. Leaves fleshy, 13–18mm
long. Flowers 5–8cm across, opening in early
morning, fading by midday. Tolerant of heat
and drought in summer. Min. −5°C. The
young buds of var. *spinosa*, which has larger
leaves to 40cm long, are the capers that are
pickled and used as flavouring. It is found in
dry areas from SE Europe, across Asia to
Nepal. *Capparis ovata* Desf. has smaller
flowers, with the upper petals much shorter
than the lower. It is probably hardier and is
found throughout the Mediterranean region.

Hibbertia pedunculata R. Br. ex DC.
(*Dilleniaceae*) A low-growing dwarf heath-like
shrub with masses of small flowers, native of
New South Wales and E Victoria in Australia,
growing in moist places, flowering mainly in
spring–summer (August–March). Plant to 2m
tall and 150cm across but often prostrate,
spreading and rooting at the nodes. Leaves

Isomeris arborea

Cadaba aphylla near Oudtshoorn

Capparis acutifolia subsp. *bodinieri* in the Dali valley in May

rolled under at the edges, 4–12mm long.
Flowers 12–16mm across, on stalks to 15mm
long. Easily grown in well-drained sandy soil
and suitable for ground-cover. Min. −5°C.

Hibbertia scandens (Willd.) Dryander
A robust evergreen woody climber, native of
New South Wales and Queensland, growing in
forests at low altitudes and on coastal dunes,
flowering in spring–summer. Plant twining, to
2m. Leaves simple ovate, leathery, 5–10cm
long. Flowers 5–6cm across. Five follicles open
to reveal seeds with a red fleshy aril. Tolerant
of heat but needs water. Suitable for clothing a
fence or wall. Min. −5°C for short periods.
Can be grown from cuttings or seed.
Commonly grown in coastal and S California.

Illicium floridanum Ellis (*Illiciaceae*)
An evergreen shrub or small tree with deep
red or purple starry flowers, native of SE
North America from W Florida to Alabama,
Mississippi and Louisiana, grows along
streams and rivers, beneath large trees,
flowering in spring. Tree to 3m, sometimes
sprouting from distant roots. Young shoots
purplish. Leaves narrowly elliptic to obovate,
5–15cm long. Flower stalks slender to 10cm
long; flowers 3–6cm across. Seed pods starry,
of 10–20 carpels. For any good soil, with shade
and water in summer. Min. −10°C.
Illicium henryi Diels from C and W China has
pinkish flowers with shorter petals. *Illicium
anisatum* L. from Japan and Korea has creamy-
white flowers and is often planted in temple
gardens. Both survive −5°C.

Isomeris arborea Nutt. (*Capparidaceae*)
A small shrub with trifoliolate leaves, native of
S California, Colorado and Baja California
(part of Mexico), growing in dry places,
coastal bluffs and dunes and along water
courses in deserts, flowering most of the year.
Stems to 1.5m. Leaflets variable in shape,
oblong to elliptic-oblanceolate, 1–3.5cm long.
Inflorescence to 15cm long. Petals 10–16mm
long. Capsule variable in shape, narrow to
subglobose. For dry places, with rain mostly in
spring. We saw this plant being visited by
hummingbirds in Palm Springs. Min. −5°C if
dry.

Hibbertia pedunculata in Canberra

Capparis spinosa var. *aegyptia* on the ruins of
Phaselis

Hibbertia scandens

Illicium floridanum

Dry grassland and marshy hollows near Nottingham Road, Natal, habitat of *Anemone fanninii* and several Dieramas

Anemone fanninii near Nottingham road

Anemone fanninii

Clematopsis villosa subsp. *uhehensis*

Anemone caffra Harvey *(Ranunculaceae)*
A perennial with a creeping rootstock, leathery deeply-lobed leaves and white flowers, native of South Africa in the NE Cape, growing in peaty, grassy places at about 2500m, flowering in October–November (spring). Leaves to 15cm across, bristly hairy on the veins beneath, 5–7-lobed, on stalks about15cm high.

Flowers about 7cm across. For peaty soil, moist in summer, drier in winter. Seen here high on the Winterberg. Min. −10°C.

Anemone fanninii Masters   A large perennial with hairy peltate basal leaves (like a small *Gunnera*) and branching stems of flowers, native of South Africa in Natal, mainly

in the Drakensberg at up to 1950m, growing in moist, grassy, peaty places and in streams, flowering from October–November (spring). Rhizome thick and solid; leaves with hairy stalks to 60cm and blades to 30cm across, brown-silky beneath. Flowering stems to 1m or more with 1–3 flowers; sepals narrow, about 7cm long. Easily grown in peaty soil, if given

Aquilegia skinneri in my woodland garden in Devon

Anemone caffra

Anemone tenuifolia

ample water in summer, kept rather dry in winter. Propagate by seed or by division, which is not easy as the rhizome is very compact. Min. −5°C or perhaps less.

Anemone tenuifolia (L. fil.) DC.
A perennial with dissected basal leaves and a single pink or white flower on a slender stem, native of South Africa in the Cape, east to Humansdorp, growing in moist, peaty places in fynbos in the mountains, flowering June–February (winter–summer). Flowering stems 25–40cm; flowers about 7cm across. Min. −5°C.

Aquilegia skinneri Hook. (*Ranunculaceae*)
A delicate perennial with striking green and orange flowers, native of Mexico in the Sierra Madre Occidentale, growing in open pine woods in the cloud forest zone, flowering in summer. Stems to 1m; leaves glaucous, the leaflets deeply 3-lobed, remaining green through the winter. Flowers with sepals to 2.8cm, green, lanceolate; petals green with straight orange spurs, swollen then narrowly pointed, 3.5–5cm long. Style and stamens projecting from the flower. Best in rich leafy soil in partial shade, cool in summer. Min. −10°C, perhaps. A double-flowered form is recorded. Named after George Ure Skinner, (b. Newcastle-upon-Tyne 1804, d. Panama 1867) who collected orchids and other plants for W. J. Hooker.

Clematopsis villosa (DC.) Hutch. subsp.
uhehensis (Engl.) J. Reynal & Brummitt syn.

C. scabiosifolia (DC.) Hutch. (*Ranunculaceae*)
A robust herbaceous perennial, native of S Tanzania, N Malawi and N Zambia, growing in mountain grasslands, often in its thousands among bracken, with *Impatiens* species, *Geranium incanum* and *Pentas decora*, flowering in summer (December–January). Stems 45–60cm, with a pair of ovate bracts and 1 or sometimes 2 nodding flowers. Sepals about 3cm long, pink or white. Subsp. *kirkii* (Oliv.) J. Reynal & Brummitt, which is widespread from Tanzania and Mozambique to Angola and Zimbabwe, has branched, many-flowered stems. *Clematopsis* are lovely plants, between *Anemone* and *Clematis*, but seldom seen in cultivation. Prefers peaty soil, moist in summer, dryish in winter. Min. −3°C, perhaps less. Photographed on the Nyika plateau in Malawi.

Knowltonia capensis (L.) Huth
(*Ranunculaceae*)   A spindly perennial with numerous narrow-petalled flowers, native of South Africa in the Cape around Worcester and on the Cape Peninsula, growing in shady places at low altitudes, flowering in late winter (June–September). Stems to 3m, much branched. Leaves deeply lobed. Flowers about 15mm across. Min. −3°C. A genus of about 8 species in southern Africa. Some of the other species have fewer and larger white or pinkish flowers and of these *K. transvaalensis* Szyszyl. which grows on Mt Mulanje in Malawi and as far north as S Tanzania is probably the hardiest and most attractive, with flowers about 3cm across.

Knowltonia capensis

Clematis indivisa at Greenway Gardens, South Devon

Clematis yunnanensis from Tienchuan

Clematis napaulensis

Clematis grandiflora in Madeira

Clematis cirrhosa var. *balearica* 'Freckles'

Clematis brachiata on the Sani Pass, Natal

Clematis cirrhosa L. (*Ranunculaceae*)
A delicate climber, woody at the base, with evergreen leaves and nodding creamy-yellow flowers, native of the Mediterranean region from Portugal and Morocco east to Syria, scrambling over evergreen shrubs at up to 1800m, flowering in winter–early spring. Stems to 6m; flowers to 4.5cm long. Two varieties are recognized; var. *cirrhosa* has simple to trifoliate leaves and often unspotted flowers; var. **balearica** (Rich.) Willk. & Lange, has deeply dissected leaves and always red-spotted flowers. '**Freckles**' is a particularly fine clone with simple toothed leaves and reddish-purple spotted flowers, raised by Raymond Evison from seed collected in the Balearic Islands. It begins to flower in October. 'Wisley Cream' and 'Ourika Valley' both have unspotted flowers, similar to the plants shown here in S Turkey. Min. −10°C.

Clematis brachiata Thunb.   A woody
climber with evergreen trifoliate leaves and
scented, creamy-white flowers, native of
southern Africa from the S Cape north to the
tropics, at up to 2200m in the Drakensberg,
growing in scrub and on the edges of forest by
streams, flowering in summer. Stems to 3m;
petals about 1cm long. Min. −5°C.
Photographed on the Sani Pass.

Clematis grandiflora DC.   A rampant
woody climber, native of central Africa from
Ethiopia and Uganda to Sierra Leone, Zaire
and Angola, growing over scrub and into forest
trees, flowering in winter (January–March in
Ethiopia) where it grows at up to 2000m.
Leaves short-stalked with 3 or 5 leaflets, dark
green and leathery, with golden-brown hairs
and prominent veins beneath. Flowers
glistening with silky hairs, greenish-yellow to
light golden, the sepals 3.5–4.5cm long, 1.5–
2.5cm wide. Styles feathery and prominent in
fruit. Min. 0°C. Herklots (1976) describes this
species from Ethiopia. Cultivated in England
in 1829. Photographed in Madeira in March.

Clematis indivisa Willd., syn. *C. paniculata*
Gmel.   A rampant woody climber with
numerous white flowers, native of New
Zealand on both North and South Islands,
growing on the margins of lowland and lower
montane forests, flowering in spring (August–
November). Stems to 10m or more. Leaves
evergreen with 3 broadly ovate to oblong dark
green, leathery leaflets, 5–10cm long, entire or
slightly toothed at the apex. Flowers white with
6 sepals; in the male sepals are 4 × 1cm, in the
female smaller. Styles feathery, 3–5cm in fruit.
Min. −5°C.
C. forsteri Gmel., also from New Zealand, is a
slenderer plant with thinner, toothed and
lobed bright green leaflets and flowers, 3–4cm
across. Seedlings of both these species have
simple linear leaves.

Clematis napaulensis DC.   A delicate
climber to 8m, deciduous in late summer,
native of Nepal, NE India, Bhutan, Sikkim
and SW China in Yunnan, growing in warm
evergreen forest at 1760–2000m, flowering in
December–January. Leaves bright green with 3
glabrous leaflets, 2–5cm long. Flowers scented
in clusters in the leaf axils, with yellowish-
green sepals 1.5–2cm long and purple glabrous
filaments. Silky styles conspicuous, about 5cm
long. For a warm protected position, growing
well in shade and good for winter flowering in
a cool greenhouse. Min. −5°C.

Clematis yunnanensis Franch.   A delicate
evergreen climber flowering on hanging stems,
native of W China in SW Sichuan, and in
Yunnan, growing in warm, moist, sheltered
ravines at 1500–2300m, flowering in autumn
to mid-winter. Leaves on stalks about 5cm
long, with 3 lanceolate leaflets about 8cm long,
3.5cm wide, 5-veined at the base with few
hairs. Flowers on woolly stalks 2cm long,
unscented, born singly or in threes in the leaf
axils; 4 white fleshy sepals, shiny inside, about
3.5cm long, 1.5cm wide; stamens with long
silky-white hairs. For a sheltered and partially
shaded position, flowering under glass in
December and January. It will drop its buds if
it gets too dry at the root. Min. −5°C. Source:
C.D. & R. 591 collected near Tien-Chuan in
1989. The Himalayan *C. acuminata* DC. is
also winter-flowering and has similar leaves,
but longer-stalked smaller flowers with sepals
hairy inside.

Clematis cirrhosa var. *cirrhosa* in March on the road to Termessos above Antalya, Turkey

A pale form of *Clematis cirrhosa* var. *cirrhosa* on the road to Termessos, Turkey

Epimedium pubescens

Holboellia grandiflora in late April in the Wolong valley, W Sichuan

Holboellia grandiflora, male flowers

Mahonia gracilis in the Sierra Madre Orientale, NE Mexico

Mahonia confusa in Sichuan

Mahonia nevinii in California

Habitat of *Mahonia mairei*

Mahonia mairei in Yunnan

Mahonia siamensis in January in Lawrence Johnston's old garden at La Serre de La Madonne

Epimedium pubescens Maxim.
(*Berberidaceae*) An evergreen perennial with bristly leaves and masses of small greyish flowers, native of W China in Sichuan, growing on damp cliffs in partial shade at about 1000m, flowering in spring–summer. Stems 30–60cm. Leaflets usually 3, ovate to acuminate, with long spreading and curled hairs beneath. Flowers about 1cm across, with minute petals and sepals 5–7mm. Close to *E. sagittatum*, another small-flowered species, which has leaves glabrous or appressed hairy beneath. Both need moist leafy soil, shade and shelter. Min. −5°C.

Holboellia grandiflora Réaubourg
(*Lardizabalaceae*) A strong, woody climber, native of W China in W Sichuan, growing over scrub and rocks in limestone ravines at 1300–1600m, flowering in April–May. Leaves evergreen, leathery with 3–7 leaflets 7–15cm long, oblong to oblanceolate, acuminate, glaucous beneath. Flowers 2.5–3cm long, scented; the male in large corymbs, white, purple inside, the female few greenish or purplish. Fruit purple, 7.5–12cm long. For moist, rich, well-drained soil, in shade and shelter. Hardy to −5°C, perhaps.
H. coriacea Diels grows outside in W France and SW England; it has 3 leaflets and smaller well-scented purplish and greenish flowers in spring. Native of W China, in W Hubei (*see Shrubs p. 86*). *H. latifolia* Wall. from the Himalayas is less hardy, with 3–9 leaflets and flowers 1–1.5cm long.

Mahonia confusa Sprague (*Berberidaceae*)
An upright shrub with neat green leaves and short dense spikes of yellow flowers, native of W China, Guizhou, Hubei and Sichuan, especially on Omei shan, growing in wet, shady ravines and woods, flowering in autumn. Shrub to 1.5m. Leaves 40–50cm with 11–15 leaflets, 7–10cm long. Flowers about 5mm across. For a shady position and leafy soil. Min. −10°C.

Mahonia gracilis (Hartw.) Fedde
A sprawling shrub with dark green leaves and long, lax spikes of pale yellow flowers, native of Mexico, especially in the limestone Sierra Madre Orientale south of Saltillo, growing in dry ravines in open pine forests, flowering in autumn and winter. Shrub to 1.5m. Leaves with 5–13 leaflets, about 5cm long, often overlapping. Flowers about 6mm across. For a dry shady position and well-drained soil. Min. −5°C, perhaps less.

Mahonia siamensis in Menton

Mahonia mairei Takeda An upright few-stemmed shrub with a terminal rosette of large compound leaves and lax spikes of yellow flowers, native of SW China in the limestone area to the east of Kunming, growing in rocky partially shaded crevices, flowering in spring. Stems to 2m; leaves to 30cm long, with 4–7 pairs of rather thin but stiff and spiny leaflets. Flower spikes to 20cm, reported by Harry Hay to be rather insignificant. Min. −5°C.

Mahonia nevinii (Gray) Fedde A large rounded shrub with grey-green leaves and loose clusters of yellow flowers, native of a few scattered places in S California, growing in dry, sandy and gravelly soils in chaparral and sagebush scrub below 600m, flowering in March–April. Shrub to 4m. Leaves 4–8cm with 3, 5 or 7 leaflets, 2–4cm long, 6–10mm wide, with numerous small spines. Flowers about 6mm across. Berries orange to red when ripe. For a hot, sunny and dry position and well-drained soil. Min. −5°C. This is one of a group of greyish, small-leaved species from SW USA and N Mexico.

Mahonia siamensis Takeda A robust branching shrub with large green leaves and long spikes of deep yellow flowers, native of Thailand, near Chiang Mai and SW Yunnan, near Tengyueh growing in evergreen forest at about 2000m, flowering in mid-winter. Stems to 4m; leaves about 50cm, the leaflets widely spaced. Inflorescence about 20cm long. This fine species was discovered by Kerr in Thailand but the specimens in cultivation in the garden of Lawrence Johnson near Menton were collected in Yunnan by his bearer. In Menton it flowers in January–February.

Nymphaea mexicana

Nymphaea mexicana naturalised on the Dal lake in Kashmir

Nelumbo nucifera Gaertn. (*Nelumbonaceae*)
Sacred Lotus   A waterlily with mature leaves
on tall stalks above the water and large pink
flowers, native of Asia from the Volga delta
eastwards to China and Japan and south to
Australia, growing in ponds and lakes,
flowering in spring and summer. Plant with a
creeping and jointed yellowish edible rhizome.
Leaves waxy, glaucous, peltate, floating when
immature; when mature, leaves 1m across on
stalks to 2.5m above the water. Flowers
scented, pinkish, white or purplish-pink in
some cultivars, about 30cm across, held well
above the water. Capsules corky, flat-topped,
the seeds sunk in holes, opening from the top.
For shallow water, about 25cm deep; water
23–27°C is needed for good growth. In Beijing
I have seen the plants growing well in large
ginger jars. The rhizomes need to be kept
frost-free in winter.
The American lotus *Nelumbo lutea* (Willd.)
Pers. is rarely cultivated; it is smaller with
leaves to 60cm across and yellow flowers
10–25cm across. Native of N America from
New York and S Ontario southwards to
Mexico, the West Indies and Colombia,
growing in ponds, slow streams and estuaries,
flowering in July–September.

Nymphaea mexicana Zucc. (*Nymphaeaceae*)
A spreading yellow-flowered waterlily, native of
Mexico, S Texas and Florida south to Miami
and Palm Beech, growing in lakes, lagoons and
slow-flowing rivers, flowering in summer.
Plant spreads by suckers. Leaves green,
marked with purple above, purplish beneath
with indistinct veins; sinus often with
overlapping lobes. Flowers 7–10cm across,
little scented. Min. 0°C. Needs water
15–30cm deep.
Nymphaea stuhlmannii (Schwein.) Gilg. from
E Africa (*not shown*), has larger scented flowers
to 15cm across and leaves ribbed and green
beneath. *Nymphaea burttii* Pring & Woodson
from Tanzania, is similar and was much used
in breeding new tropical varieties at Missouri.
It grows in seasonal ponds and swamps,
flowering in March–May and has starry, pale
yellow scented flowers.

Victoria 'Longwood Hybrid'
(*Nymphaeaceae*)   This huge waterlily with
leaves turned up at their edges is the hybrid
between the two species and is often grown in
botanic gardens. It is named after the great
gardens near Philadelphia, formerly home of
the Du Pont family, where it was raised in

Victoria 'Longwood Hybrid' at the Royal Botanic Gardens, Kew

Nelumbo nucifera on the Dal lake in Kashmir

1961. *Victoria amazonica* (Poeppig) Sowerby, native of the Amazon, Guyana and Surinam, grows in backwaters and slow-flowing rivers, flowering in summer–autumn in cultivation. Its juvenile leaves are flat; the mature leaves have raised margins of about 10cm and are up to 2m across, reddish-purple and spiny beneath. Flowers 30–40cm across; sepals reddish, prickly; petals opening white, becoming pink on the second day, scented of pineapple. This species needs great heat to do well and is usually grown as an annual. Temperature of 30°C is needed for germination, 26°C for satisfactory growth. *Victoria cruziana* (Orbigny) is similar in general appearance, but has leaves green beneath, with a raised margin 15–20cm high. Sepals green, prickly at the base only. Native of Brazil (in the Parana River), N Argentina and Paraguay, growing in lagoons, lakes and marshes. This species needs less heat than *V. amazonica* – only 20°C for germination, 25°C for growth, and grows well outdoors on the Mediterranean coast and in the warmer states of North America.

Nelumbo nucifera

25

Nymphaea capensis in Malawi in January

Nymphaea capensis

Nymphaea rubra

Nymphaea capensis Thunb.
(*Nymphaeaceae*)   A robust and variable
waterlily, native of Africa from the Cape north
to Zanzibar, growing in pools, lakes and
seasonal ponds, flowering in spring–summer
(September–February). Leaves very wavy-
edged, 25–40cm across, marked with purple
beneath. Flowers held well above the water,
15–20cm across, bright blue, open in the day,
scented. Stamens yellow. Easily grown from
seed; for water 45–60cm deep, and does not
need great heat. Photographed in Malawi near
Zomba. Var. *zanzibariensis* (Caspary) Conard
has large deep blue flowers with violet anthers
and is the parent of many hybrids. *Nymphaea
caerulea* Savigny, the Blue Nile Lotus, has been
confused with *N. capensis*, but differs in its
leaves which are not wavy-edged, and flowers
7–15cm across.

Nymphaea elegans Hook.   A delicate
waterlily, native of Texas, Mexico and
Guatamala, growing in ponds and lagoons at
low altitudes, flowering in May–October.
Leaves 15–18cm across, green spotted with
black above, reddish purple beneath, with
smooth or slightly wavy edges. Flowers 7–
13cm across, open in the day, pale blue, white
at the base; stamens yellow, with blue tips. Will
grow in shallow water 30–45cm deep;
increases by seed.

Nymphaea lotus L.   A robust waterlily
flowering mainly at night, native from Egypt to
tropical and SE Africa (Zululand), Romania
(in the hot springs at Grosswardein and

Kaiserbade) and SE Asia, growing in lakes and
slow-flowing rivers, flowering in summer–
autumn. Leaves 20–50cm across, wavy and
toothed to spiny. Flowers 15–25cm across,
white, sometimes tinged pink, held well above
the water. Stamens yellow. Needs water 45–
75cm deep, at around 20°C.
Var. **dentata** (Schum. & Thon.) Nichols
shown here, is native of Sierra Leone. It differs
from the type in its pure white flowers with
very narrow petals and reddish stamens.
'Dentata Superba' has extra large flowers to
35cm across and hairy leaves.

Nymphaea rubra Roxb. & Salisb.   A large
red-flowered waterlily, native of NE India,
flowering in summer. Leaves spotted, reddish
to greenish-brown, with toothed edges, hairy
beneath. Flowers about 20cm across, dark
purplish-red, opening mainly at night, slightly
scented. Stamens red. The cv. 'Rosea' shown
here, with paler flowers is the form usually
cultivated. Both need water 45–75cm deep
and hot temperatures. Easily raised from seed.

Nymphaea 'American Beauty'   Raised by
George Pring in the Missouri Botanical
Garden in 1941. Flowers opening in the day,
15–25cm across, purplish-pink with yellow
stamens. A cross between *N.* 'William Stone'
and *N. colorata*. Needs water 60–90cm deep.

Nymphaea 'Pink Platter'   Raised by
George Pring in 1934. Leaves light green,
splashed with brown, producing new plants in
the sinuses. Needs water 60–90cm deep.

Nymphaea 'Pink Platter'

Nymphaea elegans near Tepic, W Mexico

Nymphae 'American Beauty' at Pepsico, Purchase, New York

Nymphae 'American Beauty'

Nymphaea lotus at Kew

The shrubby perennial white stock, *Matthiola incana*, growing wild by the sea on Tresco

Matthiola incana

Iberis gibraltarica on the rock of Gibraltar

Bocconia frutescens L. (*Papaveraceae*)
A shrub or small tree with large lobed leaves, native of Mexico and Central America, growing in dry rocky places on limestone at about 1000m, flowering in late summer. Plant with a yellow juice, to 7.5m but usually less, around 3m in gardens. Leaves 15–30cm long, 10–20cm wide, greyish-green, lobed; the lobes usually acute in specimens cultivated in Europe, but rounded in the Mexican plant shown here. Flowers numerous and small, without petals, but with purple-tinted sepals about 1cm long; 16 stamens. For well-drained soil and full sun. Min. −5°C, if dry. Related to

the herbaceous *Macleaya cordata* (syn. *Bocconia cordata*) from Japan and E China.

Crambe strigosa L'Hérit. (*Cruciferae*)
A small shrub with clouds of minute white flowers, native of Tenerife, Gomera and Hierro, growing on cliffs and open places in the laurel forest at 400–1000m, flowering in spring. Stems to 1.5m; leaves stalked, rough, unlobed with crenate-dentate margins, less than 20cm across, with a pair of auricles. Fruits weakly 4-ribbed. Min. −3°C, perhaps. *Crambe gigantea* (Ceb. & Ort.) Bramwell is even larger, to 4m, with thin, not rough leaves;

from ravines in the laurel forest of NE La Palma.

Dendromecon rigida Benth. (*Papaveraceae*)
A spreading shrub with bright yellow poppy-like flowers, native of California from Sonoma and Shasta Cos., south to Baja California and Tulare Co., growing on dry slopes in chaparral below 1800m, flowering in February–June. Stems usually 1–3m; leaves glaucous, lanceolate, 2.5–10cm long. Flowers with 4 petals, 2–3cm long. Capsule curved, 5–10cm long. Good for dry, poor soils and tolerant of summer drought. Min. −5°C or less for short

Crambe strigosa in the Temperate house at the Royal Botanic Gardens, Kew

periods if dry or against a wall. Prune hard after flowering to keep in good shape.
D. harfordii Kell. from Santa Cruz and Santa Rosa islands off Ventura, has broader, more rounded, deep green leaves and often larger flowers. It makes a small tree to 6m.

Erysimum bicolor DC. syn. *Cheiranthus virescens* Webb ex Christ. (*Cruciferae*)
A small, much-branched shrub like a pale mauve wallflower, native of Madeira and the Canary Islands, growing on damp cliffs in the forest at up to 1000m, flowering in winter and early spring. Stems to 90cm. Leaves lanceolate to oblanceolate, sharply toothed, 7–11mm wide; flowers slightly scented with petals 8–10mm long. Not commonly cultivated, but valuable for flowering in late winter and tolerant of some shade. Min. −3°C, perhaps less.

Eschscholzia mexicana Greene (*Papaveraceae*)   A tufted annual or short-lived perennial, native of S Utah, W Texas, Arizona, SE California and NE Mexico, growing in deserts, plains and dry hills, flowering in February–May and again in autumn. Leaves glaucous, finely divided. Flowers 3–6cm across, usually orange, but yellow late in the year, rarely white or pink. Min. −5°C or less if dry. Close to *E. californica*, but differing mainly in its smaller size, more tufted habit and narrower outer rim of the hypanthium. Most forms of the very variable *E. californica* are perennials in warm dry climates and killed by the combination of cold and wet in N Europe.

Iberis gibraltarica L. (*Cruciferae*)   A dwarf shrubby perennial with flat heads of white or pale mauve flowers, native of Gibraltar and Morocco, growing in crevices in limestone cliffs by the sea, flowering in early spring (February–May). Plants woody at the base with flowering stems to 30cm. Leaves fleshy, sometimes with 1–4 pairs of teeth near the apex. Flower heads 4–6cm across; outer petals 15–18mm long. For well-drained soil and a cool position in summer. Min. −5°C. It grows here with *Scilla peruviana* L., a variable species native of the western Mediterranean, with purple or pale blue flowers and often growing in marshy fields. *Iberis semperflorens* L. from sea cliffs in Sicily and W Italy is also cultivated; it has white flowers throughout the winter.

Matthiola incana (L.) R. Br. (*Cruciferae*)
A shrubby perennial with sweetly-scented flowers, native of the coasts of Arabia, W Europe and the Mediterranean and naturalized on the coast of California, growing in rocky and sandy places by the sea, flowering in April–July. Plant to 1m, often branched near the top. Leaves greyish-green, soft, linear-lanceolate, to 35mm wide. Flowers sweetly scented, with petals 2–3cm long, reddish-purple, to pink or white. Grows best in sandy soil in a warm sheltered place. Min. −5°C. This species is the ancestor of several of the cultivated stocks; the Ten-Week Stock is an annual selection. The Brompton Stock is a biennial, sown one summer to flower the next. Double flowers are common in the cultivated varieties and both are suitable for a cold greenhouse where they can be protected from frost and excessive winter rain.

Bocconia frutescens in Mexico

Erysimum bicolor on Madeira

Dendromecon rigida in California

Eschscholzia mexicana

29

Ochna serrulata in Madeira in March

Ochna serrulata in fruit

Actinidia coriacea (Finet & Gangep.) Dunn
(*Actinidiaceae*) An evergreen climber with
small red flowers, native of China in Sichuan
on Mount Omei and Baoxing, growing in
forests, flowering in May–August. A unisexual
shrub to 3m or climbing to 8m. Leaves to
15cm long, leathery, glabrous, oblong to
lanceolate. Flowers scented, to 2cm across, the
male larger than the female. Fruit to 2cm
across, brown. A handsome shrub for a
partially shaded position, but must be grown
on a warm wall in cold areas. Introduced by E.
H. Wilson in 1908. Min. −5°C.
Actinidia callosa Lindl. from forest and scrub at
1500–3000m in the Himalayas from NE India
east to SW China and SE Asia, has broader
leaves and white flowers 2.5cm across.

Neolitsea levinei Merrill syn. *N. lanuginosa*
(Nees) Gamble var. *chinensis* Gamble
(*Lauraceae*) An upright evergreen shrub or
small tree with handsome leaves, native of W
China in Sichuan, growing in woods and scrub
at 900–1800m, flowering in March. Tree to
9m. Leaves 12–20cm long, 3.5–5.5cm across,
glaucous beneath. Flowers small, yellowish;
fruits black. For good, preferably acid soil,
with ample summer water. Min. −5°C.
Neolitsea sericea (Bl.) Koidz. from Japan,
Korea, Taiwan and China makes an evergreen
tree and has beautifully silky young growth.
The leaves, with three main nerves from the
base are typical of *Neolitsea* and many other
Lauraceae.

Saurauia griffithii Dyer (*Saurauiaceae*)
A multi-stemmed shrub or small tree with
parallel-veined leaves, brown hairy beneath,
and branching panicles of open flowers, native
of the Himalayas in Bhutan and Sikkim,
growing in subtropical forests at 900–1500m,
flowering in June. Leaves to 40cm long; petals
pale purple to white, about 8mm long,
obovate. Min. −3°C.

Saurauia nepaulensis DC. A shrub or
small tree, its large leaves have parallel veins,
native of the Himalayas from NE India to SW
China, Burma and SE Asia, growing in forests
and near villages at 600–2100m, flowering in
March–October. A large many-stemmed shrub
or small tree. Leaves 18–36cm long with rusty
hairs beneath and sharp glandular teeth.
Flowers cup-shaped, about 1.3cm across,
pinkish, with 5 fringed petals, in hanging
clusters. For any good soil. Min. −3°C. A fine
tree of this species at Tresco was cut to the
ground by cold but is now springing up
strongly from the root.

Ochna serrulata (Hochst.) Walp.
(*Ochnaceae*) A small twiggy shrub with yellow
flowers and strange fruits with black seeds on
persistent red sepals, native of much of South
Africa, growing on the edges of forest,
flowering from April–October, with the fruit
persistent through the winter. Shrub or small
tree to 3m. Leaves narrowly elliptic, toothed,
shining pale green. Flowers with yellow
obovate petals, about 2cm across. Fruits of 5
green, then black, fleshy 1-seeded drupes, 1cm
across, on the base of the swollen red
persistent sepals. Easily grown in a cold
greenhouse or in a warm garden outside.
Prune in spring. Min. −3°C.

Actinidia coriacea at Paignton Zoo

Saurauia griffithii in January at Les Cèdres, Cap Ferrat

Saurauia nepaulensis at Kew

Neolitsea levinei wild near Baoxing

Oncoba kraussiana in Natal

Oncoba kraussiana (Hochst.) Planch. syn. *Xylotheca krassiana* Hochst. (*Flacourtiaceae*) A small much-branched tree or large shrub, native of South Africa on the Zululand coast, flowering in January (summer). Tree to 4.5m. Leaves evergreen, downy, elliptic oblong, about 6cm long, 2.5cm wide. Flowers about 5cm across. Fruit orange, 5cm across. For any soil, with water in summer. Min. 0°C.

Viola hederacea Labill. (*Violaceae*) A mat-forming dwarf violet with flowers for most of the year, native of E Australia and Malaysia, growing in damp places in forests. Stems creeping and rooting, forming wide-spreading mats. Leaf blades to 35mm across. Flowers about 10mm across, blue and white or sometimes all white. For moist soil. Min. −3°C for short periods but killed by prolonged freezing.

Viola hederacea at La Mortola

Oncoba kraussiana

31

Habitat of *Camellia granthamiana* in Hong Kong

Camellia crapnelliana in the Shing Mun arboretum

Camellia granthamiana fruit

Camellia crapnelliana

Camellia crapnelliana fruit

Camellia granthamiana flowering in October

Camellia grijsii at Trehane's Nurseries

Camellia irrawaddiensis at Nuccio's nurseries, Altadena, California

Camellia salicifolia in the Shing Mun arboretum

Gordonia axillaris wild in Hong Kong

Camellia nitidissima at Nuccio's nurseries, Altadena

Camellia crapnelliana Tucher (*Theaceae*)
A small upright tree with beautiful chestnut-brown mat bark and small white flowers, native of Hong Kong, where it was first found on Mt Parker, flowering from October–December. Tree to 7m. Leaves 9.5–12cm long, obovate-elliptic, with conspicuous nerves. Flowers white, about 9cm across. Fruits large and spherical, hanging on the tree until autumn. For acid soil. Min. 0°C.

Camellia granthamiana Sealy   A shrub with large veined leaves and white flowers, native of Hong Kong, near Shing Mun in the New Territories, growing in a wooded rocky ravine at 600m, flowering from October–December. A shrub or small tree to 4m; leaves leathery, reticulate with impressed veins above, hairy on the midrib and with corky warts beneath, 8–10cm long, 2.7–4cm wide. Buds large, rounded, dark brown and hairy. Flowers white, with pink edges as they fade, 12–14cm across with 8 indented petals. Ovary and style hairy. This spectacular species was discovered in 1955, when a single tree was found by a Chinese forester, C. P. Lau. It is easily grown in a cool greenhouse. Min. 0°C.

Camellia grijsii Hance   A shrub with small white flowers with deeply lobed petals, native of C China in Hubei (though described from Fujian), growing in ravines and glens near Ichang, flowering in January–March. Shrub to 3m; leaves elliptic to ovate, 4–8cm long, 2–3cm wide with numerous fine teeth, dark green, leathery, with the veins indented on the upper surface. Flowers white, 4–6cm across, the petals obcordate, with a wide sinus. Ovary hairy; styles and stamens very short. This species is now in cultivation and should be almost hardy to −5°C. Related to *C. sasanqua*, but differing in its spring flowering and very short styles.

Camellia irrawaddiensis P. K. Barua
A many-stemmed shrub with small white flowers, native of Burma in the Irrawady Valley at around 2500m, flowering probably in December–March. Stems to 7m. Leaves 8–14cm long, 3–5cm wide, rather thin, acuminate and cuneate at the base. Flowers white, about 4cm across with long stamens 1–1.6cm long. Related to the tea plant but differing in its long stamens and deeply divided style. Min. 0°C.

Camellia nitidissima Chi syn. *C. chrysantha* (Hu) Tuyama   An upright shrub with large, rather thin leaves and bright yellow flowers, native of N Vietnam and S Guangxi around Nanning (a very wet, hot and humid area), from whence it was described only in 1965, growing in rich, acid, porous soil, flowering in November–March. A quick-growing shrub to 3m or more, with two flushes of new growth, in spring and in autumn. Leaves to 8–17cm long, 4.5cm wide, narrowly ovate, acuminate, shining and with impressed veins above, with numerous shallow teeth. Flowers pendulous, 4–5cm across. Styles free to the base. Not difficult to grow in a cool greenhouse but shy to flower. Min. −3°C for short periods if kept dry.

Camellia salicifolia Champion ex Benth.
A shrub or small tree with arching branches, narrow lanceolate leaves and small white flowers, native of S China in Fujian, Guangxi and Hong Kong, growing in woods and rocky ravines, flowering in November–January. Twigs and midrib of leaves bristly hairy; leaves 5–10cm long. Sepals acuminate. Flowers 1.5–2cm long. Stamens silky-hairy, joined into a tube for 2 3 of their length. Ovary hairy. Min. −5°C, perhaps.

Gordonia axillaris (Roxb.) D. Dietr. (*Theaceae*)   An evergreen shrub or small tree with white flowers in the leaf axils near the apex of the shoot, native of Taiwan and S China west to Yunnan and SW Sichuan, growing in scrub and open woods at up to 2800m, flowering in October–March (or to May in cold areas). Tree to 8m. Leaves leathery, rather crowded, usually obtuse, 6–18cm long. Flowers 8–15cm across, lasting only one day. Petals notched. Fruits hard and woody. For acid soil and a mild climate. Min. −3°C. This species will survive outdoors in Cornwall.
Gordonia lasianthus (L.) Ellis Loblolly Bay, is a large evergreen tree to 20m, with smaller short-stalked white flowers, native of the hot parts of SE North America from S Virginia southwards. Min. −5°C.

Franklinia altamaha near New York

Camellia sinensis in Sichuan

Camellia yunnanensis at Nuccio's

Camellia transarisanensis

Camellia fraterna Hance   A spreading shrub with bristly-hairy twigs and small white flowers, native of SE China in Fujian, Jiangsu, Zhejiang, Anhui and Jiangxi, growing in glens and shady ravines at 500–1500m, flowering in April–May. Shrub to 5m. Leaves to 4–8cm long, 1.5–3.5cm wide, elliptic, shortly acuminate, shining, smooth, bristly-hairy above when young, with numerous shallow teeth. Calyx bristly-hairy. Flowers 3.5cm across, white, scented. Free-flowering under glass or outside. Min. −3°C. Plants from the Ichang gorges and Sichuan which were recorded under *C. fraterna* were described as *C. dubia* Sealy. They differ in their glabrous pedicels and usually glabrous calyx.

Camellia luchuensis Itô   A small shrub with hairy twigs and numerous small white flowers, native of the Liu Kiu Islands including Okinawa, off the south of Japan, growing in woods at up to 500m, flowering in March. Shrub to 3m. Leaves 2–4cm long, 1–1.8cm wide, elliptic to oblong, acute, shining, smooth, hairy beneath when young. Calyx smooth. Flowers about 3cm across, white, with rounded petals. Style 11.5mm long, divided only at the apex. Ovary glabrous. Heat tolerant. Min. 0°C for short periods.

Camellia nokoensis Hayata   A shrub or small bushy tree with acuminate leaves and small white flowers, native of Taiwan, growing in forests, flowering in March. Tree to 8m; twigs puberulose, becoming glabrous; leaves 3–4.5cm long. Flowers 9–12mm long. Stamens villose, 9mm long. Min. −5°C, perhaps.

Camellia sasanqua Thunb.   A large shrub with small white flowers and narrow lobed petals, native of S Japan in Kyushu and the islands south to the Liu Kiu islands, growing in openings in the forest, flowering in September–December. Shrub to 6m; leaves elliptic to ovate, 3–5.5cm long, 1.5–2 cm wide with numerous shallow rounded teeth, dark green, leathery. Flowers white, 4–7cm across, the petals obovate with a shallow sinus. Ovary hairy; style 11–14mm, divided to about 1 2 Many cultivars are in cultivation with single and double flowers varying from red to pink. Min. −7°C, but needs summer heat to flower well. Very popular in S Japan and good in western USA and in the southern Alps in N Italy where a fine collection is grown at the Villa Taranto. In colder areas it needs a warm wall to flower well.

Camellia sinensis (L.) O. Kuntze   This is the tea plant, widely grown in the subtropics and on mountains in the tropics. Two varieties were recognized by J. R. Sealy in his account of *Camellia*, published in 1955. Var. *sinensis* is a shrub with rather small thin leaves and small white flowers, probably native of W China in W and SW Yunnan (though widely naturalized elsewhere), growing in openings in the forest, in scrub and on rocky hillsides at 2000–2800m, flowering mainly in October. Shrub to 6m; leaves elliptic to ovate, 5–9cm long, 2–3cm wide with blunt teeth, dark green, thin in texture. Flowers white, nodding on thin stalks, 2–4cm across, the petals rounded. Ovary hairy; styles divided only at the apex. Stamens 8–13mm long. Easily grown in sun or partial shade in areas with warm, wet summers and mild winters. Hardier and hardier forms are being selected in China, so that tea can be grown further north. Var. *assamica* (Masters) Kit. is a tree to 17m, with larger, thinner, more acuminate leaves, probably native of NE India and Burma, south to Thailand and possibly to Hainan Island. It needs more tropical conditions.

Camellia transarisanensis (Hay.) Cohen Stuart   A shrub or small tree with hairy twigs and small white flowers, native of Taiwan, growing in forests in the mountains at 2000–3200m. Tree to 9m; leaves lanceolate, acuminate, with shallow blunt teeth. Flowers white, about 2cm long. Stamens glabrous, joined at the base for 1–1.3m. Min. −10°C.

Camellia yuhsienensis Hu   A shrub with large white scented flowers and large elliptic leaves, native of S China in Hunan, growing in scrub and on the edges of forests, at 1300–2500m, flowering in February–April. Shrub to 3m with branches and twigs densely pubescent when young. Leaves elliptic, 6–9cm long, 3–4cm wide, dull green. Flowers white, 5–7cm across. Min. 0°C. Close to *C. grijsii*, but with larger leaves and larger, scented flowers.

Camellia yunnanensis (Pitard ex Diels) Cohen Stuart   An autumn-flowering shrub with ovate leaves and white flowers, native of SW China where it is widespread in Yunnan, including the Cangshang and rare in S Sichuan, growing in scrub and pine forest at 1700–2000m, flowering in July–November. Shrub or small tree to 7m. Leaves to 4–8cm long, 1.5–3.5cm wide, elliptic to ovate-elliptic, smooth with numerous shallow teeth. Calyx with a broad scarious margin. Flowers 2.5–4cm across, white, with overlapping petals. Styles 5. Min. −10°C.

Franklinia altamaha Marsh (*Theaceae*)   A large deciduous shrub or small tree with simple leaves and scented white flowers, native of Georgia in woods and on sand dunes along the Alatamaha River, where it was discovered by John Bartram in around 1765 and introduced to cultivation by his son William in 1778. It has not been seen in the wild since 1802 and so is probably extinct, but it has been preserved in cultivation. Tree to 10m. Leaves oblanceolate, 12–15cm long, downy beneath, turning a good scarlet and purple in autumn. Flowers terminal, white, about 7–9cm across, in late summer and autumn. Fruit a woody capsule, splitting into 10 segments. This interesting tree is hardy as far north as New York City, but grows slowly in Britain and NW Europe because of the cool summers. To thrive, it needs very well-drained soil but ample water in summer.

Camellia sasanqua 'Crimson King'

Camellia sasanqua white form

Camellia nokoensis at Nuccio's, California

Camellia sasanqua 'Crimson King' at Coleton Fishacre, S Devon

Camellia luchuensis at Marwood Hill

Camellia yuhsienensis at Trehane's, Dorset

Camellia fraterna at Marwood Hill, N Devon

Camellia japonica 'Brilliant' at the Huntington Gardens, California

Camellia japonica 'Berenice Boddy'
Raised at Rancho del Descanso, introduced by Jones in California, 1946. Vigorous upright growth.

Camellia japonica 'Brigadoon' (*saluenensis* × *japonica* 'Princess Bacciocchi') Armstrong, USA, 1960. Compact upright growth.

Camellia japonica 'Brilliant' Originated by Blackwell, USA. Known since at least 1939. Bushy upright growth.

Camellia japonica 'Coed' Bred by Nuccio's Nurseries, Altadena, California, USA and launched in 1963. Vigorous compact growth.

Camellia japonica 'Desire' ('Dr. Tinsley' × 'Debutante') Bred by David Feathers, Lafayette, California, USA in 1973. Vigorous dense growth.

Camellia japonica 'Emily Wilson' Bred by Arthur T. Wilson, Batesburg, South Carolina, USA in 1949. Upright rapid compact growth.

Camellia japonica 'Emmett Barnes' A seedling grown by Ingleside Nursery, Georgia, USA in 1945 from seed that originated in Japan. Compact vigorous growth.

Camellia japonica 'Finlandia' Probably a white sport of 'Finlandia Variegated'. Propagated by Jannoch Nurseries, Pasadena, California, USA in 1937. Medium growth.

Camellia japonica 'Kamo-honnami' An old camellia from Kansai District, Japan. Bushy growth.

Camellia japonica 'Mollie Moore Davis' A sport of 'Big Beauty'. Originated in Jungle Gardens, Louisiana, USA. Launched commercially in 1945.

Camellia japonica 'Monte Carlo' A sport of 'Finlandia'. Originated by Barney Goletto, USA. Launched in 1950.

Camellia japonica 'Senator Duncan U. Fletcher' Launched by Gerbings, USA in 1941. Slow upright growth.

Camellia × williamsii 'Shocking Pink' Seedling of *C. saluenensis*, grown by Prof. E. G. Waterhouse, Gordon, NSW, Australia. Launched in 1955. Compact upright growth.

Camellia japonica 'Virgin's Blush' A seedling of 'Orandagasa' bred by McIlhenny at Jungle Gardens, Avery Island, Louisiana, USA. Launched in 1945. Medium growth.

Camellia japonica 'Kamo-honnami'

Camellia japonica 'Berenice Boddy'

Camellia × williamsii 'Shocking Pink'

Camellia japonica 'Desire'

'Virgin's Blush'

'Coed'

'Finlandia'

'Emily Wilson'

'Mollie Moore Davis'

'Emmett Barnes'

'Brigadoon'

'Senator Duncan U. Fletcher'

'Monte Carlo'

Specimens from Marwood Hill Gardens, N Devon, February 15th, 1/2 life size

'Tip Top'

'Margaret Waterhouse'

'Jennifer Turnbull'

'Jean Lyne'

'Snow Goose'

'Genji-guruma'

'Le Lys'

'Betty Sheffield'

'Silver Anniversary'

Specimens from Eccleston Square, 2nd March, 1/2 life size

Camellia japonica 'Elizabeth Cooper'

Camellia × williamsii 'Margaret Waterhouse'

Camellia japonica 'Sacco Vera'

Camellia japonica 'Kewpie Doll'

Camellia japonica 'Betty Sheffield'
Launched by Thomasville Nursery, Georgia, USA in 1949. A very variable plant. Many sports and colour forms have been named.

Camellia japonica 'Elizabeth Cooper'
A seedling discovered by Tammia Nursery, Louisiana, USA in 1973. Upright growth.

Camellia japonica 'Genji-guruma'
Originates from Japan. First mentioned in 1859. Medium growth.

Camellia japonica 'Jean Lyne' Raised at Camellia Grove, Ashfield, NSW, Australia in 1941. Average growth.

Camellia japonica 'Jennifer Turnbull'
A seedling of 'Henry Turnbull' raised by Mrs Hume Turnbull, Malvern, Victoria, Australia in 1959. Spreading habit.

Camellia japonica 'Kewpie Doll' Raised by McCaskill Gardens, Pasadena, California, USA in 1971. Average growth.

Camellia japonica 'Le Lys' Often named 'Madame Victor de Bisschop'. Originated in Belgium in 1937. Spreading growth.

Camellia × williamsii 'Margaret Waterhouse' A *C. saluenensis* seedling raised by Prof. E. G. Waterhouse in Gordon, NSW,

Australia in 1955. Vigorous upright growth.

Camellia japonica 'Sacco Vera'
Originated by Paolina, Milan, Italy in 1843. Strong growth.

Camellia japonica 'Silver Anniversary'
Launched by Nuccio, Altadena, California, USA in 1960. Vigorous upright growth.

Camellia japonica 'Snow Goose'
Anonymous 1953, exhibited by Loder – given an Award of Merit at the RHS. Open growth.

Camellia japonica 'Tip Top' Launched by Mealing, USA in 1981. Slow upright growth.

'Chandler's Victory'

'Helenor'

'Alison Leigh Woodroof'

'Laurie Bray'

'Betty Cuthbert'

Camellia japonica

Specimens from Marwood Hill Gardens, N Devon, February 15th, 1/2 life size

Camellia japonica 'Christmas Beauty'

Camellia japonica 'Laurie Bray'

An ancient *Camellia japonica* in Wang Shi Yuan (Master of the Fishing Nets Garden) in Suzhou, E China

Camellia japonica 'Kingyo-tsubaki'

The Wang Shi Yuan Camellia This free-flowering double camellia shows the way the Chinese use flowering plants in their gardens as single specimens that are shown off against the stark white walls, just the way a water colour artist would have painted them against a white ground or a pale mist-grey tint.

Camellia japonica Was labelled **'Lillian Rickets'** but this is a misnomer as 'Lillian Rickets' has large blush-pink semi-double flowers. To date we have not been able to name it.

Camellia japonica **'Alison Leigh Woodroof'** Raised by McCaskill Gardens Camellia Nursery, California, USA in 1955. Flowers in profusion on an upright plant.

Camellia japonica **'Christmas Beauty'** Bred by V. Howell, USA in 1859. Lax growth, will need support.

Camellia japonica **'Betty Cuthbert'** A seedling of 'Yoibjin' from E. G. Waterhouse, Gordon, NSW, Australia in 1962. Spreading growth.

Camellia japonica **'Chandler's Victory'** Raised by B. Chandler in Australia. Launched 1947. Average growth.

Camellia japonica **'Laurie Bray'** Probably a seedling of 'Edith Linton', found by G. Linton, Australia in 1955. Tall growth habit.

Camellia japonica **'Helenor'** First published by the Botanical Society of Sydney, 1848. Mentioned in Taylor and Sangster's catalogue, 1877.

Camellia japonica **'Kingyo-tsubaki'** syn. 'Fishtail' First mentioned by Shirai Bunko in 1789. Grown for the extraordinary foliage with a divided apex like a fish's tail.

41

'Elegans Supreme'

'Cynthia Kuyper'

'Salab'

'Erin Farmer'

'Laurie Bray'

'Paul Jones Supreme'

'Diddy's Pink Organdie'

'Tomorrow Parkhill'

Specimens from Marwood Hill Gardens, N Devon, March 5th, 1/2 life size

Camellia japonica 'Tomorrow Parkhill'

Specimens from Marwood Hill Gardens, N Devon, February 15th, 1/3 life size

Camellia japonica **'Coronation'**
A seedling of 'Lotus' bred by McCaskill
Pasadena, California, USA, 1954. Vigorous
spreading growth.

Camellia japonica **'Cynthia Kuyper'**
As yet this name has not been registered in
the Camellia Register.

Camellia japonica **'Diddy's Pink
Organdie'**   A sport of 'Diddy Mealing'. Bred
by Mealing in Georgia, USA in 1953.
Pendulous growth.

Camellia japonica **'Elegans Supreme'**
A sport of 'Elegans' originated by Bray,
Florida, USA in 1960. Spreading open growth.

Camellia japonica **'Erin Farmer'**
Originated by Ashby, South Carolina, USA in
1956. Upright growth.

Camellia × *williamsii* **'E. T. R. Carlyon'**
syn. 'Rupert Carlyon' ('J. C. Williams' ×
'Adolphe Audusson')   Raised by Gillian
Carlyon, Cornwall, UK in 1972. Vigorous
upright growth.

Camellia japonica **'Hana Fuki'** (Hanafûki)
Reported to have been raised from seed at
Sakura-shi, Japan in about 1882. Slow upright
growth.

Camellia japonica **'Laurie Bray'**
A seedling found under a plant of 'Edith
Linton' by Linton Somersby, Australia in
1952. Erect growth.

Camellia japonica **'Nuccio's Gem'**
A seedling found by Nuccio's Nursery,
Altadena, California, USA in 1965. Dense
upright growth.

Camellia japonica 'Hana Fuki'

Camellia japonica **'Paul Jones Supreme'**
A seedling of 'Paul Jones' found by Prof. E. G.
Waterhouse, Gordon, NSW, Australia in 1958.
Vigorous growth.

Camellia **'Salab'** ('Apple Blossom' × *C.
saluenensis*)   Originated by Feathers,
Lafayette, USA in 1971. Compact growth.

Camellia japonica **'Tomorrow Parkhill'**
A sport of 'Tomorrow Variegated' found by
Mrs Peer, Hollywood, California, USA in
1960. Upright open growth.

Camellia japonica **'White Nun'**
A seedling found by McCaskill, Pasadena,
USA in 1959. Vigorous upright growth.

43

Camellia japonica 'Elegans Variegated' underplanted with azaleas at the Huntington garden, California

Camellia japonica 'Guest of Honor'

Camellia japonica 'Vittorlo Emanuele II'

44

Camellia japonica 'Pink Pagoda'

Camellia japonica 'H. M. Queen Elizabeth II'

Camellia japonica 'Elegans Variegated'
A white blotched form of 'Elegans'. First published by the Southern California Camellia Society in 1946. Open spreading growth.

Camellia 'Francie L.' (*C. saluenensis* × *C. reticulata*)   Originated by Marshal, Huntington Gardens, San Marino, USA in 1960. Open growth.

Camellia japonica 'Guest of Honor'
A seedling of 'Lotus' bred by Short, Ramona, USA in 1953. Open growth.

Camellia japonica 'HM Queen Elizabeth II'   A seedling planted by Rubel, later taken over by Harris, USA in 1953. Dense upright growth.

Camellia × williamsii 'Jubilation'
A 'Betty Sheffield' cross bred by Jury, New Zealand in 1978. Upright growth.

Camellia × williamsii 'Margaret Waterhouse'   A *C. × williamsii* seedling raised by Prof. E. G. Waterhouse, Gordon, NSW, Australia in 1955. Tall open growth.

Camellia japonica 'Nuccio's Carousel'
Bred by Nuccio's Nursery, Altadena, USA in 1988. Medium upright growth.

Camellia japonica 'Pink Pagoda'
A seedling of 'Pink Star'. Originated by Moore, Los Gatos, USA in 1965. Compact upright growth.

Camellia japonica 'Tiffany'   Grown from Japanese seed by Urabec, La Canada, USA in 1962. Vigorous upright growth.

Camellia japonica 'Vittorio Emanuele II'
Originated by Madoni, Brescia, Italy in 1861. Vigorous growth.

Camellia japonica 'Elegans Variegated'

Camellia japonica 'Nuccio's Carousel'

'Jubilation'

'Francie L'

'Pink Pagoda'

'Guest of Honor'

'Tiffany'

Specimens from Eccleston Square, 2nd March

Camellia japonica 'Purity'

Camellia japonica 'Snow Chan'

Camellia japonica 'Ivory Tower'

Camellia japonica 'Eleanor Martin Supreme'

Camellia japonica 'Jean Clere'

Camellia japonica 'Campari'

Camellia japonica 'Kumasaka'

Camellia japonica 'Mercury Variegated'

Camellia japonica 'Shuchûka'

Camellia japonica 'Elizabeth Weaver'

Camellia japonica 'Tom Thumb'

Camellia japonica 'Prima Ballerina'

Camellia japonica 'Ivory Tower'
Originated by Shackelford, Albany , USA.
First published by the S. California Camellia
Society in 1968. Medium compact growth.

Camellia japonica 'Kumasaka'
Recognized since 1695. Modern cultivar
photographed in *American Camellia Catalogue*

in 1945. Originated in Kanto, Japan. Sports:
'Kumasaka White' and 'Hanatachibana'.

Camellia japonica 'Prima Ballerina'
A chance seedling, first bloomed 1972.
Originated by Nuccio's Nurseries, Altadena
California, USA. Slow dense growth.

Camellia japonica 'Purity'   Originated in
Australia. Noted in the International Camellia
Register, 1993 as probably extinct. We found
this clearly labelled in Descanso Gardens, near
Los Angeles, 1994.

Camellia japonica 'Snow Chan'   A sport
of 'Shiro Chan'. Originated by Nuccio's
Nurseries, Altadena, California, USA in 1957.

Camellia japonica 'Campari'   Published
by the Southern California Camellia Society in
1972. Originated by Armstrong, USA.
Vigorous upright growth. Sports: 'Campari
White' and 'Campari Rose'.

**Camellia japonica 'Eleanor Martin
Supreme'**   A sport of 'Eleanor Martin', first
observed 1959. Originated by Caesar Breschini,
San Jose, USA. Vigorous upright growth.

Camellia japonica 'Elizabeth Weaver'
('Elizabeth Boardman' × 'Clarise Carleton')
Originated by Dr W. Homeyer, Jr., Macon,
USA. First bloomed in 1967. Medium upright
growth.

Camellia japonica 'Jean Clere'   A sport of
'Asapasia Macarthur'. Found on an old tree at
Taranaki, New Zealand and propagated by
R. H. Clere, Hawara, New Zealand. Published
in *New Zealand Camellia Bulletin*, 1969. Slow
upright growth.

Camellia japonica 'Mercury Variegated'
Described in *McCaskill Gardens Newest
Camellias*, 1957. A virus-variegated form of
'Mercury'. Originated in the USA. Dense
growth.

Camellia japonica 'Shuchûka'   First
recorded in 1789. Originated in Kanto area,
Japan. Bushy and spreading.

Camellia japonica 'Tom Thumb'
Recorded in 1964 by the Southern California
Camellia Society. Originated by A. Kreuger,
San Gabriel, California, USA. Medium
upright growth.

Camellias in the national collection at Mount Edgcumbe, Cornwall

Camellia **'Black Opal'** (*C.* hybrid 'Ruby Bells' × *C. japonica* 'Kur-tsubaki') Originated by O. Blumhardt, Whangarei, New Zealand. Won champion seedling at 1984 New Zealand National Camellia Show. Dense slow growth.

Camellia japonica **'Elegans'** syn. 'Chandleri Elegans' Originated from the seed of 'Anemoniflora' (brought to England from China in 1806 and much used as a seed parent by 19th-century hybridists). Planted in 1823 by Alfred Chandler of Vauxhall, England. Spreading open vigorous growth.

Camellia japonica **'Ginyô-tsubaki'** syn. 'Terada Foliage' Originated in Izu Ohshima,

Japan. Recognized by the Japanese Camellia Society in 1979. Slow-growing upright compact.

Camellia japonica **'Mrs Tingley'** Originated by J. H. Ward Hinkson, Chester, Pennsylvania, USA. First published by Nuccio's Nurseries in 1948. Upright open growth.

Camellia japonica **'Nuccio's Jewel'** Originated by Nuccio's Nurseries, Altadena, USA. First bloomed in 1974. Slow dense growth.

Camellia japonica **'Purpurea'** We photographed this upright dark-flowered

specimen at Nuccio's nurseries in California, eventually it will probably get another name as the name 'Purpurea' has been used before and is rather muddled up.

Camellia japonica **'Red Candles'** Originated by Harvey Short, Ramona, USA. First published by the Southern California Camellia Society in 1962. Vigorous upright growth.

Camellia japonica **'Tinsie'** syn. 'Bokuhan' Originated in Kantô District, Japan. First published in 1719. Exported to the USA by the Star Nursery, California in about 1930. Vigorous upright growth.

48

Camellia japonica 'Elegans'

Camellia japonica 'Mrs Tingley'

Camellia japonica 'Nuccio's Jewel'

Camellia japonica 'Ginyô-tsubaki'

Camellia japonica 'Red Candles'

Camellia japonica 'Tinsie'

Camellia japonica 'Purpurea'

Camellia 'Black Opal'

49

'Debbie's Carnation'

'Wildfire'

'Can Can'

'Yours Truly'

'Dr Burnside'

'Innovation'

Specimens from Eccleston Square, 2nd March, 1/2 life size

'Gauntlettii'

'Candissima Pink'

'Roza Harrison'

Specimens from Marwood Hill Gardens, N Devon
February 15th, 1/2 life size

Camellia japonica 'Yours Truly' at Eccleston Square

Camellia japonica **'California'**   Purchased from a Japanese sailor in 1888 by Harlem Cate at Redondo Pier, Los Angeles, California, USA. The original plant still grows in the grounds of Park Hill, Hollywood. Introduced commercially by E. H. Carter, California in 1942. Vigorous growth.

Camellia japonica **'Can Can'**   A sport of 'Lady Loch' found by Camellia Grove Nursery, Australia in 1961. Strong upright growth.

Camellia japonica **'Candidissima Pink'**   A sport of the white 'Candidissima' (1832), originated in England in 1966. Slow growth.

Camellia japonica **'Claudia Phelps'**   A sport of 'Duchess of Sunderland'. Published in *Fruitland Nursery Catalogue* in 1949.

Camellia × *williamsii* **'Debbie's Carnation'** (*C. saluenensis* × *C. japonica* 'Debutante')   Originated by Felix Jury Tikorangi, Taranaki, New Zealand. First flowered in 1971. Dense upright and spreading growth. Free-flowering.

Camellia japonica **'Debutante'** syn. 'Sarah C. Hastie'   First published in *House and Garden* in 1930. Slow growth. Sports: 'Gladys Marie' and 'Debutante Blush'.

Camellia japonica **'Destiny'**   A sport of 'Lady Clare'. Introduced to the USA by Domoto in 1955.

Camellia japonica **'Dr Burnside'**   A chance seedling, first blooming in 1959. Originated by Dr A. F. Burnside, Columbia, USA. Upright growth. Sport: 'Dr Burnside Variegated'.

Camellia japonica **'Gauntlettii'** syn. 'Lotus' and 'Sodekakushi'   Published in *Gauntlett Nursery Catalogue* in 1909. Originates from Kantô area of Japan. Slow growing, upright when young, forming an open-branched plant, scant foliage.

Camellia **'Innovation'** (a hybrid of *C. saluenensis* 'William's Lavender' × *C. reticuiata* 'Crimson Robe')   First bloomed in 1957. Originated by David L. Feathers, Lafayette. Open rapid growth.

Camellia **'Monticello'** (a hybrid of 'Sylvia May')   Originated by David L. Feathers, Lafayette, USA. Published in the *American Camellia Yearbook* in 1959. Upright rapid growth.

Camellia japonica **'Roza Harrison'**   Published in the *RHS Rhododendron and Camellia Yearbook* in 1969.

Camellia japonica **'Wildfire'**   Originated by Nuccio's Nurseries, Altadena, USA. First bloomed in 1955. Vigorous upright growth.

Camellia japonica **'Yours Truly'**   A sport of 'Lady Vansittart' syn. 'Lady Vansittart Pale' and 'Lady Vansittart Shell'. First published in *Fruitland Nursery Catalogue* in 1947–8. Medium bushy growth.

Camellia japonica 'Claudia Phelps'   *Camellia japonica* 'Destiny'

Camellia japonica 'Debutante'

Camellia 'Monticello'   *Camellia japonica* 'California'

'Centenary'

'The Czar'

'Cathy Becher'

'Alexander Hunter'

'Winter Cheer'

'Burwell's Primus'

'Margaret Crozier'

'Great Eastern'

'Prince Frederick William'

Specimens from Marwood Hill Gardens, N Devon, February 15th, 1/2 life size

Camellia japonica 'Apollo'

Old camellias along the drive at Quinta de Palheiro Ferreiro in Madeira

Camellia japonica 'Alexander Hunter'
Raised by Alexander Hunter at Camellia
Grove, Ashfield, NSW, Australia. First
published in *Hazlewood Nursery Catalogue* in
1941. Upright moderate growth.

Camellia japonica 'Apollo' There are a
confusing number of plants with this name;
this, the correctly named one, originates from
Italy. First published in *Rovelli Nursery
Catalogue* in 1874. Strong growth, free-
flowering.

Camellia 'Burwell's Primus' (*C. ×
williamsii*) Originated in New Zealand by
Henry Burwell. Published in the *International
Camellia Journal* in 1982.

Camellia japonica 'Cathy Becher'
Originated from a seedling of 'Constance' by
Mrs D. M. Andrew, Lindfield, NSW,
Australia. First flowered in 1954.

Camellia japonica 'Centenary'
Originated at Chandler's Nursery, Victoria,
Australia in 1860. Bushy upright growth.

Camellia japonica 'Great Eastern'
Probably a seedling of 'Chandleri' and may
have originated at Camden Park. An
Australian variety. First published in 1872 in
Shepherd and Co. Nursery Catalogue.

Camellia japonica 'G. W. Ellis'
Originated in the USA by Huested. First
published by the Pacific Camellia Society in
1946. Medium compact growth.

Camellia japonica 'Katie' Originated by
Nuccio's Nurseries, Altadena, California,
USA. First flowered in 1976. Upright dense,
rapid growth.

Camellia japonica 'Margaret Crozier'
A hybrid, 'Spencer's Pink' × 'Elegans',
originated by C. F. Cole, Canterbury, Victoria,
Australia in 1946. Vigorous upright growth.

Camellia japonica 'Great Eastern'

Camellia japonica 'G. W. Ellis'

**Camellia japonica 'Prince Frederick
William'** syn. 'Early Prince' Originated by
Sheather, Paramatta, NSW, Australia. First
published in *Sheather and Co. Nursery
Catalogue*, 1872. Vigorous upright growth.

Camellia japonica 'The Czar' Originated
by Neil Breslin, East Camberwell, Victoria,
Australia. First published in *Hodgins Nursery
Catalogue*, 1913. Erect compact growth.

Camellia japonica 'Winter Cheer'
Found as a seedling at the foot of 'Tricolor' at
Treseder's Nursery, Ashfield, NSW, Australia.
First published in *Hazlewood Nursery
Catalogue*, 1945. Compact bushy growth.

Camellia japonica 'Katie'

Camillia japonica 'William Bull'

Camellia japonica 'Bernice Perfection'

Camellia japonica 'C. M. Hovey'

Camellia japonica 'Eiraku'

Camellia japonica 'Marchioness of Exeter'

Camellia japonica 'Berenice Perfection'
Originated at Nuccio's Nurseries, Altadena, California, USA. First published in *Nuccio's Catalogue*, 1965. Vigorous upright growth.

Camellia japonica 'Bob Hope' Originated at Nuccio's Nurseries, Altadena, California, USA. First bloomed in 1969. Bushy compact upright growth.

Camellia japonica 'C. M. Hovey' syn. 'Colonel Firey', 'Firey King', 'William S. Hastie' Originated by C. M. Hovey, Massachusetts, USA and first published in Haggerston's *Magazine of Horticulture*, 1850. Robust vigorous growth, free-flowering.

Camellia japonica 'Conquistador'
Originated at Nuccio's Nurseries, Altadena, USA. First published in *Nuccio's Catalogue*, 1959. Vigorous upright compact growth.

Camellia japonica 'Eiraku' syn. 'Kuro Wabisuke' Originated in Ikeda City, Osaka Prefecture, Japan by Katayama, 1957. Slow upright growth.

Camellia japonica 'Fire Falls' A seedling of 'Professor Sargent'. Originated by Harvey Short, Ramona, California, USA. First published in the *American Camellia Yearbook*, 1953. Vigorous open upright growth.

Camellia 'Harold L. Paige' (*C. japonica* 'Adolphe Audusson' × *C. reticulata* 'Crimson Robe') Originated by Jack Osegueda, Oaklands, California, USA. First bloomed in 1969. Upright vigorous growth.

Camellia japonica 'Marchioness of Exeter' syn. 'Marquisa', 'Bright Pink' and 'Candy Pink' Raised by James Priaulx, Guernsey from a seed of 'Middlemists'. First published in *Floricultural Cabinet*, 1838. Free-flowering vigorous growth.

Camellia japonica 'Miss Charleston'
Originated by W. I. McGill, Adams Run, South Carolina, USA from a chance seedling which first flowered in 1958. Upright growth.

Camellia reticulata 'Miss Tulare'
Originated by M. W. Abramson, Tulare, USA. A chance seedling of 'Crimson Robe' which first bloomed in 1951. Upright rapid growth.

Camellia japonica 'Sultana' A sport of 'Julia Drayton'. Originated at McCaskill Gardens, Pasadena, USA. First published by the Southern California Camellia Society, 1956.

Camellia 'Virginia W. Cutter' A hybrid of *C. japonica* 'Bertha Harms' × *C. lutchuensis* 'Ackerman 6332'. Originated by Dr R. K. Cutter, Berkeley, USA. First published in the *American Camellia Yearbook*, 1973.

Camillia japonica 'William Bull'
Originated in Australia. First published in Shepherd and Co.'s nursery catalogue, 1878. Upright growth. Sports: 'Wrightii' and 'Kayel'.

'Bob Hope'

'Miss Charleston'

'Harold L. Paige'

'Miss Tulare'

'Conquistador'

'Fire Falls'

'Sultana'

'Virginia W. Cutter'

Specimens from Marwood Hill Gardens, N Devon, February 15th, 1/2 life size

Camellia reticulata 'Captain Rawes' in the conservatory wall at Chatsworth

***Camellia* 'California Sunset'** (*C. sasanqua* × *C. reticulata*)   Originated by Nuccio's Nurseries, Altadena, California, USA. First bloomed in 1981. Fairly open, upright rapid growth.

***Camellia reticulata* 'Captain Rawes'** syn. 'Guixia'   Of unknown parentage. Originated in China. Imported to England in the 1820s. Open growth, forming a small tree.

***Camellia* 'Francie L.'** (*C. saluenensis* 'Apple Blossom' × *C. reticulata* 'Buddha') Originated by Ed Marshall, Huntingdon Gardens, San Marino, California, USA and first published in *Nuccio's Catalogue*, 1964. Vigorous growth, free-flowering. Excellent for training against a wall. Sports: 'Francie L. Surprise' and 'Francie L. Variegated'.

***Camellia reticulata* 'K. O. Hester'** Originated by K. O. Hester, Laguna Hills, California, USA and released by Nuccio's Nurseries, Altadena. A chance seedling of *C. reticulata* 'Tali Queen'. First published in the *American Camellia Yearbook*, 1973. Medium upright growth. Sport: 'K. O. Hester Variegated'.

***Camellia* 'Interval'** (*C. japonica* × *C. reticulata*)   Raised by David Feathers, Lafayette, California, USA. First published in *Trehane Nursery Catalogue*, 1972–3. Compact bushy growth.

***Camellia reticulata* 'Nuccio's Ruby'** A chance seedling, originated at Nuccio's Nurseries, Altadena, USA, which first bloomed in 1973. Upright dense growth.

***Camellia* 'Otto Hopfer'** (*C. reticulata* 'Crimson Robe' × *C. japonica* 'Lotus') Originated by D. Hopfer, San Francisco, USA in 1970. Vigorous upright growth. Sport: 'Otto Hopfer Variegated'.

Camellia reticulata 'Nuccio's Ruby'

Camellia 'Francie L.'

Camellia 'Lila Naff'

***Camellia* × *williamsii* 'Angel Wings'**
(*C. japonica* 'Dr Tinsley' × *C. saluenensis*)
Originated by Kramer Bros. Nursery Upland,
California, USA and first published in its
catalogue in 1970. Medium loose growth.
Sport: 'Angel Wings Variegated'.

***Camellia* × *williamsii* 'Holland Orchid'**
(*C. saluenensis* × *C. japonica*)   First published
by the Southern California Camellia Society in
1964. Compact upright growth.

***Camellia* 'Lila Naff'**   A seedling of
C. reticulata 'Butterfly Wings', originated by
Mrs Ferol Zerkowsky, Slidell, Louisiana, USA.
First bloomed in 1958. Upright dense, rapid
growth. Free-flowering. Sport: 'Lila Naff
Variegated'.

Camellia 'Otto Hopfer'

Pale wild form of *Camellia japonica*

Camellia × *williamsii* 'Holland Orchid'

Camellia 'California Sunset'

Camellia × *williamsii* 'Angel Wings'

Camellia 'Interval'

Camellia reticulata 'K. O. Hester'

Camellia reticulata 'Liuye Yinhong' at Berkeley Botanic Garden, near San Francisco

Camellia reticulata 'Liuye Yinhong' syn. 'Willow Wand', 'Narrow-leaved Shot Silk' Widely grown in the Kunming district of Yunnan. First published by Fang in *Diannan Chahua Xiaozhi* in 1930 and cultivated in U.S.A. since 1948. Free-flowering, vigorous, upright growth. It will quite rapidly form a small tree.

Camellia 'Arbutus Gum' (*C. reticulata* × *C. japonica*) Originated by Frank Maitland, Sylmar, California, USA. A chance seedling which first bloomed in 1964. Rapid upright, fairly dense growth. There is also a variegated form.

Camellia reticulata 'Crimson Robe' syn. 'Dataohong', 'Daye taohong', 'Large Crimson', 'Great Peach Bloom' Originated in Yunnan, China. First published in *Diannan Chahua Xiaozhi* (an account of Diannan camellias) by Fang Shu-Mei, 1930. Vigorous spreading growth.

Camellia reticulata 'Houye Diechi' syn. 'Butterfly Wings' Cultivated in Kunming, Yunnan, China. A specimen in the Golden Temple, Kunming is 15m high and is probably over 300 years old. Slender open growth.

Camellia reticulata 'Mildred Pitlkin' Originated by Frank Maitland, San Fernando, California, USA. A chance seedling which first bloomed in 1968. Medium open upright growth.

Camellia 'Royalty' (*C. japonica* 'Clarise Carlton' × *C. reticulata* 'Chang's Temple') Originated by T. E. Croson, Simi, California, USA. First published in the *American Camellia Yearbook*, 1970. Medium upright growth.

Camellia 'Royalty'

Camellia reticulata 'Mildred Pitlkin'

Old japonica camellias in the park at Wuxi, China

Camellia reticulata 'Crimson Robe'

Camellia 'Arbutus Gum'

Camellia reticulata 'Houye Diechi'

Old camellias and palm trunks at Mount Edgcumbe, Cornwall

Camellia 'Carousel' A seedling of *Camellia* 'Sylvia May'. Originated by V. R. James, California, USA. First published by the Northern California Camellia Society in 1858.

Camellia 'Fragrant Pink' (*C. japonica* var. *rusticana* 'Yoshida' × *C. lutchuensis*) Originated by Dr William Ackerman, Glenn Dale, Maryland, USA. First bloomed in 1964. Fragrant. Upright spreading growtth.

Camellia 'High Fragrance' (*C. japonica* 'Bertha Harms' × *C.* 'Scentuous') Originated by J. R. Finlay, Whangarei, New Zealand. First bloomed in 1985. Strong fragrance. Vigorous open growth.

Camellia 'Night Rider' (*C.* 'Ruby Bells' × *C. japonica* 'Kuro Tsubaki') Originated by O. Blumhardt, New Zealand. First bloomed in 1980. Upright growth.

Camellia 'Osaraku' Originated in Kumamoto Prefecture, Japan. First mentioned by Taniguchi in *Chinka Kyôkan*, 1912. Upright growth.

Camellia 'Scentuous' Originated by F. R. Finlay, Whangarei, New Zealand. A seedling of *C. japonica* 'Tiffany' × *C. lutchuensis* which first bloomed in 1976. Upright fairly open growth. It has the *C. lutchuensis* fragrance.

Camellia 'Shunpû' (*C. saluenensis* × *C. lutchuensis*) Originated in Niigata Prefecture, Japan. Compact growth and strong fragrance.

Camellia 'Spring Mist' (*C. japonica* 'Snow Bells' × *C. lutchuensis*) Originated by A. E. Longley and C. R. Parks, Los Angeles State and County Arboretum, USA. First bloomed in 1965. Open spreading growth. Free-flowering.

Camellia 'Tarôkaja' syn. 'Pink Wabisuke', 'Wabiske', 'Judith' First mentioned by Jukyû Itô in *Honzô Hanamakie* in 1739. In the *Journal of Japanese Botany*, 1910, Makino described the 'Wabisuke' group as a species, but it is now thought to be a hybrid related to *japonica*. The original cross was probably between *C. japonica* and *C. sinensis*. A large and very old 'Tarôkaja', known as 'Wabisuke' (hence the use of the name for this cultivar) grows in the garden of the Buddhist Temple Tôji-in, in Sakyô-ku, Kyôto, Japan. 'Tarôkaja' is common on mainland China. Slow compact bushy growth.

Camellia 'Tiny Princess' (*C. japonica* 'Akebono' × *C. fraterna*) Originated by K. Sawada, Mobile, Alabama, USA. First bloomed in 1956. Free-flowering and fragrant. Slow growth.

Camellia 'Shunpû'

Camellia 'Tiny Princess'

Camellia 'Osaraku'

Camellia 'Carousel'

Camellia 'Tarôkaja'

Camellia 'Night Rider'

Camellia 'Spring Mist'

Camellia 'Fragrant Pink'

Camellia 'High Fragrance'

Camellia 'Scentuous'

A single *Camellia japonica* in Liu Yuan (the Lingering Garden) in Suzhou, E China

Camellia rusticana 'Otome'

Camellia reticulata seedling

Camellia 'Arcadia Variegated' (*C. reticulata* 'Mouchang' × *C. sasanqua* 'Bonanza') A virus-variegated form of 'Arcadia'. First published by the American Camellia Society, 1981. Upright rapid fairly dense growth.

Camellia reticulata 'Dayinhong' syn. 'Shot Silk' Originated in Kunming, Yunnan, China in the 1920s. Probably a seedling of the cultivar 'Liuye Yinhong' in the Black Dragon Pool Park. The original 'Dayinhong' plant is on the hillside behind the Golden Temple in Kunming.

Camellia 'Howard Asper' (*C. reticulata* 'Damanao' × *C. japonica* 'Coronation') syn. 'Howard Asper (Peony)' and 'Howard Asper

Pink' Originated by Howard Asper, Escondido, California, USA. First flowered in 1962. Upright spreading rapid growth.

Camellia rusticana 'Otome' syn. 'Pink Perfection', 'Pink Pearl' First mentioned by Ihei Itô in *Hyakka Tsubaki Nayose Irotsuki* in the late 18th century. Free-flowering bushy compact growth.

Camellia 'Trophy' A hybrid of *C. reticulata*, originated by Nuccio's Nurseries, Altadena, California, USA. First bloomed in 1976. Upright dense rapid and robust growth.

Camellia reticulata 'William Hertrich' A seedling of *C. reticulata* 'Damanao'. First

published in the *American Camellia Yearbook*, 1962. Vigorous bushy growth.

Camellia reticulata 'Wanduocha' syn. 'Ten-thousand-flower camellia' Originated near Lijiang, Yunnan in the courtyard of the Yufeng lamasery where the tree may still be seen. It is said to be five hundred years old, and has flowers both single and semi-double on the same tree, which has been trained on a trellis. A picture of the whole tree in its setting can be seen in our book *Shrubs*, page 57.

Camellia reticulata seedling A semi-double seedling photographed in the Descanso Gardens, La Canada, just outside Los Angeles, California.

Camellia reticulata 'Wanduocha' in the Yufeng lamasery, Lijiang, Yunnan

Camellia 'Howard Asper'

Camellia reticulata hybrid 'Trophy'

Camellia 'Arcadia Variegated'

Camellia reticulata 'Dayinhong'

Camellia reticulata 'William Hertrich'

Passiflora antioquiensis

Passiflora alata

Passiflora vitifolia

Passiflora mollissima

Specimens from John Vanderplank's National *Passiflora* collection, Clevedon, Avon, August 10th, 1/2 life size

There are about 450 species of passion flower, of which a selection is illustrated below, divided into subgenera given after the species name. Most species have edible fruits – those worth eating are noted in the text.

Cultivation

Passion flowers need well-drained soil as their roots are liable to rot if they become waterlogged, so a compost containing equal parts of sand or gravel, coarse peat and loam is more suitable than a peat-based compost. Many species (especially those members of subgenus *Tacsonia* which are used to this kind of climate in the wild) can stand short periods of quite sharp frost, but if prolonged frozen conditions are expected, it is worth burying an electric heating cable near the roots. Passion flowers thrive on regular feeding with a high potash liquid fertilizer during the growing season, and when growing well they need feeding frequently. As they are vigorous plants, they are likely to become tangled with dead growth in the centre and may need to be pruned annually once they are established, cutting unwanted branches back to the base.

Propagation

Passion flowers are usually easily rooted from tip cuttings which should be taken in early spring. They can also be grown from seed, although this is not always so easy. Use fresh seed and soak before sowing. Germination may be slow, but can be speeded up by keeping the temperature at 20°C for 16 hours a day and then 30°C for the remaining 8 hours. For further details see John Vanderplank's excellent book *Passion Flowers*.

Passiflora alata Dryand. (*Passiflora*)
A rampant woody climber with dark brownish-red flowers, native of Brazil but now found throughout the tropics, flowering through the year, mainly in summer in cultivation. Stems to 10m or more, 4-angled and winged. Leaves simple, unlobed, ovate, 8–15cm long. Flowers fragrant, 10–12cm across; sepals and petals dark brownish-crimson inside; outer corona filaments 4cm long, wavy, banded purple, red and white. Fruit edible, 10–15cm long, orange or yellow when ripe. Close to *P. quadrangularis* which has larger leaves, outer corona filaments 6cm long and huge fruits to 30cm long. 'Ruby Glow' (*not illustrated*) is a good clone, with larger fragrant flowers to 15cm across and tolerates cooler conditions. Min. 2°C.

Passiflora antioquiensis Karst. (*Granadillastrum*) A slender woody climber to 5m with pinkish-red flowers, native of the mountains of Columbia at up to 2000–3000m, flowering mainly in summer in cultivation. Stems to 5m. Leaves 3-lobed, sometimes unlobed with fine sharp teeth, to 15cm long, 8cm wide. Solitary flowers pendent, up to 14cm across; sepals and petals 5–6.5cm long, 1.5–2.5cm wide, bright rose-red, sometimes pink inside; outer corona filaments only 2mm long, purple tipped with white. Fruit edible, like a small banana, yellow when ripe. Min. −3°C for short periods, as long as the root is protected. Has survived outside in the Isles of Scilly and is cultivated for its fruit in Australia and New Zealand.

Passiflora mollissima (HBK.) Bailey (*Tacsonia*) A rampant climber to 10m or more with pale pink flowers, native of the Andes from W Venezuela and E Columbia to SE Peru and W Bolivia at 2000–3200m,

Passiflora quadrangularis

Passiflora tripartita

Passiflora mollissima covering a tree near Anguangeo, Mexico

flowering in summer–autumn in cultivation. Grown for its fruit and naturalized elsewhere in the tropics. Stems to 10m or more. Leaves 3-lobed with fine sharp teeth, to 12.5cm long, 15cm wide, softly hairy. Flowers pendent, 6–9cm across, with a narrow green pink-tinged calyx tube up to 8cm long; sepals and petals 2.5–3.5cm long, 1–1.5cm wide, pale pink, sometimes coral-pink inside; outer corona filaments reduced to pinkish warts. Fruit 7–10cm long, edible, like a small banana, yellow and downy when ripe. Easily grown and increased by seed or cuttings; requires cool, humid conditions in summer. Min. −3°C for short periods, as long as the root is protected.

Passiflora quadrangularis L. syn. *P. macrocarpa* Mast. (*Passiflora*) A huge woody climber with dark crimson flowers, native of Central America and the West Indies, but now found throughout the tropics, at up to 2500m, flowering throughout the year, mainly in summer in cultivation. Stems to 15m or more, 4-angled and broadly winged. Leaves simple, unlobed, broadly ovate, 10–25cm long, 8–15cm wide. Flowers pendent, 12cm across; sepals and petals pale red to deep brick red inside; outer corona filaments 6cm long, wavy, banded purple and white towards the base and mottled on the upper half. Fruit edible, the largest of any passion flower, to 30cm long, greenish-orange when ripe. (Fruit is rarely

produced in greenhouse-grown plants.) Min. 10°C or lower for short periods, if kept dry.

Passiflora tripartita Breit. A species recently collected in cool mountain forest in N Ecuador by Jim Archibald and at present rare in cultivation. Closely related to *P. mollissima*.

Passiflora vitifolia HBK. syn. *P. sanguinea* Smith (*Distephana*) A vigorous woody climber with bright scarlet upright flowers, native of Nicaragua, Costa Rica, Columbia, Ecuador and Peru, growing in forest margins and open woodland at up to 900m, widely cultivated elsewhere in the tropics, flowering in summer–autumn in cultivation. Stems tomentose, to 15m or more. Leaves dark green, broadly 3-lobed with shallow teeth, to 15cm long and 18cm wide, with fine brown hairs beneath. Flowers fragrant, 12.5–19cm across, with a short calyx tube. Sepals scarlet, 6–8cm long, 1–2cm wide; petals scarlet 4–6mm long, 8–15mm wide, narrowly lanceolate. Outer corona filaments scarlet or yellow, 1.2–2cm long, inner filaments shorter, white, pink or reddish at the base. Fruit ovoid, to 6cm long, dark green, mottled with white, edible. Min. 10°C. 'Scarlet Flame' (*not illustrated*) is a vigorous clone with large scarlet flowers up to 15cm across; particularly popular in the USA where it was raised. Min. 8°C.

Passiflora 'Mauvis Mastics'

Passiflora 'Incense'

Passiflora × allardii Lynch   A vigorous climber with pale mauve and greenish flowers appearing mainly in summer and autumn, raised by E. J. Allard at the University Botanic Garden, Cambridge around 1900, by crossing *P. caerulea* 'Constance Elliott' with *P. quadrangularis.* Stems to 5m. Leaves 3-lobed for much of their length, up to 16cm long and wide. Flowers 7–9cm across, well scented. Sepals white edged with mauve; petals mauve-pink. Corona filaments the same length as the petals, outer two rings tipped white, then banded white and violet, purple-red at base. Inner series purple-red. Fruit orange when ripe. Min. −3°C. Increase by cuttings.

***Passiflora* 'Amethyst'** syn. *P. amethystina* Mikan., *P. onychina* Lindl., *P. violacea* Vell., *P.* 'Lavender Lady', *P.* 'Star of Mikan'   A very confusing species or hybrid, native of eastern Brazil; it is common in cultivation throughout Britain and Europe where it is grown commercially as a pot plant, and in the USA. John Vanderplank thinks that the plant we call 'Amethyst' (itself known as *P. amethystina* in the UK and *P. violacea* in the rest of Europe) probably originated from plants of *P. onychina* imported during the late 19th or early 20th century. In any case it is very variable with flower colour depending to a large extent on growing conditions. Stems to 3m. Leaves 3-lobed, 6–8cm long, 10–12cm wide. Flowers purple or blue, to 11cm across; blooms of plants grown under glass are lighter in colour than those grown outside. Sepals purple or purple-blue inside, 1–1.5cm long; petals the same colour but slightly larger. Corona filaments in five rows, purple, with single band of white. Fruit 5–6cm long, orange when ripe. Will tolerate a small amount of frost in well-drained soils. Min. −2° C.

Passiflora × alato-caerulea Lindley syn. *P. belotii* Pépin., *P. × pfordtii* Mast., *P.* 'Empress Eugenie', *P.* 'Kaiserin Eugenia'   This hybrid of *P. alata* and *P. caerulea* was raised by William Masters of Canterbury, Kent, but it is better known and widely grown in the USA., and is also cultivated in some Mediterranean areas, Tenerife, Hawaii and Australia. The fragrant flowers are freely produced during summer and autumn. Stems to 4m, 4- or 5-winged. Leaves large, glabrous, 3-lobed to 14cm long. Flowers fragrant, to

13cm across. Sepals to 5cm long, white on inner surface; petals 5cm long, 2.5cm wide, white speckled pinkish-purple on inner side. Corona filaments in 5 series, outer two rings 2.5 cm long, banded white and purple; inner rows very short, deep purple. No fruit. Min. −5°C, but will sprout from the root in colder areas. Increase by cuttings.

Passiflora caerulea L. (*Passiflora*)   One of the best known and most widely cultivated species (often called the Blue Passion Flower), this vigorous climber is a native of South America, from east-central Brazil to Argentina, flowering there throughout the year. Stems to 10m. Leaves often palmate, but can be 5–7 lobed, 10–16cm across. Flowers solitary, to 10cm across, slightly fragrant. Sepals to 3.5cm long, 1.5cm wide, white; petals to 4cm long, 1.5cm wide, white inside and out. Corona filaments arranged in 4 rows, the outer ones up to 2cm long, purple at the base, blue at the top, with a white band in the middle. Inner series of filaments very short, thread-like, white, with purple tips. Herklots, in his fascinating book *Flowering Tropical Climbers,* notes that the flowers are open all night, starting to close gradually in the morning, and that the best time to see them is between 7.30 and 8am. Fruit ovoid, bright orange when ripe, with red seeds, edible, but rather insipid, tasting slightly of blackberries. Easily grown indoors or out, but prefers a well-drained soil and a sheltered position. One of the hardiest passion flowers, this has been known to survive temperatures as low as −15°C for short periods; in such cold conditions the plant may lose all its top growth, but will rejuvenate from the base. It was introduced into Britain in 1609 and is hardy there and in the milder parts of Europe and the USA, flowering in summer. It makes an excellent free-flowering plant for the conservatory.

***Passiflora caerulea* 'Constance Elliott'**
This variety of *P. caerulea* was raised by Lucombe and Pince in Exeter, Devon and was awarded a First Class Certificate by the RHS in 1884. It will survive outside in mild areas if given the protection of a wall but is best kept frost-free. It has fragrant creamy-white flowers.

***Passiflora* 'Incense'**   A new American cultivar, a hybrid between *P. incarnata* and *P. cincinnata,* raised at the Subtropical Horticulture Research Station in Florida. This variety is very vigorous and blooms prolifically with fragrant deep purple flowers produced throughout summer and autumn. Leaves 5-lobed, deeply divided to 20cm long and wide. Flowers fragrant, to 13 cm across, sepals and petals deep mauve inside to 4cm long. Corona filaments in several rows: the outer two series to 4cm long, striped white and violet at the base, shading to mauve spotted with white at the tips; inner series shorter, mauve. Fruit edible, egg-shaped, light olive green when ripe. Can survive temperatures as low as −8°C for short periods if the root is protected, although the top growth will die off; new shoots will appear from the roots during the summer. 'Incense' is particularly vulnerable to a die-back virus and if this manifests itself all affected shoots, and in severe cases the entire plant, should be burnt.

***Passiflora* 'Mauvis Mastics'** syn. 'Mavis Massicks'   A cultivar of *P. caerulea × P. racemosa,* often included under *P. violacea.* Leaves 3–5-lobed, deeply divided. Sepals and petals deep maroon, corona filaments white, purple at base.

Passiflora caerulea 'Constance Elliott' at John Vanderplank's collection

Passiflora 'Mauvis Mastics'

Passiflora 'Amethyst'

Passiflora caerulea

Passiflora × allardii

Passiflora × alato-caerulea

Passiflora 'Incense'

Specimens from John Vanderplank's National *Passiflora* collection, Clevedon, Avon, August 10th, 1/2 life size

Passiflora racemosa at the Royal Botanic Garden, Edinburgh

Passiflora racemosa

Passiflora × exoniensis

Passiflora edulis Sims (*Passiflora*) Passion Fruit   Native of Brazil, Paraguay and N Argentina, where it flowers in summer. Naturalized in Malawi and widely cultivated for its fruit throughout the tropics and subtropics. Stems rounded, to 8m. Leaves 3-lobed, deeply toothed, light yellow green, to 10cm wide, 20cm long. Flowers to 8cm across; sepals to 3cm long, 1cm wide, white on the inside. Petals to 3cm long, 7mm wide, white. Corona filaments in 4 or 5 ranks, the two outer series longer, white, purple at the base. Fruit ovoid or globose, 5–6cm long, about 5cm wide, deep purple and fragrant when ripe; delicious when used to make drinks and sorbets. There is a yellow-fruited form, *flavicarpa*, which is found naturally in Brazil, and this, together with many other named varieties and hybrids of the two forms, is grown commercially. Some of these forms can be grown for ornamental use also. Min. −3°C or less for short periods; will tolerate slight frost.

Passiflora × exoniensis hort. ex Bailey A vigorous climber with pale scarlet hanging flowers, produced mainly in summer and autumn, raised by Messrs Veitch in Exeter, England in 1870, by crossing *P. antioquiensis* with *P. mollissima*. Stems to 5m or more. Leaves finely hairy, narrowly 3-lobed with sharp teeth, up to 10cm long, 12cm wide. Flowers 10–12.5cm across, bright pink or rose-red, with a calyx tube 6.5cm long. Sepals and petals ovate-lanceolate. Corona filaments very small, white. Fruit is banana-shaped, yellow when ripe, of very good flavour. Min. −3°C or less for short periods. This lovely hybrid can be grown outside in warm parts of the British Isles, in the Mediterranean and in much of coastal California.

Passiflora jamesonii (Mast.) Bailey (*Tacsonia*)   A rare species from the mountains of Peru and Ecuador, at up to 4000m. Stems glabrous, angular. Leaves deeply 3-lobed, shiny, spiny-toothed, to 8cm long, 11cm across. Flowers deep rose-pink, up to 11cm across. Sepals deep pink, to 5cm long, 2cm across; petals the same colour as sepals, slightly shorter. Corona filaments warty, purple. Fruit oval, green when ripe. Min. temperatures unknown, but should be quite hardy in view of its native habitat.

Passiflora × kewensis Nicholson A variable hybrid, probably between *P. caerulea* and *P. raddeana*, named after the Royal Botanic Gardens, Kew. A vigorous and free-flowering climber. Stems 3m. Flowers up to 9cm wide. Sepals pink or purple; petals red or pink. Corona filaments white or violet flecked white. Min. −5°C. Propagate by cuttings.

Passiflora mixta × manicata   This hybrid, often sold as *P. manicata*, grows in southern Europe and is common in the Mediterranean area where it flowers nearly all year round. It requires frost-free conditions.

Passiflora platyloba Killip (*Passiflora*) This handsome species is native of Central and South America, from Guatemala to Costa Rica, growing at or near sea level. Stem stout. Leaves 3-lobed, with a very broad middle lobe,

Passiflora jamesonii in the Santa Cruz Botanic Garden, California

to 14cm long, 18cm wide. Distinctive large green ovate bracts completely envelope the flower, which is small, fragrant, purple and white, to 5cm across. Sepals to 2cm long and 8mm wide, keeled; petals linear-lanceolate, mauve, to 1.7 cm long, 5mm wide. Corona filaments in several series: outer rank to 8mm long; second series wider, longer, banded white and purple; inner series all minute. Fruit to 3.5cm across, edible. Suitable for the frost-free or heated conservatory. Min. 10°C. It is a popular plant for the conservatory and warm gardens in the USA and is not yet common in Britain or Europe, although it deserves to be, as it flowers freely from spring to late summer.

Passiflora racemosa Brotero (*Calopathanthus*) syn. *P. princeps* Lodd.   A very beautiful evergreen vine, with hanging racemes of red flowers, native of Brazil in the state of Rio de Janeiro, flowering most of the summer and autumn. Stems slender, to 10m or more outside in warm countries but nearer to 5m under glass. Leaves glossy, ovate, sometimes lobed on one or both sides to below the middle, to about 9cm long and wide; wavy edged. Flowers red, usually borne in pairs in pendulous terminal racemes, 30cm or more long. Sepals bright red, to 4cm long, 1cm wide; petals similar but smaller. Corona filaments in three series: outer rank purple with white tips; inner shorter. Fruit narrowly ovoid to 7cm long and 3cm across, pale green when ripe. Min. 7°C for short periods. Introduced into cultivation in 1815 and much used in hybridizing. RHS Award of Garden Merit as a plant requiring unheated glass.

Passiflora mixta × manicata

Passiflora × kewensis

Passiflora edulis

Passiflora platyloba

Passiflora capsularis

Passiflora foetida

Passiflora citrina

Passiflora foetida pink form

Passiflora rubra

Passiflora × adularia
'Colour of Moonstone'

Passiflora gracilis

Specimens from John Vanderplank's National *Passiflora* collection, Clevedon, Avon, August 10th, 1/2 life size

Passiflora incarnata

Passiflora foetida f. *hirsuta* unripe fruits

Passiflora subpeltata in India

***Passiflora × adularia* 'Colour of Moonstone'** A new hybrid, raised by John Vanderplank in about 1994 with small starry peach-coloured flowers with a deeper centre, freely produced almost throughout the year. The leaves are deeply veined. Plant small-growing, only 120–180cm tall. Min. 5°C for short periods. Parentage: *P. citrina × P. sanguinolenta* 'Colour of Blood'.

***Passiflora capsularis* L.** (*Plectostemma*) Native of Nicaragua, C Brazil and Paraguay, up to about 1900m. Flowers during the summer months in the conservatory. Stems vining, 3–5 angled, to 4m. Leaves deep green, 2-lobed, to 7cm long, 10cm wide, lanceolate. Flowers greenish-white or pale yellow to 6cm across. Sepals linear-lanceolate, green-white, to 3cm long; petals to 1.5cm long, 0.5cm wide, cream, narrow. Corona filaments in 1 or 2 series, greenish-white or yellow green. Fruit to 6cm long, 2cm wide, ellipsoid, brownish-red when ripe. Often confused with *P. rubra* (*see below*). Min. −3°C. Will tolerate slight frost for short periods.

***Passiflora citrina* MacDougal** (*Plectostemma*) A newly introduced species, found in the pine-covered hills of central western Honduras and E Guatemala by John MacDougal. The small vine produces little yellow flowers, an unusual colour in the passion flowers. Stem pubescent. Leaves 2- or 3-lobed, deep green, velvety, to 8cm long. Flowers bright yellow or greenish-yellow, to 6.5cm across. Sepals oblong lanceolate, to 3cm long, yellow inside; petals same shape, size and colour as sepals. Corona filaments in a single series, to 1.5cm long, pale yellow with darker yellow tips. Fruit ellipsoid or obovoid, to 3.5cm long, red when ripe. Min. −3°C, perhaps.

***Passiflora foetida* L.** (*Dysosmia*) A very variable species, with numerous synonyms and over 50 named varieties, native of South and Central America and the West Indies, and naturalized in many tropical countries where it is often considered a weed. There are, generally speaking, two groups: those with white or pale pink flowers and yellow fruits; and those with pink, purple or blue flowers and pinkish-red fruit. This unpleasant-smelling but beautiful vine is extremely vigorous and easy to grow outside in tropical and subtropical areas and will also do well under glass, flowering during summer and autumn. Stems to 2.5m, hairy. Leaves 3–5-lobed, usually cordate at the base. Flowers 2–5cm wide, white to purplish, surrounded by feathery bracts. Sepals ovate to ovate-oblong to ovate-lanceolate, to 2.5cm; petals similar to the sepals but usually shorter. Corona filaments in several series, the outer two about 1cm long, the others much shorter. Fruit edible, yellow, pink or red when ripe, bracts persistant. The yellow-fruited varieties are self-pollinating and produce small fruits quite freely. Easy to grow. Min. 5°C or lower for short periods. Propagate by cuttings, or seed if you want a surprise!

Passiflora foetida* L. f. *hirsuta A form from the Amazon, with large 3-lobed leaves, white flowers and yellow, edible fruit.

***Passiflora gracilis* Jacq. ex Link** (*Plectostemma*) A climbing annual with very small greenish flowers, native of S Florida to Brazil and Costa Rica, flowering throughout the summer. Stems to 2m; leaves with three lobes, the middle the smallest. Flowers to 2cm across, with 4 sepals and no petals. Corona filaments in 2 series, white and mauve at the base. Fruit ripening bright red, 2.5cm long. An easily grown annual, a curiosity for a warm place outside or in a conservatory. Min. −3°C.

***Passiflora incarnata* L.** (*Passiflora*) Commonly known as May Pops because of the sound of the ripe fruit falling to the ground, this is an herbaceous species, native of the eastern part of North America, as far north as S Ohio and West Virginia and therefore one of the hardiest of all passion flowers, flowering throughout summer and early autumn. Stems vining, to 10m. Leaves 3-lobed, to 15cm long, 12cm wide. Flowers 6–9cm across, variable in colour, but usually white, pinkish or pale lilac, very fragrant. Sepals to 3cm long; petals shorter than sepals. Corona filaments in several series, outer rank to 2cm long, inner rank much shorter. Fruit ovoid, to 6cm long; sweet, edible, greenish-yellow when ripe. A good plant for the unheated conservatory, it can also be grown outside in Britain, but considerable care is needed as it requires a warm, sheltered position and a very well-drained soil to avoid waterlogging. It is reputed to be able to survive temperatures as low as −16°C, though it dies back to the ground at the onset of cold weather. Normal recommended min. −7°C.

***Passiflora rubra* L.** (*Plectostemma*) A vigorous climber, native of tropical South America and the West Indies. Can be grown outside in the milder parts of Britain if given a sheltered position, but the roots must be completely protected from frost. Flowers prolifically during summer and autumn in Britain and will also set fruit here. Stems to 4m, 3–5 angled. Leaves 2- or 3-lobed, to 10cm long, downy, light green, often variegated. Flowers to 5cm across. Sepals to 3cm long, white or pale yellow inside; petals same colour as sepals, to 1.5cm long. Corona filaments in 1 or 2 series, outer rank to 1cm long, pink or mauve towards the base, shading to white or yellow at the tip. Fruit variable in shape, often ovoid, pink or red, to 5cm long. Min. 0°C.

***Passiflora subpeltata* Ortega** syn. *P. alba* Link & Otto (*Passiflora*) A well-known species with many other synonyms, this vigorous climber is native of Mexico, Colombia and Venezuela, at up to 2800m and is also naturalized in the West Indies, Hawaii, Australia and Malaysia. It does well under glass, flowering freely throughout the summer. Stems slender, glabrous, to about 3m. Leaves 3-lobed to the middle, to 9cm long, 12cm wide. Flowers pure white, to 5cm across. Sepals oblong, white inside; petals white, slightly shorter than sepals. Corona filaments in 5 series, all white, outer 2 rings to 2.5 cm long, others shorter. Fruit ovoid, white, to 6cm long with an unpleasant smell. Easy to propagate from seed or cuttings and easily grown, even on a light, warm windowsill. Min. 0°C

Passiflora 'Sunburst'

Passiflora nelsonii at John Vanderplank's

Passiflora bryonioides at La Mortola

Passiflora coriacea

Passiflora bryonioides HBK (*Plectostemma*)
syn. *P. inamoena* A. Gray   Native of Arizona
and Mexico, from sea level to 1700m, this very
variable species is frequently confused with
P. morifolia, from which it differs chiefly in its
yellow fruit (purple in *P. morifolia*). Stems
stout, angular. Leaves to 9cm wide, 7cm long,
3-lobed. Flowers greenish-yellow or white and

lilac, to 3cm across (may be more when grown
in good soil). Sepals greenish-yellow or
greenish-white, to 1.3cm long and 5mm wide;
petals white, shorter and narrower than sepals.
Corona filaments in single row, filiform, to
8mm long, white tinged mauve at base. Fruit
ovoid, to 3.5cm long, 2.5cm wide, pale yellow
when ripe. Easy to propagate from seed or
cuttings. Min. −3°C.

Passiflora coriacea Juss. (*Plectostemma*)
A vigorous vine with exceptionally large
variegated leaves, native of much of South
America from N Peru, N Bolivia and Guyana
to Mexico, at up to 2000m. The small flowers
are freely produced throughout the year. Stems

to 6m. Leaves medium green, mottled with
pale yellowish-green; usually 2–3-lobed, to
7cm wide, 30cm long. Flowers to 3.5cm
across, solitary or in pairs in the leaf axils and
in terminal racemes to 6cm. Sepals yellowish-
green, to 1.5cm long; there are no petals.
Corona filaments in 2 series, both yellow,
outer rank to 8mm long, inner to 5mm long.
Fruit globose, deep blue to 2cm across. Easy
to grow and remarkably free from pests and
diseases. Propagate from seed or cuttings.
Min. 5°C for short periods.

Passiflora holosericea L. (*Plectostemma*)
A tall vine found in Central and South
America from S Mexico to Colombia,
Venezuela and Cuba at up to 700m, flowering
in summer in cultivation. Stems cylindrical,
corky below. Leaves 3-lobed, softly tomentose,
to 7.5cm wide, 10cm long. Flowers fragrant,
white, yellow or orange, to 4cm across, in
axillary double clusters of 2–4. Sepals to 5mm
wide, 1.5cm long, white spotted with pink on
the inside; petals the same size, white. Corona
filaments in 2 ranks, outer to 8mm long,
purple at base, yellow or orange at tip; inner
capillary to 5mm long. Fruit globose, to 1.5cm
across. Suitable for the large heated
conservatory. Propagate by seed or cuttings.
Min. 10°C.

Passiflora morifolia Mast. (*Plectostemma*)
A vigorous vine, native throughout much of
South America from Argentina to Colombia,
at up to 2800m; also naturalized in Java and
Malaysia. Flowers produced throughout the
year both in the wild and in the well-heated
greenhouse. Stem 4-angled. Leaves 3-lobed,
occasionally 5-lobed, to 7cm long, 9cm wide.
Flowers white and mauve, to 3cm across.
Sepals sometimes green, sometimes white
mottled with purple, to 5mm wide, 1.2cm
long; petals white, to 4mm long, 1cm across.
Corona filaments in a single row, filiform,
mauve at base. Fruit to 4cm long, 2.5cm wide,
oblong, deep rich purple, with bright orange
pith; said to be good to eat, but we have not
tried it. Frequently cultivated as a food plant
for heliconiine butterflies. Easy to propagate
from seeds or cuttings. Min. 0°C.

Passiflora nelsonii Mast. & Rose (*Passiflora*)
A glabrous stout climber with ovate leaves and
mauve and white flowers, native of S Mexico
in Chiapas and N Guatamala, growing in
forests at 1300–1600m, flowering in summer.
Leaves to 12cm long, 9cm wide, rounded at
the base, with sessile, saucer-shaped glands on
the petiole. Bracts broadly ovate, 5–6cm long.
Flowers 5–7cm across. Close to *P. ligularis*.
Suitable for the warm conservatory. Min. 0°C,
but is also said to dislike high temperatures.

Passiflora standleyi Killip   Native of Costa
Rica, leaves narrow, 2-lobed with blue and
white flowers to 4cm across.

Passiflora 'Sunburst'   Recently raised by
Patrick Worley and introduced in 1983, this
cultivar is a cross between *P. gilbertiana* and *P.
jorullensis*. The attractive but rather unpleasant-
smelling small flowers are produced
prolifically. Stem slender. Leaves medium
green, variegated along the veins. Flowers
bright orange, to 2.5cm across. Sepals
greenish-yellow; no petals. Corona filaments in
single rank, bright orange, to 1cm long. Fruit
unknown as yet. Easy to propagate by cuttings.
Min. 5°C, perhaps.

Passiflora
'Sunburst'

Passiflora standleyi

Passiflora morifolia

Passiflora coriacea

Passiflora holosericea

Specimens from John Vanderplank's National *Passiflora* collection, Clevedon, Avon, August 10th, 1/2 life size

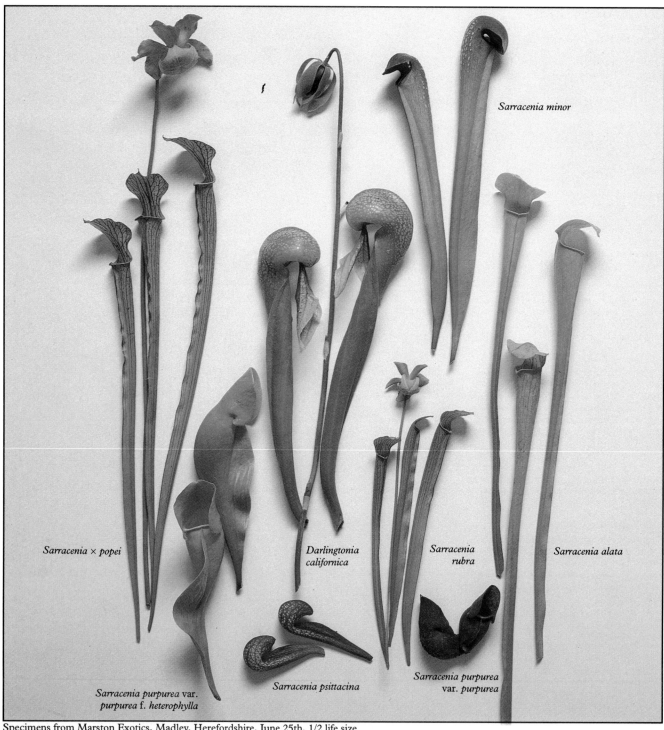

Sarracenia minor

Sarracenia × popei

Darlingtonia californica

Sarracenia rubra

Sarracenia alata

Sarracenia purpurea var. purpurea f. heterophylla

Sarracenia psittacina

Sarracenia purpurea var. purpurea

Specimens from Marston Exotics, Madley, Herefordshire, June 25th, 1/2 life size

Sarracenia flava var flava

Sarracenia purpurea flower

All the members of the *Sarracenia* family are carnivorous, with leaves modified into pitchers to catch insects. There are 3 genera. *Heliamphora*, with 2 species, is found in the mountains of Venezuela and on Mt Roraima in Guyana, and requires very humid tropical conditions, with regular misting. *Darlingtonia*, with one species is confined to California. *Sarracenia*, with 8 species, is found throughout eastern North America. All grow wild in wet, acid bogs and pine barrens, and require continually wet conditions with a loose compost of sphagnum peat, live sphagnum and coarse acid sand. They can be grown successfully in a plastic basin or in a pot kept standing in a deep saucer of water. Flowers are produced in spring followed by the new pitchers.

Darlingtonia californica Torr.
(*Sarraceniaceae*) A tufted perennial with
hooded pitchers and nodding flowers, native
of California from Plumas and Nevada Co.,
north to Oregon, growing in open bogs in
coniferous forest at 100–1800m, flowering in
April–June. Pitchers to 60cm, usually about
30cm, with a hooded mouth from which hang
two spreading lobes. The upper part of the
hood has transparent patches. Flower stems
longer than the leaves, to 120cm; sepals
4–6cm; petals dark purple, 2–4cm long.
Min. −10°C for short periods, but normally
grown under glass.

Sarracenia alata Alph. Wood Plant with
tall slender, light green pitchers with maroon
veins inside the hood and creamy-yellow
flowers, native of Alabama through to Texas,
growing in pine barrens and bogs, flowering in
April–May. Pitchers to 75cm; flower stems
about 30cm. Min. −10°C.

Sarracenia × catesbyi Elliott A hybrid
between *S. flava* and *S. purpurea* var. *venosa*,
found in the wild where the parents grow
together. Pitchers to 75cm, with a well-veined
lid. Flowers large, brick-red. Min. −10°C.

Sarracenia flava L. var. ***flava*** Plant with
tall yellow pitchers and yellow-green flowers,
native of Florida through to Alabama and
north to SE Virginia, growing in pine barrens
and bogs, flowering in April–May. Pitchers to
1m, sometimes veined inside; flower stems
about 30cm; flowers 10cm across, with long
drooping yellow petals. Short, flat curved
leaves are formed in winter. Min. −10°C.

Sarracenia flava 'Red Burgundy' A form
of *S. flava* with reddish or claret-coloured
pitchers.

Sarracenia minor Walter A medium-sized
plant with narrow hooded pitchers and deep
yellow flowers, native of South Carolina
through to Florida, growing in wet sphagnum
bogs. Pitchers with translucent patches on
the back, up to 25cm tall, or to 120cm in a
large form from the Okefenokee Swamp in
S Georgia. Min. −5°C.

Sarracenia leucophylla Raf. Plant with
tall, white red-veined pitchers and ruby-red
flowers, native of Florida, Georgia and N
Missouri, growing in pine barrens and bogs,
flowering in April–May. Pitchers to 1.2m,
heavily veined inside. Flowers 10cm across,
with long drooping red-purple petals. A
second crop of pitchers is sometimes formed
in autumn. This is possibly the most exciting
of all the species, noted for the striking and
unusual colour of its leaves. Min. −5°C.

Sarracenia × popei hort. A hybrid between
S. flava and *S. alata*, with rather small (about
30cm), greenish-yellow pitchers, veined
maroon. Flowers freely produced, buff
coloured, scented. Min. −5°C.

Sarracenia psittacina Michx. A low
evergreen plant with spreading, almost
prostrate pitchers and red-purple flowers,
native of Georgia, Florida and Louisiana,
growing in very wet bogs and often submerged
in wet weather. Pitchers to 15cm long, whitish,
veined reddish above, with translucent
patches. Flower stems to 30cm. Min. −3°C.

Sarracenia purpurea L. var. ***purpurea***
Plant with short red to purple pitchers and

deep red-purple flowers, native of NE North
America from Newfoundland and Labrador,
west to Saskatchewan, south to Maryland and
Ohio, and naturalized in C Ireland near
Tullamore, and in W Switzerland, growing in
sphagnum bogs, flowering in April–May.
Pitchers to 20cm, usually glabrous outside,
with narrow wings; flower stems about
30cm, with drooping reddish-purple petals.
Min. −20°C. Forma **heterophylla** (Eat.)
Fern. A rare variant in the wild, differs in its
green leaves and yellow flowers.

Sarracenia purpurea L. var. ***venosa*** (Raf.)
Fern. Differs from var. *purpurea* in having
shorter and fatter pitchers, hairy on the outside
and with the edges of the hood extending
beyond the broad wings of the pitcher. It is
found south of var. *purpurea*, from Florida to
Louisiana, north to New Jersey and Tennessee,
where it flowers in May–June. Min. −10°C.

Sarracenia rubra Walt. A medium-sized
plant with reddish veined pitchers and deep
red scented flowers, native of the Carolinas
and Georgia. Pitchers to 45cm. Stems to
25cm, with flowers to 4.5cm across. Subsp.
alabamensis has taller, green pitchers with little
or no red veining. Subsp. *jonesii* has taller
pichers to 60cm with a wider lid. Min. −5°C.

Sarracenia flava 'Red Burgundy'

Sarracenia leucophylla

Sarracenia flava var *flava*

Sarracenia × catesbyi

Sarracenia flava var *flava*

Sarracenia purpurea var. *venosa*

From Marston Exotics, 1/2 life size

Sarracenia purpurea wild in Maine

75

Drosophyllum lusitanicum from seed collected near Ronda S Spain

Drosera aliciae in the Cape

Drosera nitidula at Marston Exotics

Drosera pulchella × nitidula

The Sundew family, *Droseraceae,* is carnivorous. *Drosera,* the main genus has around 125 species, the other genera are monotypic. *Drosera* and *Drosophyllum* catch and digest small insects with very conspicuous, sticky glandular hairs on the leaves, which often curl over and enclose their victim. In *Dionaea,* the Venus' Fly Trap, however, the leaf hairs are modified into stiff bristles which line the rim of the trap; it springs shut when the 3 or 4 trigger hairs in the middle of the trap are touched. The fourth genus in the family is the rare, minute floating aquatic *Aldovandra,* which catches swimming animals in its tiny traps. It is found from C Europe to SE Asia and N Australia.

Drosera aliciae Raym. Hamet. (*Droseraceae*) A dwarf perennial with a rosette of reddish spathulate leaves and slender stems with pink to magenta flowers, native of South Africa in the Cape from near Clanwilliam to Port Elizabeth, growing in wet peaty sandy places, flowering in November–January (summer). Rosettes about 5cm across; leaves covered almost to the base with glandular hairs. Stem to about 45cm; flowers 1.3cm across. Min. −3°C.

Dionaea muscipula Ellis (*Droseraceae*) **Venus' Fly Trap** A dwarf perennial with a rosette of traps and branched stems with white flowers, native of North America in North and South Carolina, growing in bogs and pine barrens along the coast, flowering in late spring. Plant forms a resting bud in winter. Leaves to 16cm, usually about 7cm long. Flowering stems to 45cm; flowers white, about 1.5cm across. Needs wet peaty soil with coarse acid sand, preferably with live sphagnum moss. Min. −5°C.

Drosera capensis L. A perennial with long leaves and magenta, pink or rarely white flowers in f. **alba**, native of South Africa in the Cape from Clanwilliam to Uniondale, growing in wet peaty places, flowering in November–January (summer). Leaves 3–6cm long on a petiole to 10cm. Stem to about 30cm with flowers 2cm across. Min. −3°C.

Drosera cistiflora L. A soft dwarf perennial with a leafy stem and large flowers of mauve, white, yellow or red, native of South Africa in the Cape from Clanwilliam to Port Elizabeth, growing in wet peaty and sandy places, flowering in August–October (spring). Leaves

5–10cm long, with a short petiole. Stem to about 30cm, with 1–3 dark-eyed flowers 5cm across. Min. −3°C.

Drosera binata Labill. A delicate perennial with forked or branching leaves and branched stems of white or rarely pink flowers, native of E Australia from Queensland to Tasmania and throughout New Zealand at up to 700m, growing in wet peaty places, flowering mainly in September–April (summer). Leaves 5–60cm long, with a long petiole and glandular blades which uncurl like a fern. Stem to about 80cm branching at the top, with many scented flowers 5cm across. Min. −3°C. Several cultivars are grown: **'Dichotoma'** has yellowish-green leaves, forked twice. **'Extrema'** from Stradbroke Island, has leaves repeatedly forked, with 14–40 points in a fully developed leaf. **'Multifida'** has dark red leaves, divided 3 or 4 times; this variety keeps growing throughout the year and sometimes has pink flowers. Min. 4°C, though some of the New Zealand forms should be frost-hardy.

Drosera filiformis Raf. A delicate plant with a bulbous base, upright, very slender leaves covered nearly to the base with

Drosera cistiflora in the Cape

Drosera pulchella

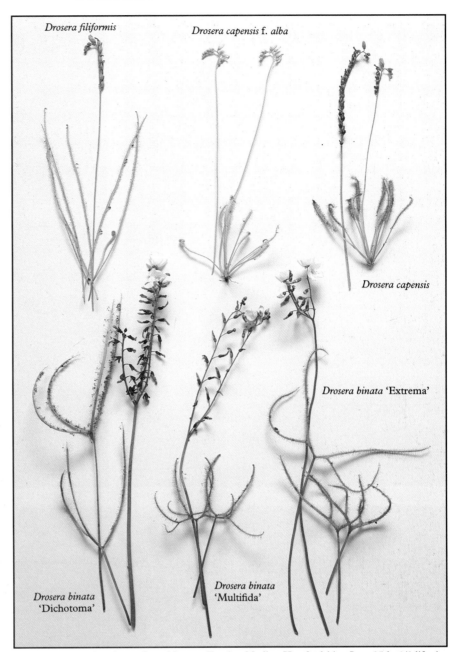

Drosera filiformis

Drosera capensis f. *alba*

Drosera capensis

Drosera binata 'Extrema'

Drosera binata 'Dichotoma'

Drosera binata 'Multifida'

Specimens from Marston Exotics, Madley, Herefordshire, June 25th, 1/2 life size

glandular hairs and pink flowers, native of North America from Florida through to Massachusetts, growing in damp sandy and peaty places on the coastal plain, flowering in June–September. Leaves to 30cm long; flowers 7–15mm across. Min. −15°C.

Drosera nitidula Planch.   A pygmy sundew with tiny tight rosettes and white flowers, native of W Australia, common in wet sandy heathland near Perth, flowering in November–December (summer). Rosette about 1cm across; leaves with a round lamina about 1mm across. Stem 2–4cm with flowers about 4mm across, with crimson stigmas. Keep a little drier in winter. Min. 5°C.

Drosophyllum lusitanicum (L.) Link (*Droseraceae*)   An almost shrubby sundew with stiff stalks, numerous thread-like leaves covered with sticky glands and branched flowering stems with rich yellow flowers, native of S and C Portugal and S Spain, growing in hot heathy places near springs, on sandstone rocks, often in cork oak forests, flowering in April–May. Stems woody, clothed at the base with dead leaves; leaves 10–30cm long, coiled when young. Flower stalk thick and branching,

to 30cm; flowers about 2.5cm across, cup-shaped and sometimes not opening. A difficult plant to keep happy; it needs very sandy acid soil, needs to be kept moist, wet beneath, dry on top. One method recommended is to grow the young plant in a small clay pot, which is plunged in a larger pot; once established only the outer pot is watered and that is kept moist. I raised one seedling to flowering, but it then rotted from the top and died, I beleive, from being watered overhead in summer. Min. 0°C.

Drosera pulchella Lehm.   A pygmy sundew with tight rosettes and bright pink or rarely red flowers, native of W Australia, growing by springs and in swamps, flowering in November–January (summer). Rosette about 2cm across; leaves with a narrow petiole and a round lamina about 3mm across. Stem about 5cm, with flowers 1–1.2cm across. Keep moist at all times. Min. 5°C.

Drosera pulchella × nitidula   Intermediate between the parents with freely produced pink flowers.

Dionaea muscipula

Abutilon 'Cerise Queen'

Abutilon 'Louis Marignac'

Abutilon 'Boule de Neige'

Abutilon × hybridum hort. (*Malvaceae*)
A group of hybrids between *A. darwinii* and *A. striatum*, with softly hairy, unlobed or shallowly lobed leaves and bell-shaped flowers with incurving petals. 'Golden Fleece' is typical of this group. Other hybrids involve *A. megapotamicum* as well and produce more flared flowers, such as are seen in 'Canary Bird'. Colours in this group now range from darkest red and pink, to yellow and white. Most are upright shrubs with soft stems up to 3m or more if supported. All the abutilons of this group should be pruned in late winter, just as the new growth is beginning. Most will survive −5°C for short periods in dry soil and are good in warm gardens in central London, in Cornwall and on the West Coast to N California and Oregon.

Abutilon 'Apricot' Flowers pale orange with darker red veins, bell-shaped. 'Tangerine' is similar, but said to have brighter orange-yellow flowers. Shown here growing in S California.

Abutilon 'Boule de Neige' Flowers white, in summer flushed with pale pink, narrowly bell-shaped. A tall leafy plant with rather small flowers, dating from before 1850.

Abutilon 'Canary Bird' Flowers clear yellow, open bell-shaped. Leaves glossy. A reliable, free-flowering variety. Raised in 1890.

Abutilon 'Canary Bird'

Abutilon 'Apricot' in Jo Stromei's garden in Sunland, California

Abutilon 'Silver Belle'

Abutilon 'Moonchimes' at Green Farm Plants, Farnham

Abutilon 'Cerise Queen' Flowers rich pink, with spirally overlapping petals. 'Ashford Red' (*shown in Shrubs p. 254*) has soft red flowers.

Abutilon 'Golden Fleece' Flowers rather pale yellow, bell-shaped, with incurved petals. Raised in 1930.

Abutilon 'Louis Marignac' Flowers pale pink, petals incurved and overlapping. Raised by Lémoine of Nancy before 1878, when it was awarded an FCC by the Royal Horticultural Society.

Abutilon 'Moonchimes' A small plant with large yellow, open bell-shaped, or sometimes almost flat flowers. Leaves 3-lobed.

Abutilon 'Nabob' Flowers dark reddish-purple, petals incurved; leaves dark green. 'Cannington Peter' has similar dark crimson flowers and yellow-mottled leaves.

Abutilon 'Silver Belle' Flowers white, with wide-spreading petals; stamens dark yellow.

Abutilon 'Golden Fleece'

Abutilon 'Nabob'

79

Abutilon × *milleri*

Abutilon 'Cynthia Pike'

Abutilon pictum

Abutilon insigne

The *Abutilon* hybrids shown on this spread have smaller, more flared flowers and are mostly forms and hybrids of *A.* × *milleri*, the hybrid between *A. megapotamicum* and *A. pictum*, named after Philip Miller, curator of the Chelsea Physic Garden from 1722–70. Flowers either pale orange or yellow with reddish calyx, the petals spreading to form a flared bell.

Abutilon 'Cynthia Pike' Calyx red with orange-yellow slightly spreading petals. Leaves shallowly lobed.

Abutilon 'Daffy' Flowers yellow with spreading petals, very numerous. Plant low and spreading. Leaves 3-lobed.

Abutilon 'Hinton Seedling' Flowers red with spreading petals. Leaves almost unlobed. 'Patrick Synge' has orange flowers with spreading petals.

Abutilon pictum (Gillies ex Hook. & Arn.) Walp. A small tree or shrub with leaves like a Japanese maple and flowers with protruding stamens, hanging on long slender stalks, native of Brazil and naturalized elsewhere in C and S America to the Argentine, flowering in summer. Stems to 5m. Leaves toothed, deeply 3, 5 or 7-lobed, the lobes broadly based with acuminate tips. Flower stalks to 15cm. Flowers 2.5cm across; petals orange-yellow, veined with dark crimson, 2–4cm long. Stamens and styles protruding. For any good soil and a damp position; suitable for planting outside in summer. Min. 0°C. Several forms are cultivated with golden-spotted leaves, caused by virus-infection which can spread to other abutilons. 'Thompsonii' is the commonest, used in tropical bedding schemes; its central leaf lobe narrows at the base.

Abutilon insigne Planch. A shrub with entire or shallowly-lobed leaves and small heavily veined flowers, native of Colombia and Venezuela, flowering spring–autumn. Shrub to 1.2m. Leaves unlobed or the lower 3-lobed, to 15cm long. Flower stems slender, pendulous, covered with brown hairs which extend onto the calyx. Flowers open bell-shaped; petals 4–5cm long, white to purplish-pink with dark purple veins. For good soil and a sheltered position. Min. 0°C. Photographed in the Temperate House at Kew.

Abutilon × milleri hort. Most forms sold under this name have red calyces and pale orange flowers. Leaves with short side lobes and a long central lobe. 'Kentish Belle' is similar, with rather larger, red-veined flowers.

Abutilon 'Wisley Red' A hybrid between *A. megapotamicum* and (probably) a red cultivar, with flowers larger and more open than *A. megapotamicum*. Plant often tall-growing. Calyx large, dark reddish.

Abutilon unidentified species A tall shrub with lobed leaves, a large swollen calyx and rather small, brownish-orange veined flowers. We photographed this unusual plant in an old garden in Marin Co., California.

Abutilon venosum Walp. A small tree or shrub with leaves like a Japanese maple and flowers hanging on long slender stalks, native of Brazil, flowering in summer. Stems to 5m. Leaves toothed, deeply 5 or 7-lobed, the lobes narrow-based with acuminate tips. Flower stalks to 20cm. Flowers 5cm across; petals orange-yellow, veined with brown, 5.5cm long. Stamens and styles not protruding. For any good soil and a damp position; suitable for planting outside in summer. Min. 0°C.

Abutilon 'Daffy'

Abutilon 'Wisley Red' at Trengwainton

Abutilon species in California

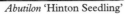

Abutilon 'Hinton Seedling'

Abutilon venosum in the Huntington garden, California

Abutilon × suntense

Abutilon × suntense 'Gorer's White' at Sellindge, Kent

Abutilon vitifolium 'Tennant's White'

Alyogyne huegelii 'Santa Cruz' in Beverley Hills

Abutilon vitifolium 'Veronica Tennant'

Alyogyne huegelii 'Mood Indigo'

Alyogyne hakeifolia in a cold greenhouse

Alyogyne cuneiformis in Palos Verdes, California

Alyogyne hakeifolia (Giord.) Alef.   A lax shrub with fleshy narrow divided leaves and mauve flowers with a red centre, native of S Western Australia and the Eyre Peninsula in South Australia, growing in sandy soils, flowering November–March (summer). Stems to 3m. Leaves glabrous, fleshy, 5–10cm long, divided into narrow segments 1–2mm thick. Flowers opening only in hot sun, 5–6cm long with a dark centre, mauve, rarely pale yellow and unmarked. (The colour film here exaggerates the pink colour.) Needs a warm position, full sun and well-drained sandy soil. In a greenhouse this species can grow very fast and produces rather few flowers. Easily grown from cuttings. Min. 0°C.

Alyogyne huegelii (Endl.) Fryxwell   A tall open shrub with hairy lobed leaves and bluish-lilac flowers with a white centre, native of SW Western Australia and the Lofty Ranges in South Australia, flowering mainly October–March and on and off throughout the winter. Stems to 2.5m and inclined to become straggly unless carefully pruned. Leaves roughly hairy on both sides, 2–7cm long and wide, deeply 5-lobed, each lobe with shallow rounded oak-like lobes. Flowers 7–10cm across, usually bluish-mauve, but sometimes deep purple, white or yellow (the beautiful shade of silvery bluish-mauve of the form shown here, called **'Santa Cruz'**, seems impossible to show on colour film) **'Mood Indigo'** has deep purplish-blue flowers. Very tolerant of heavy soils, hardy and free-flowering. Easily grown from cuttings. Min. − 5°C.

Abutilon × suntense C. Brickell (*Malvaceae*) A tall shrub with loose bunches of open flowers, usually bright mauve, but often white as shown here. Stems to 5m; flowers 5–6cm across, produced mainly in spring. A cross between two species from Chile, *A. vitifolium* and the smaller, hardier and darker-flowered *A. ochsenii*. It was first raised in 1969 and comes true from seed.
'Gorer's White' is named after the original raiser of the cross, Geoffrey Gorer of Sunte House, Sussex. 'Jermyns" and 'Violetta' are two good deep purplish forms. For moist, good soil and a sheltered position. Min. − 10°C.
Abutilon vitifolium (Cav.) Presl. syn. *Corynabutilon vitifolium* (Cav.) Kearney A fast-growing tall shrub or small tree with softly felty leaves and pale violet flowers, native of S Chile, growing in open places in warm temperate forest, flowering in spring and early summer. Stems to 10m; leaves 10–15cm long, 3 or 5-lobed, soft white-felty beneath. Flowers in groups of 3–4, about 7.5cm across, pale lilac or white.
'Veronica Tennant' is a large-flowered pale selection.
'Tennant's White' is its white counterpart. These are hardy to a minimum of − 5°C or lower if protected by a wall. They require shelter in windy climates, and are likely to be damaged or the soft branches broken by wind-rock. In hot summer climates they need partial shade, ample humidity and water in dry weather, and are best in coastal climates in N California and W Europe.

Alyogyne cuneiformis (DC.) Lewton (*Malvaceae*)   A lax shrub with narrow leaves and creamy-white tubular flowers, native of W Australia, growing in sandy places near the coast, flowering in November–March (summer). Stems to 3m. Leaves 5–8cm long, 8–15mm wide, thick and fleshy, entire, cuneate to spathulate. Flowers not opening wide, 5–6cm long, whitish with a dark centre. Needs a warm position and well-drained sandy soil. Min. 0°C.

Sphaeralcea angustifolia in the semi-desert of the San Jacinto mountains above Palm Springs, California

Callirhoe involucrata in Mexico

Malvastrum lateritium

Anisodontea scabrosa in Palos Verdes, California

Sphaeralcea ambigua in Mexico

Malacothamnus fasciculatus var. *nesioticus*

Malacothamnus fasciculatus var. *fasciculatus*

Anisodontea × hypomandarum (Sprague) Bates (*Malvaceae*) An upright shrub with small 3-lobed leaves and small pinkish flowers, of uncertain parentage (possibly *A. capensis* × *A. scabrosa*). Stems to 3m; leaves to 3.5cm, 3-lobed; flowers pinkish purple, veined at the base, about 3cm across. The genus *Anisodontea* is confined to southern Africa, with about 20 species in the Cape, and north to Namibia and Lesotho. *A. capensis* (L.) Bates has smaller leaves, to 2.5cm long, and magenta flowers.

Anisodontea scabrosa (L.) Bates
A spreading (or erect) shrub with rounded leaves and pale pink flowers, native of South Africa from the W Cape east to Natal, growing in scrub along the coast, flowering most of the year. Stems 1–2m; leaves often sticky and scented. Leaves variable, 3- or 5-lobed, 2–7cm long. Flowers 3–4cm across, pinkish, often deeper at the base. For a sunny bank in well-drained soil and tolerant of summer drought.

Callirhoe involucrata (T. & G.) A. Gray (*Malvaceae*) A thick-rooted perennial with a rosette of deeply cut, stalked leaves and prostrate flowering stems, native of North America from Minnesota and Iowa south to Texas, Utah and central Mexico, growing in dry open soils, flowering in April–October. Plant to 1m across, usually less. Leaves geranium-like, deeply palmately dissected. Stipules ovate. Flowers born singly in the leaf axils, long-stalked, 3–6cm across, purplish-red. For dry well-drained soil on a sunny bank. The Mexican form, shown here, is sometimes called 'Tenuissima'. Min. −10°C.

Malacothamnus fasciculatus (Nutt.) Greene (*Malvaceae*) A slender arching shrub with wand-like branches and round, shallowly-lobed leaves, native of S California from Riverside Co. south to Baja California, growing on dry hills and canyons below 800m, flowering in April–July. Stems 1–5m; leaves 2–4cm across, crenate, whitish beneath; flowers mauve, with petals 12–18mm long, usually in head-like clusters. Tolerant of summer drought. Min. −5°C.
Var. *fasciculatus* has small leaves less than 4cm long, grey on both surfaces, and flowers in head-like clusters. Var. *catalinensis* (Eastw.) Kearn.

from Santa Catalina Island has larger, deeply-lobed leaves, 5–7cm long, darker green above. Var. **nesioticus** (Rob.) Kearn., has similar leaves, but a loose inflorescence. It is found on Santa Cruz Island flowering June–July.

Malvastrum lateritium Nichols (*Malvaceae*) A spreading sub-shrubby perennial with maple-like leaves and pale orange flowers with a ring of pink near the centre, native of South America in Uruaguay, flowering in summer. Plant to 1m across; leaves 4–7.5cm, 3 or 5-lobed. Flowers about 5cm across. For well-drained soil in a sunny position. Min. −5°C, perhaps less if dry.

Sphaeralcea ambigua Gray (*Malvaceae*)
A many-stemmed perennial, shrubby at the base with orange or more rarely pinkish flowers, native from SW Utah to S California, Arizona and N Mexico, growing in stony and rocky places in the desert at up to 1500m, flowering in April–October. For well-drained soil in a dry position. Drought-tolerant. Min. −5°C or less if dry.

Sphaeralcea angustifolia (Cav.) G. Don
An upright, many-stemmed perennial with narrow leaves and red, orange or pinkish flowers, native of North America from W Kansas and Colorado to W Texas, California and N Mexico, growing on wasteland, especially on roadsides, at 1000–2000m, flowering in May–November. Stems 80–180cm; leaves white-felty, rather thick, linear-lanceolate, 2–7cm long, with small spreading lobes at the base. Flowers 7–12mm long. Min. −5°C or less if dry. There are about 60 species of *Sphaeralcea* in North America, mostly very similar, differing in leaf shape and fruit details.

Sphaeralcea munroana (Dougl.) Spach
A perennial with spreading stems from a central root and deeply toothed 5-lobed leaves, native from NE California to British Columbia, Montana and Wyoming, growing in dry bare soils, flowering in May–August. Stems to 90cm; leaves 1.5–5cm long. Flowers pinkish-red, 2–3.5cm across. For poor well-drained soil. This species is hardy as far as cold is concerned, but is usually short-lived in cultivation. Min. −10°C or less if dry.

Anisodontea × hypomandarum

Sphaeralcea munroana

Lavatera maritima 'Bicolor' at Dr Ernest Scholtz's garden in Palos Verdes, California

Lavatera assurgentiflora Kellogg syn.
Saviniona assurgentiflora Greene (*Malvaceae*)
Misson Mallow   An erect or spreading shrub
or small tree with purplish flowers half-hidden
among the pale green maple-like leaves, native
of California on the Santa Barbara Islands and
naturalized on the mainland, growing on sandy
flats and rocky places, flowering mainly in
March–November. Stems fast-growing to 4m.
Leaves 5–15cm long and wide, with 5–7
toothed lobes, on petioles 5–15cm long.
Flowers 5–8cm across; petals pink with dark
purple veins, narrow at the base, with a pair of
hairy tufts. For any good soil in a hot sunny
position. Min. −5° C. Easily propagated from
seed. Wind- and salt-tolerant, but I have found
it becomes leafy and floppy in greenhouse
conditions. This species was cultivated by the
Spanish in the 18th century and is said to have
been found originally on Anacapa Island.

Lavatera maritima Gouan   A soft
spreading shrub with pale pink flowers, veined
purple at the base, native of the W
Mediterranean from Corsica, Sardinia and N
Africa, west to Spain, growing in dry rocky
places, usually near the sea, flowering in
February–June or October in cool climates.
Stems to 1.8 m. Leaves white-tomentose with
stellate hairs, to 7cm long and 8cm wide,
suborbicular, with 5 shallow lobes on petioles
0.6–3cm long. Flowers 3–6cm across, opening
very flat, usually pale silvery-pink with a purple

centre. For poor well-drained soil in a hot
sunny position. Soil that is too good and shade
make the plant leafy and soft. Min. −5°C.
'Bicolor' syn. *L. bicolor* Rouy is the name
often given to the large cultivated form, shown
here.

Phymosea rosea (DC.) Kearney syn.
Sphaeralcea rosea (DC.) Standl. (*Malvaceae*) A
spreading leafy shrub, with upright pinkish
flowers in pairs, native of Mexico and
Guatemala, flowering most of the year. Large
shrub or small tree to 5m; leaves to 25cm long,
usually deeply 3–7 lobed; flowers cup-shaped,
about 6cm long, pink to dark red. For good
well-drained soil in sun or partial shade.
Min. −3°C.

Phymosea umbellata (Cav.) Kearney syn.
Sphaeralcea umbellata (Cav.) D. Don
A spreading leafy shrub with upright purple,
red or scarlet flowers in branched heads, native
of Mexico, flowering in early spring. Large
shrub to 6m; leaves to 20cm long, shallowly 5–
7-lobed; flowers tightly cupped, about 4cm
long, long- or short-stalked, usually in 3's,
rarely in pairs or 5's. For good well-drained
soil in sun or partial shade. Min. −3°C.

Sidalcea malachroides (Hook. & Arn.) Gray
(*Malvaceae*)   A tall sub-shrubby perennial
with roughly hairy vine-like leaves and tight
heads of white flowers, native of coastal

Lavatera maritima wild in S Spain

C California north to Oregon, growing in open
places in redwood and mixed evergreen forests
below 600m, flowering in April–July. Stems to
2m; leaves shallowly 7-lobed, 2–10cm across.
Flowers about 2cm across. For any good soil
in partial shade. Min. −3°C or less for short
periods.

Lavatera assurgentiflora at Harry Hay's

Phymosea umbellata in S France

Lavatera maritima 'Bicolor'

Phymosea rosea

Sidalcea malachroides in Berkeley Botanical Garden

Sida fallax

Malvaviscus arboreus var. *mexicanus* at the Huntington garden, California

Pavonia schrankii

Abutilon molle

Abutilon molle (DC.) syn. *Sida mollis* DC. (*Malvaceae*) A shrub or small tree with cordate, softly-hairy leaves and small yellow flowers, native of Peru. Stems to 6m. Leaves cordate; flowers 5cm across. For a sheltered position. Min. −3°C.

Malvaviscus arboreus Cav. (*Malvaceae*) A very variable much-branched shrub with red flowers that never open, native of Florida, Texas and Mexico south to Peru and Brazil, flowering in summer. Stems to 4m. Leaves unlobed or shallowly 3-lobed, coarsely toothed, downy. Flower stalks to 7cm. Flowers 2.5–5cm long; petals red, remaining twisted, with the style and stamens protruding. For any good soil and a sunny position, kept rather dry in winter and well-watered in summer. Min. 0°C.
Var. **mexicanus** Schldl. syn. *M. penduliflorus* hort., *M. conzatti* Greenman, from Mexico south to Colombia has almost glabrous lanceolate to ovate, shallowly toothed leaves and large nodding flowers.

Pavonia hastata Cav. (*Malvaceae*) A small evergreen shrub with hairy leaves, dark green on top and white flowers with a red eye, native of tropical South America and naturalized in Georgia and Florida; apparently native also in Queensland and New South Wales and naturalized in Victoria and South Australia, flowering in summer and autumn. Stems to 2m. Leaves 4–7cm long, 1–4cm wide, widest at the base with 2 shallow lobes, the centre tapering to a blunt point. Flowers 4–6cm across, usually white, rarely pink, with a dark centre. I have found that cleistogamous flowers are also produced, possibly under poor light conditions and some clones are said to be more free-flowering than others. For good soil in a hot sunny position. Min. −5°C.

Malvaviscus arboreus in Hong Kong

Pavonia spinifex

Pavonia schrankii Spreng.   A shrub with hairy leaves and upright red flowers, native of Brazil, flowering in spring and summer. Erect shrub to 2m with coarse yellowish hairs. Leaves about 8cm long, 2.3cm wide; flowers 3.5–4cm long, open only in the morning. Best in partial shade. Min. −3°C.

Pavonia spinifex (L.) Cav.   A shrub with hairy leaves and small yellow flowers, native of South and Central America and Bermuda, and naturalized in SE USA, flowering in summer and autumn. Stems to 4.5m. Leaves 3–10cm long, 2–8cm wide, ovate to ovate-lanceolate, toothed. Flowers 4–7cm across, yellow. For good soil in a sunny position. Min. −5°C. *Pavonia multiflora* Juss. (not shown), is a distinct plant with several upward-pointing flowers clustered at the top of the stems and numerous narrow spiky red calyx segments; petals to 4cm; stamens and style exserted.

Sida fallax Walp. (*Malvaceae*)   A large and sometimes spreading dense twiggy shrub with greyish leaves and semi-double yellow, orange or red flowers, native of the Pacific islands. Shrub to 2m or more. Leaves ovate, crenate. Flowers 3cm across. Dr Alfred Graf, in *Exotica*, records that on Oahu the flowers of this species, called Ilima, are used to make leis. Min. 0°C.

Malvaviscus arboreus

Pavonia hastata

89

Abelmoschus manihot in the humid hills near Ya-an, SW Sichuan

Abelmoschus manihot 'Cream Cups'

Hibiscus moscheutos 'Disco Belle'

Hibiscus moscheutos 'Southern Belle'

Hibiscus moscheutos in a summer bedding scheme at Wisley

Abelmoschus manihot

Abelmoschus esculentus

Hibiscus calyphyllus

Abelmoschus esculentus (L.) Moench syn. *Hibiscus esculentus* L. (*Malvaceae*) Okra, Gumbo   An attractive, heat-loving annual with yellow, red-centred flowers and edible fruit. A series of complex hybrid annuals of uncertain origin, long grown in India and Africa. Cultivars vary greatly in height from 1–4m. Leaves lobed and vine-like or deeply divided. Flowers about 8cm across, short-lived. **'Dwarf Green Longpod'** with stems about 80cm and the red-stemmed **'Burgundy'** are both attractive and useful. All need warm conditions above 25°C.

Abelmoschus manihot (L.) Medick. syn. *Hibiscus manihot* L.   A large perennial with 3–7-lobed leaves and large white to yellow flowers, native of SE Asia and N Australia, growing on wasteland and humid rocky hillsides, flowering in summer and autumn. Stems to 2m; leaves to 45cm across; epicalyx segments 4–8, ovate. Flowers about 10cm

across. Plant often flowering in the first year from seed, so may be grown as an annual in a warm greenhouse. **'Cream Cups'** is a large-flowered, pale yellow selection. *Abelmoschus moschatus* Medik. (not shown) is similar but has 6–10 linear epicalyx segments; it is normally pinkish-flowered but may be sulphur-yellow or red. Min. −5°C.

Hibiscus moscheutos L. Swamp Rose Mallow   A tall perennial with huge flowers, native of NE America from Massachusetts south to Florida and east to W Ontario, Indiana and Missouri, growing in saline marshes and on lake shores, flowering in August–September. The wild form has stems to 2m and pink to white flowers to 16cm across. Subsp. *moscheutos* has a dark eye; subsp. *palustris* (L.) R. T. Clausen has unmarked flowers. Cultivated forms have even larger flowers and shorter stems and can be grown as annuals if started early and kept

growing in heat. **'Southern Belle'** raised by Sakata in Japan, has flowers white, pink or red, about 25cm across. Stems 1–1.5m. **'Disco Belle'** has slightly smaller flowers, pink or white with a scarlet eye, on stems only 50cm tall.

Hibiscus calyphyllus Cav. syn. *H. calycinus* Willd. (*Malvaceae*)   A shrubby perennial with toothed leaves and large yellow flowers, maroon in the centre, native of southern Africa from the coast of Natal to Mozambique and on Madagascar and the Mascaene Islands, flowering in summer. Stems to 3m. Leaves about 12cm, toothed, sometimes 3 or 5-lobed. Flowers 8–15cm across. For any good soil. Min. −3°C, perhaps.

91

Hibiscus mutabilis growing wild on the coast of Yakushima Island, S Japan

Hibiscus pedunculatus

Hibiscus tiliaceus in Hong Kong

Hibiscus mutabilis

Hibiscus denudatus

Hibiscus elatus in Florida

Hibiscus elatus Sweet (*Malvaceae*)   Similar to *H. tiliaceus* (below) with orange flowers fading to crimson, native of Jamaica and Cuba. Tree to 25m; leaves glabrescent, flowers with petals 8–12cm long, not overlapping. Tropical. *Thespesia populnea* (L.) Sol. ex Corr. (*not shown*) is a very similar tree, but has smaller leaves 6–12cm long and smaller solitary flowers with reflexing petals.

Hibiscus denudatus Benth.   A bushy perennial or sub-shrub with pinkish flowers, red in the throat, native of California, Texas and south into N Mexico, growing on rocky slopes and in canyons in creosote bush scrub in desert areas, flowering in February–May in California, January–October in Arizona. A low bush, 30–100cm, covered with dense yellowish, stellate hairs; leaves ovate, 1–2.5cm long, finely toothed. Flowers 3–4cm across, pinkish-purple to white. Best grown outside in hot dry places and well-drained soil. Min. −3°C.

Hibiscus mutabilis L.   A large deciduous shrub with softly hairy leaves and flat pink flowers, native of S Japan and the coasts of S China, growing in scrub, flowering in August–October. Stems to 3m. Leaves softly hairy beneath, 10–20cm long and wide, shallowly 3 or 5-lobed, each lobe acuminate from a broad base. Flowers 10–13cm across, usually pink, with a dark spot at the base of each petal, but white changing to pink in 'Versicolor' and red in 'Rubra', deep pinkish in 'Rasberry Rose'. For any good soil in a sheltered position, warm and wet in summer. Min. 0°C. In colder areas it is said to cut to the base in winter and sprout again from the rootstock. Commonly cultivated in the southern USA where it is called Confederate Rose Mallow.

Hibiscus pedunculatus L. fil.   A large perennial or sub-shrub with pale pinkish flowers on long ascending stalks, native of South Africa in coastal forest in the E Cape, north through Natal to Mozambique, growing in scrub and on the edges of woods, flowering in summer, November–April in South Africa. Plant to 2m; leaves deeply 3-lobed, fig-like. Epicalyx segments spreading, hairy. Flowers about 6cm across. For moist soil in partial shade with water in summer. Photographed in the Weza Forest of Natal in January. Min. −5°C.

Hibiscus tiliaceus L. Mahoe   An evergreen tree to 12m, with leathery leaves and flowers which open yellow, reddening as they fade, native of coastal areas from S Japan to Malaysia and Australia, flowering most of the year. Leaves cordate-orbicular, 7–16cm long, untoothed or sometimes wavy-edged. Petals 4–7cm long. Often planted near the coast. Min 0°C.

Hibiscus rosa-sinensis 'Cooperi'

Hibiscus rosa-sinensis 'Lady Bird'

Hibiscus rosa-sinensis 'Stoplight'

Hibiscus rosa-sinensis L. **Chinese Hibiscus** An evergreen shrub thought to be native of tropical Asia, but with a confusing history. Philip Miller, curator of the Chelsea Physic Garden, London, introduced double and other forms of *H. rosa-sinensis* (under the name *H. javanica*) to England as early as 1731. Shrub or tree up to 5m high in the tropics and to about 2.5m in cultivation. Leaves to 15cm long, 9cm wide, ovate to broadly lanceolate, serrate, glossy green. Flowers solitary, showy, in leaf axils. Petals 6–12cm, generally red or deep red, darker towards the base.

Cultivars of *Hibiscus rosa-sinensis* There are numerous showy cultivars, some of which are illustrated on the next two pages. There is no international registration authority for hibiscus, so some plants will be found under different names in different catalogues. The American Hibiscus Society (*see appendix*) produces illustrated catalogues of names which are useful.

Plants require good drainage, protection from draughts and frost, and plenty of warmth and sun if they are to flower satisfactorily, but they can be grown in conservatories in northern Europe as long as the temperature is not allowed to fall below 5°C. Do not be discouraged if many of the leaves drop off in the winter; the plants will regenerate in the spring. It is also worth remembering that the length of the flowering season and the pigmentation of individual blooms can be affected by extremes of temperature, the orange-red and white varieties being the most susceptible. The flowers of most cultivars last for only one day but some of the older types such as 'Ross Estey' keep their flowers for 48 hours.

'Brilliant' A vigorous branching variety with single bright red blooms to 18cm across.

'Cooperi' Notable chiefly for its foliage which is variegated; the narrow leaves are splashed with pink and white. Bright red flowers to 10cm across are borne on a small bushy shrub.

'Diamond Head' Large dark red double flowers, to 15cm across, produced over a long season on compact plants.

'Lady Bird' An upright bush of average height bearing single red blooms with prominent white or yellow veins, to 20cm across.

'Ross Estey' A vigorous grower up to 3m, with large shiny leaves and very large single flowers to 15cm across. Variable in colour but usually pinkish-red blooms edged with apricot or yellow. Petals are crinkled and overlap.

'Stoplight' A single red variety photographed in the intermediate glasshouse at the RHS Garden, Wisley.

'Sunset' An attractive single variety from Bermuda.

Hibiscus rosa-sinensis 'Sunset'   *Hibiscus rosa-sinensis* 'Brilliant'   *Hibiscus rosa-sinensis* 'Diamond Head'

Hibiscus rosa-sinensis 'Ross Estey'   *Hibiscus rosa-sinensis*

Hibiscus rosa-sinensis in the 17th century garden on Isola Bella, Lake Maggiore

Hibiscus rosa-sinensis 'Bermuda Pink' in the Botanic Garden in Bermuda

Hibiscus rosa-sinensis 'Painted Lady'

***Hibiscus arnottianus* 'Ruth Wilcox'**
A cultivar of *H. arnottianus* which is a small evergreen tree or shrub, native of Hawaii. In the species, leaves are dark green, to 25cm. Flowers slightly fragrant, solitary, usually white, sometimes having pink veins.

'Bermuda Pink'   A delightful old variety used as a hedging plant in Bermuda.

'Gray Lady'   This large-flowered variety with its attractive central pink flush has been used successfully by breeders as it seeds well and is also good as a male parent.

'Painted Lady'   This is **not** the 'Painted Lady' that won an Award of Merit from the RHS back in 1897, although I hoped it might be! It is very beautiful, however.

'Peggy Walton'   We photographed this in Bermuda in 1995; it is a new variety that has not yet come into general cultivation.

'Tylene'   A prolific modern upright-growing hybrid with single flowers, to18cm across. The main colour is hyacinth blue, zoned and veined with white; it has a small pink eye. Raised by Boss.

'White Wings'   Large white flowers to 15cm across, with red throat. Frequently used for hedging in tropical climates although it also makes a very satisfactory potplant as it has a compact habit.

Hibiscus rosa-sinensis 'Peggy Walton'

Hibiscus rosa-sinensis 'White Wings'

Hibiscus arnottianus 'Ruth Wilcox'

Hibiscus rosa-sinensis 'Tylene'

Hibiscus rosa-sinensis 'Gray Lady'

97

Yellow *Hibiscus rosa-sinensis* in the Huntington garden, California

'All Aglow' A spectacular, tall (up to 5m) single variety with orange flowers to 15cm across, edged with red-orange, centred with pink and white and a blotch of yellow on each petal. The petals overlap and are slightly ruffled. Raised by Estelle Kanzier.

'Butterfly' Single bright yellow flowers. Up to 2.5m tall.

'Carnival' A beautiful single-flowered cultivar, photographed here in the Huntington Garden, Los Angeles.

'Cherie' A vigorous upright grower with single pale orange blooms with rose-red eye and veins.

'Florida Sunset' Flowers to 10cm across. Petals orange-red, shading to gold at the edges. A compact plant; good in containers.

'Hula Girl' Very free-flowering with single flowers to 16cm across, with crinkled petals and red centre. Bushy plants.

'Kate Sessions' Large single flowers with broad red petals tinged with gold underneath. Upright growth to 3m.

'Norman Lee' A vigorous variety of medium height that blooms profusely. Single-flowered, about 20cm across with ruffled overlapping petals. Red centre, pink zone, shading to orange and a yellow edge. Raised by Brube Acres.

'Santana' A vigorous variety, the result of crossing 'Miss Liberty' and 'Aussie II'. Single dark orange flowers, edged and veined with yellow. Raised by D. Conrad.

Hibiscus schizopetalus (Mast.) Hook. Japanese Lantern, Coral Hibiscus   This species is native of Kenya, Tanzania and N Mozambique. It makes an evergreen or semi-deciduous shrub to 4m. It has leaves to 12cm and bears delicate pendulous flowers with long styles, on slender drooping stalks. It is a popular ornamental plant throughout the tropics and can be grown in a greenhouse in Europe, provided the temperature does not drop below 5°C. As the flowers are borne on the previous year's wood, pruning must be done sparingly, immediately after flowering.

Hibiscus schizopetalus

Hibiscus rosa-sinensis 'Kate Sessions'

Hibiscus rosa-sinensis 'Florida Sunset'

Hibiscus rosa-sinensis 'Santana'

Hibiscus rosa-sinensis 'Carnival' in the Huntington garden, California

Hibiscus rosa-sinensis 'Hula Girl'

Hibiscus rosa-sinensis 'Butterfly'

Hibiscus rosa-sinensis 'Cherie'

Hibiscus rosa-sinensis 'Norman Lee'

Hibiscus rosa-sinensis 'All Aglow'

Chorisia speciosa in the Jardin exotique du Val Rameh, Menton, S France

Chorisia speciosa

Chorisia speciosa A. St Hil. (*Bombacaceae*)
Floss Silk Tree   A tall tree, upright when
young, with scattered thick spines on the trunk
and palmately compound leaves, native of
Brazil and Argentina, flowering in autumn–
winter, usually after the leaves have fallen. A
fast-growing tree to 10–20m, growing 1–1.5m
in its first few years. Bark yellowish, smooth,
with very stout short spines. Leaves with 5–7
leaflets, each about 12cm long, 3cm wide,
lanceolate. Flowers about 10cm across, pink,
red or purplish with a white or cream base.
Seeds surrounded by silky fibres. For any good
soil; water well in summer, less in autumn to
encourage flowering. Min. −3°C, for short
periods. Commonly planted in S California
and in warm parts of the Mediterranean.
Named varieties that have to be grafted
include 'Los Angeles Beautiful' with wine-
red flowers and 'Majestic Beauty' with pink
flowers. Other familiar trees in the family
Bombacaceae include the Baobab and the
Kapok tree, both common in tropical Africa,
and the Durian fruit from SE Asia.

Entelia arborescens R. Br. (*Tiliaceae*)
A shrub or small tree with large softly hairy
leaves and small white flowers, native of New
Zealand on both islands, growing in forests at
low altitudes, flowering in September–January
(spring–summer). Tree to 6m; leaves cordate,
shortly acuminate, 10–15cm long and wide;
flowers to 2.5cm across with 4–5 crumpled
petals and numerous stamens with versatile
anthers. Capsule with stiff hairs. For any good
moist soil. Min. −3°C.

Grewia occidentalis L. syn. *G. caffra* hort.
(*Tiliaceae*)   A spreading stiff shrub with small
purplish, starry flowers, native of South and
tropical Africa from the E Cape northwards,
growing on dry hillsides, flowering in
October–December (early summer). Shrub to
3m or small tree, with dense twiggy branches.
Leaves ovate, finely toothed, up to 7.5cm long.
Flowers about 2.5cm across with narrow
petals. Fruits yellow, 4-lobed. For any soil,
with water in summer; can be grown and
clipped as a hedge or trained on a wall.
Min. −3°C.

Reinwardtia indica Dumort (*Linaceae*)
A small shrub with bright yellow flowers in
autumn and winter, native of SE Asia from
Pakistan eastwards, growing in wasteland and
on field banks at up to 1800m, flowering in
November–May. Shrub to 1m, but often
prostrate. Leaves obovate to oblanceolate,
3–9cm long. Flowers with petals 1.5–3cm
long and 5 fertile and 5 sterile stamens. For
any soil, with ample water and humidity in
summer. *R. cicanoba* (D. Don) Hara from
Nepal, Bhutan and SW China has larger
leaves and more numerous flowers with petals
3–5.5cm long. Min. −3°C.

Sparmannia africana L. fil. (*Tiliaceae*)
A shrub with large leaves and small white
flowers with numerous stamens, native of
South Africa in the southern part of Cape
Province, growing in moist gulleys and on the
edges of forest, flowering in June–November
(winter–early summer). Shrub or small tree to
4m. Leaves ovate, roughly hairy, up to 20cm
long. Flowers 2.5–4cm across with white petals
and numerous fertile and sterile stamens with
purple tips, which move when touched. For
any soil, with water in summer. This is very
popular as a houseplant, called Zimmerlinden.
Min. −3°C.

Reinwardtia indica

Sparmannia africana in the wild

Sparmannia africana

Entelia arborescens

Grewia occidentalis

Grewia occidentalis wild near Swellendam, S Africa

101

Dombeya cacuminum in the Huntington garden, California

Brachychiton discolor F. Muell. (*Sterculiaceae*)   A tall tree with sycamore-like leaves, but leafless when covered with pink or red flowers, native of Queensland and New South Wales, growing in coastal scrub and rainforest, flowering in November–March. An upright tree to 30m, with a stout trunk, but smaller in cooler areas. Leaves 10–20cm across, 3–7-lobed. Flowers about 5cm across, bell-shaped on a slender inflorescence, but usually seen as here, carpeting the ground after they have fallen. Easily grown in any good soil. Min. −3°C and will recover if defoliated by light frost. *B. acerifolius* F. Muell. is the commonest species in cultivation and very striking when covered with large-branched inflorescences of red, bell-shaped flowers about 1.5cm across, produced most prolifically on leafless trees after a hot, dry period, usually May–June in California, October–March in Australia. Young trees make good pot plants with beautiful maple-like leaves.

Dombeya burgessiae Gerrard ex Harv. syn. *D. mastersii* Hook. fil., *D. tanganyikensis* Baker, *D. nyasica* Exell. (*Sterculiaceae*)   A very variable shrub with small upright, spreading or nodding heads of pink or white flowers, native of South Africa from the Natal coast, northwards to Ethiopia and the Sudan, growing in scrub and forest edges, flowering in spring. An erect shrub to 4m. Leaves usually 3-lobed, 10–20cm across, hairy. Flowers 3–5cm across, pink to white in loose upright or spreading heads. Easily grown in good soil in a warm position. Min. 0°C, but soon recovers after damage by light frosts.

Dombeya cacuminum Hochr.   A leafy evergreen tree with hanging bunches of red flowers, native of Madagascar, flowering in early spring. An erect tree to 10m. Leaves 3-lobed, about 10cm across. Flowers about 5cm across, in loose heads, hanging beneath the branches. A very striking tree when in flower. Easily grown in good soil in a warm position. Min. 0°C, but soon recovers after damage by light frosts.

Fremontodendron mexicanum

Reevesia thyrsoidea in Hong Kong

Trochetiopsis erythroxylon at Kew

Fallen flowers of *Brachychiton discolor* at La Mortola in September

Dombeya ianthotricha Arènes   A shrub
with stems and leaves covered in dense
chocolate-brown hairs, and clusters of hanging
tubular red flowers, native of C Madagascar,
around Manakazo-Ankazobe, growing in the
remnants of forest, flowering in spring. In
cultivation a coarse, spreading shrub to 5m
with long thin branches. Leaves ovate, cordate
to 30cm long, with small pointed lobes
towards the apex; flowers around 10 in an
umbel, around 3cm long, the coiled petals
remaining in a tube. Min. 0°C. This lovely
shrub, one of 200 species of *Dombeya*, grows
in the Huntington Gardens in California.

Fremontodendron mexicanum A. Davids
(*Sterculiaceae*)   A tall stiff shrub with dark
green, leathery leaves and orange-yellow
flowers, native of S California in San Diego
Co., on Otay and Jamul mountains and N Baja
California, growing in dry canyons at about
500m, flowering in March–June. Shrub or
small tree to 6m. Leaves 5–7 veined from the
base, 2.5–7cm wide, shallowly-lobed. Flowers
without petals, but with an orange-yellow calyx
6–9cm across, slightly cupped, not flat,
produced in succession among the leaves. For
well-drained soil in a hot, sunny position or
trained on a wall. Keep dry in summer. Min.
−3°C. *F. californicum* Cov., from Shasta south
to Kern Co. and Arizona, has smaller flat
flowers, bright yellow, 3.5–6cm across, mostly
open at one time; leaves 1–3-nerved at the
base. It is hardier, surviving −10°C for short
periods. 'California Glory', a hybrid between
the two species, is a fast-growing shrub or
small tree to 6m, hardier than the parents,
grown from cuttings; flowers 7.5cm across.
'Ken Taylor' is a prostrate variety; 'Pacific
Sunset' is tall-growing with long tails on the
tips of the sepals, they all flower mainly in
spring.

Guichenotia macrantha Turcz.
(*Sterculiaceae*)   A small shrub with nodding,
cup-shaped mauve flowers, native of W
Australia, growing in open sandy places,
flowering in winter–spring. A rounded shrub
to 70cm. Leaves linear, about 5cm long, with
a pair of leaf-like stipules. Flowers 2.5cm
across. Easily grown in sandy soil in a warm
position. Min. −5°C, in dry conditions.

Reevesia thyrsoidea Lindl. (*Sterculiaceae*)
A small tree with flat heads of white flowers,
native from SE China to Java, growing in
forests on low hills, flowering in May. Tree or
large shrub to 18m. Leaves evergreen, ovate to
broadly oblong, about 25cm long. Flower
heads about 8cm across; flowers 2cm across,
with a long tube on which there are 15 stalkless
anthers and the stigma. Capsules woody; seeds
with a papery wing. For well-drained, peaty
soil, wet in summer. Min. −3°C. *R. pubescens*
Mast. from Sikkim to W Sichuan, is a hardier
tree, with smaller, tighter heads of flowers (see
Shrubs p. 179, growing outside at Wakehurst
Place, Sussex).

Trochetiopsis erythroxylon (Forst. f.) W.
Marais (*Sterculiaceae*)   A hibiscus-like shrub
or small tree with white flowers, native of St
Helena. Leaves ovate, cordate, acuminate,
about 8cm. Flowers 4cm long. This rare plant
is growing in the Temperate House at Kew.

Dombeya burgessiae in Malawi

Dombeya burgessiae in the Huntington garden

Guichenotia macrantha

Dombeya ianthotricha

Euphorbia pulcherrima 'Red Sails'

Euphorbia pulcherrima 'Maren'

Euphorbia pulcherrima growing wild in the forest near Copala, above Mazatlán, W Mexico

Euphorbia pulcherrima

Beware! The spurge family can be recognized by its small, green unisexual flowers which are surrounded by coloured and sometimes petal-like bracts. All parts of the plant contain a milky juice which is usually poisonous and may be very toxic, causing blistering of the skin and intense irritation if put anywhere near the eyes.

Euphorbia pulcherrima Willd. ex Klotzsch (*Euphorbiaceae*) A large shrub with red leaf-like bracts, native of Mexico in the Sierra Madre Occidentale, growing on the margins of forest, flowering in October–January. Shrub to 3m in frost-free climates. Leaves long-stalked to 15cm long, with few shallow lobes and teeth. Bracts 10–15cm long, lanceolate in the wild, but larger and broader in modern cultivars. In frost-free climates the shrubs are easily grown in sun or partial shade, given well-drained, slightly acid soil and ample water in summer. They should be pruned after flowering and usually produce numerous small heads. Larger heads are encouraged by thinning the branches. They do well outdoors in the warm parts of California, surviving −5°C overnight if protected by buildings or a wall and kept dry at the root.
Paler-flowered varieties are said to hold their bracts into spring. Pot cultivation aims to produce a dwarf plant with large heads, flowering in mid-winter. Commercially the plants are treated with a dwarfing hormone. To keep a pot plant going a second year, prune,

Euphorbia pulcherrima 'Double Form' near Copala

Euphorbia pulcherrima 'Top White'

Euphorbia pulcherrima 'Pegirl'

water very sparingly and keep cool (10°–15°C) after flowering, when the plants may drop their leaves. In early summer, the plants should be repotted in good rich compost, kept as warm and humid as possible, and in good light until autumn. Flower buds are not produced until the long nights of the autumn equinox, at temperatures below 18°C and should then develop through the winter. For instance, at 40–45°N, the latitude of New York, Northern California or Madrid, flower buds are initiated on September 21–25th. In this period, when the buds are being formed, the plants need a minimum of 15°C. If the plants are grown where they get artificial light at night, it is necessary to put them in a dark cupboard or closet for 14 hours each night.

'Double Form' This spectacular shrub is an old Mexican garden plant first introduced to Europe in 1873 by M. Roezl, who found it in a small Indian village in Guerrero in SW Mexico. The plant shown here was growing in Sinaloa State, west of Durango. 'Plenissima' is even more double, with masses of small upright bracts surrounded by a circle of distinctly larger ones.

The following very dwarf varieties were grown at the RHS Garden at Wisley and photographed in early December. **'Marbella'** raised by Gutbers, **'Maren'** raised by Beckman, **'Pegirl'** raised by Jacobsen, **'Red Sails'** raised by Paul Ecke in California, **'Top White'** raised by Hegg in Norway.

Euphorbia pulcherrima 'Marbella'

Codiaeum variegatum 'Punctatum Aureum' in Nairobi

Codiaeum 'Veitchii' with 'Souvenir de Thomas Rochford' (behind)

Ricinus communis with pelargoniums behind, in the temperate house at Wisley

Acalypha wilkesiana 'Marginata' in Hong Kong

Acalypha wilkesiana 'Macrophylla'

Acalypha godseffiana hort. Sander ex Mast. (*Euphorbiaceae*)   A dwarf bushy shrub with bright green leaves margined with white, native of New Guinea. Flowers greenish-yellow. The cultivar **'Barbados Green'**, shown here in Kenya, seems to belong to this species.

Acalypha wilkesiana Muell.   A shrub eventually 2–3m tall, with ovate-acuminate brownish-purple leaves, often edged or streaked with pink or yellow, native of Polynesia and Fiji. Flowers reddish-brown, inconspicuous. The following old named cultivars are recognized by their leaves. **'Macrophylla'** leaves ovate, cordate, reddish-brown, introduced in 1876. **'Macafeeana'** leaves red blotched with bronzy-crimson, introduced in 1877. **'Marginata'** leaves large, greenish-brown, edged with crimson or orange. Introduced from Fiji in 1875. **'Musaica'** leaves rounded, bronzy with orange and green markings.

Codiaeum variegatum (L.) Bl. var. *pictum* (Lodd.) Muell. (*Euphorbiaceae*) A shrub with brightly coloured variegated leaves in a variety of shapes, native of S India, Ceylon and Malaya. Stems eventually to 1.8m. Leaves to 30cm long. Flowers small, the male with 5 petals, the female with 5 sepals, but no petals. Needs well-drained, fertile, lime-free soil. Min. 0°C. The following old varieties were photographed in Kenya. **'Punctatum Aureum'** leaves narrowly lanceolate, well-furnished with yellowish spots and blotches. **'Souvenir de Thomas Rochford'** has long linear leaves, named after the founder of the great firm of T. Rochford and Sons, houseplant specialists founded in 1877 which continued until 1984. **'Veitchii'** has upright lanceolate leaves with pale veins and midribs that turn pinkish with age, named after the great nursery firm of Veitch, founded in Devon in 1808 and closed down in 1914.

Acalypha wilkesiana 'Musaica'

Acalypha wilkesiana 'Macafeeana'

Ricinus communis L. (*Euphorbiaceae*) Castor Oil Plant   A robust plant with very large, often purplish lobed leaves and often with conspicuous spiny fruit, native of the SE Mediterranean area, but now found throughout the tropics, flowering in summer. A shrub to 12m, but usually smaller and often grown as an annual for foliage. Leaves to 60cm across in various shades of green, purple and red in cultivated strains. Capsules spiny or smooth, often bright red; seeds greyish, mottled with brown. 'Zanzibarensis' has the largest leaves. Requires rich soil and temperatures of over 20°C for the seedlings to grow well. The seed coat contains an extremely powerful poison which was used by the KGB to dispose of its enemies.

Acalypha godseffiana 'Barbados Green'

107

Pale green shrubs of *Euphorbia atropurpurea* light up the dark volcanic mountains in C Tenerife

Euphorbia atropurpurea

Euphorbia bravoana

Euphorbia atropurpurea Brouss.
(*Euphorbiaceae*)   A small rounded shrub with
blue-green leaves and bright maroon
inflorescences, native of W and S Tenerife,
growing on dry rocky slopes, at 300–1200m,
flowering in January–March. A much-
branched shrub to 1.5m high and wide. Leaves
mostly at the tips of the stems, oblong-
spathulate, obtuse. Inflorescence with 5–15
rays. Bracts broad, more than 1cm across.
Capsule smooth. For well-drained dry soil in a
sunny position. Min. 0°C or less if dry. An
attractive shrub in leaf and flower.

Euphorbia balsamifera by the coast of NW Tenerife

Euphorbia balsamifera Ait. Á low
rounded greyish shrub, native of all the Canary
Islands and NW Africa, growing on cliff tops
and dry slopes near the sea, flowering in
winter and early spring. Shrub eventually
reaching 2m high and much wider. Leaves
mostly at the tips of the stems, oblong-
spathulate, acute or obtuse, pale green or
glaucous. Inflorescence with a single flower.
Capsule smooth, globose. Well-drained dry
soil in a sunny position. Min. 0°C or less if
dry. *E. balsamifera* subsp. *adenensis* from
S Arabia, Somalia and Aden has shorter,
rounder and bluer leaves on a more upright
plant. It needs hotter, drier conditions.

Euphorbia bravoana Svent. A sparingly
branched shrub with very white leaves and
dark purple inflorescences, native of NE
Gomera, growing in ravines at up to 800m,
flowering in spring. Shrub to 1m; leaves
narrowly lanceolate; bracts less than 5mm
across. Umbels with 2–5 rays. A striking plant
with well-contrasting leaves and flowers like
E. atropurpurea, but has narrower leaves and
bracts and fewer rays. For well-drained dry soil
in a sunny position. Min. 0°C or less if dry.

Euphorbia lambii

Euphorbia lambii Svent. A much-
branched shrub or small tree with bright green
and yellowish inflorescences, native of NW and
C Gomera, growing on the margins of forest at
600–800m, flowering in spring. Stems to 2m;
leaves narrowly lanceolate; bracts 5mm across,
fused for at least half their length. Umbels with
2–5 rays. Glands toothed. A strong-growing
shrub, commonly cultivated in California, with
bright yellow-green flowers, like a stout
E. dendroides. For well-drained dry soil in a
sunny position. Min. 0°C or less if dry.

109

Euphorbia dendroides on the slopes above the town of Simi, in April

Euphorbia dendroides near Nice

Euphorbia hierosolymitana in Turkey

Euphorbia dendroides L.   A much-branched, rounded shrub, native of the Mediterranean coast and naturalized in coastal California, growing on limestone cliffs and rocky places at up to 400m, flowering in March–May. Stems to 2m and as much across. Leaves linear-lanceolate or narrowly elliptic, 2–6cm long. Rays usually 5; the rhombic-ovate to kidney-shaped bracts and yellow flowers. Capsule smooth. Easily grown in well-drained soil, drought-resistant in summer. Min. −5°C.

Euphorbia glauca Forst. fil.   A perennial with numerous fleshy sprawling stems, native of New Zealand and Norfolk Island, growing on rocks and sand dunes around the coast, flowering in October–April (summer). Stems to about 1m. Leaves glaucous, all up the stems, elliptic to oblong-obovate, 2–10cm long. Rays 5–6. Glands dark purple. For sandy soil with good drainage. Min. −3°C, perhaps less.

Euphorbia hierosolymitana Boiss. A shrub with wiry stiff branches and soft flowering shoots, native of the eastern Mediterranean from W Turkey to Israel, growing on limestone cliffs and rocky places, at up to 300m, flowering in January–June. Stems to 3m and as much across, the dead branchlets not becoming spiny as in *E. acanthothamnos*. Leaves elliptic to elliptic-obovate, 1–4.5cm long. Rays usually 5; the obovate bracts and flowers bright greenish-yellow. Fruit verrucose. Easily grown in well-drained soil, drought-resistant in summer. Min. −5°C. Described by Boissier as common around Jerusalem, hence the specific name.

Euphorbia mellifera Ait.   A shrub or small tree with flat heads of brownish flowers, native of Tenerife, La Palma and Madeira, growing in laurel forest in the mountains, flowering in spring. Eventually a tree to 15m, but usually seen as a multi-stemmed shrub. Leaves narrowly lanceolate, dark green, about 10cm long. Flowers scented of honey. For any moist soil in sun or partial shade in a sheltered position. Min. −10°C, but will usually sprout from the root if cut to the ground.

Euphorbia stygiana H. Wats.   A low shrub with dark green leaves, often becoming red in autumn, native of the Azores, growing in rocky bushy places, particularly in small volcanic craters, at 500–800m, flowering in spring. Stems to 1.5m; leaves about 15cm long and 4cm wide, oblong, mucronate, glaucous beneath, often becoming bright red in autumn. Rays about 4, repeatedly branching. Capsule about 6mm across, verrucose. For well-drained soil in a sheltered position. Min. −10°C. Related to *E. dendroides*.

Euphorbia mellifera in Madeira

Euphorbia stygiana

Euphorbia glauca in New Zealand

111

Euphorbia milii var. *splendens*

Euphorbia milii growing in Tenerife

Euphorbia hislopii at Kew

Euphorbia milii var. *breoni*

Euphorbia lophogona

Euphorbia milii var. *tananarivae*

Euphorbia fulgens

Euphorbia fulgens Karw. ex Klotzsch (*Euphorbiaceae*)   A slightly succulent branching, arching shrub with small red flowers, native of Mexico, flowering in winter. Stems to 2m. Leaves deciduous, lanceolate, stalked, about 8cm long. Flowers in clusters in the leaf axils, with 5 rounded red petal-like bracts, looking very unspurge-like. 'Albatross' (not shown) has pure white flowers and bluish-green leaves; 'Alba' has creamy flowers. Easily grown and propagated by cuttings. For warm, humid conditions and often seen in florists. Min. 0°C.

Euphorbia hislopii N.E. Br.   A large spreading thorn with salmon-pink bracts, native of Madagascar. Stems to 180cm, 8–10-sided; spines to 25mm long. Leaves ovate-lanceolate, to 18mm long, deciduous in hot, dry seasons. For well-drained dry soil. Min. 0°C.

Euphorbia lophogona Lam.   A slow-growing succulent without spines, but with brown hairs on the corners, native of Madagascar. Stems to 50cm. Leaves oblanceolate, to 12cm long. Bracts pink or nearly white. Easily grown in warm conditions. This is a parent of many hybrids including *E. × lomii* Rauh, and the 'Giant Christ's Thorn' raised by Ed Hummel in California. Min. 10°C.

Euphorbia milii Desmoul. syn. *E. splendens* Bojer ex Hook.   A spreading or creeping thorn with bright red flowers, native of Madagascar. Stems to 1.8m but usually less than 1m tall, 5–6-sided, about 9mm thick. Leaves deciduous, obovate, to 5cm long. Bracts red, to 1.2cm across. For well-drained dry soil. Min. 0°C. The varieties, natural and man-made hybrids and cultivars of *E. milii* and related species from Madagascar are complex and difficult to name. The plants here were photographed in cultivation and seem to be nearest to the named forms described. Var. *bojeri* is one of the shortest-leaved and most freely branching; var. **splendens** the largest.

Euphorbia milii Desmoul var. **breoni** (L. Nois.) Ursch & Leandri   A large long-leaved thorn, native of Madagascar. Stems to 1.8m. Leaves deciduous, lanceolate, 10–15cm long. Bracts red. For well-drained dry soil. Min. 0°C.

Euphorbia milii var. **tananarivae** Leandri syn. var. *alba* hort.   A creamy-yellow flowered thorn with lanceolate leaves, native of Madagascar. Vegetatively close to var. *breoni* but with flowers creamy-white to pale yellow. Var. *lutea* is said to have lemon-yellow bracts edged with red. Var. *longifolia* Rauh has leaves with the edges curved upwards and large heads of pale sulphur-yellow flowers.

Euphorbia xanthi Engleman (often spelled *xantii*)   A slightly succulent branching, upright shrub with masses of small white flowers, native of Mexico in Baja California, flowering in spring. Shrub to 2m, with green pencil-like stems. Leaves deciduous, narrowly lanceolate, about 8cm long. Flowers slightly scented, with 5 white 'petals' looking very unspurge-like. Easily grown and propagated by cuttings. For hot dry conditions. Min. 0°C.

Euphorbia milii var. *lutea* in the garden of the Carnivore restaurant, Nairobi

Euphorbia xanthi at the Living Desert Reserve, Palm Desert, California

Jatropha integerrima at Elbow Beach Hotel garden, Bermuda

Jatropha integerrima

Jatropha podagrica

Jatropha multifida

Ricinocarpos 'Bridal Star'

Pedilanthus tithymaloides

Ricinocarpos tuberculatus

Pedilanthus tithymaloides

Jatropha integerrima Jacq. (*Euphorbiaceae*)
A shrub or small tree with dark green leaves
and clusters of small bright red flowers, native
of Cuba and the West Indies, flowering spring–
summer. Tree to 6m, leafless in winter. Leaves
usually 3-lobed, with the terminal lobe largest,
the side lobes of variable size even on the same
stem. Flowers tubular at the base, about 1.5cm
across. Plants can be grown outdoors in frost-
free climates, with a winter minimum of 10°C.
If grown in pots or tubs they need a dry period
in winter and a warm, wet summer.
'**Compacta**' is a slow-growing, free-flowering
clone suitable for pot culture.

Jatropha multifida L.   A shrub or small tree
with deeply lobed leaves and upright branched
clusters of bright red flowers, native of tropical
America, flowering in spring and summer.
Tree to 7m, leafless in winter. Leaves 7–11-
lobed to the base, with narrow entire or deeply
toothed lobes. Flowers tubular at the base,
bright coral-red. Culture as for *Jatropha
integerrima*.

Jatropha podagrica Hook.   A shrub with a
swollen bulbous stem and terminal rosettes of
long-stalked, 3- or 5-lobed leaves and flat-
topped clusters of small bright red flowers,
native of Central America, flowering in spring
and summer. Plant usually about 1.5m in the
wild, to 3m in cultivation. Leaves 15–30cm, as
wide as long, with 3–5 deep lobes, whitish
beneath. Flowers flat, in groups of 5–6, one
female surrounded by four or five males. Easy
to grow in a pot; culture as for *Jatropha
integerrima*.

Ricinocarpos tuberculatus F. Muell.
(*Euphorbiaceae*) Wedding Bush   A spreading
heath-like shrub with white starry flowers,
native of Western Australia, flowering in
spring. Shrub to 2.5m; leaves to 2cm long;
flowers around 1.5cm across.

'**Bridal Star**' is a cultivar with larger flowers,
perhaps derived from the hardier *R. pinifolius*
found from Queensland to Tasmania.

Pedilanthus tithymaloides (L.) Poit. subsp.
tithymaloides   A shrubby succulent with
cylindrical stems and strange, beak-like red
flowers, native of S Mexico and Central
America to S Columbia, flowering most of the
year. Stems to 3m; leaves ovate, elliptic to
ovate-lanceolate, 1–16cm long. Bracts 12mm
long; flowers 7–14mm. For any well-drained
soil. Min. 0°C. Other subspecies are found in
the West Indies.

Geranium maderense

Geranium maderense in the Abbey Gardens, Tresco in July

Geranium rubescens in the Abbey Gardens, Tresco in July

Erodium trifolium (Cav.) Cav. syn. *E. hymenodes* L'Hérit. (*Geraniaceae*) A softly hairy and glandular perennial with white flowers veined with magenta pink, the upper petals blotched with brownish red, native of Morocco in the Atlas Mountains growing on limestone rocks, flowering most of the year. Plants evergreen, to 20cm, with branched flowering stems from a central rootstock. Leaves shallowly or deeply 3–5 lobed. Flowers about 2.6cm across; sepals 6–7cm, with a short mucro about 0.5mm long. Easily grown and self-seeding. Min. −7°C. Very close and often confused with *E. pelargoniiflorum* Boiss. & Held. from Turkey, which has a mucro 5mm long on the sepals.

Geranium canariense Reut. (*Geraniaceae*) A large fleshy short-lived rosette perennial with dark green leaves and glandular-hairy flowering stems, native of the Canary Islands of Tenerife, Palma, Gomera and Hierro, growing in shady ravines and by streams in laurel forests and pine woods, at 500–1000m, flowering in March–July. Main stem of the rosette to 30cm, with branching and spreading inflorescences to 1m tall. Leaves long-stalked, the blade to 30cm across, deeply divided into 5 segments, each further divided nearly to the midrib, with the lobes overlapping. Flowers 2–3.6cm across, deep pink; petals narrow, 6–9mm across, not overlapping. Easily grown and free-seeding in moist well-drained soil. Min. −3°C.

Geranium harveyi Briq. syn. *G. sericeum* Harvey A clump-forming silky, silver-leaved perennial with purplish flowers, native of South Africa in C and E Cape Province, growing on hot sunny rocks or among scrub on grassy slopes at 1000–2000m, flowering mainly in October–December (summer). Clumps to 60cm or more across. Leaves on slender stalks, the blades 5–30mm across, usually about 20mm, deeply 5-lobed, greyish above, white beneath. Flowers 24–30mm across, magenta to purplish-blue. A good silver cushion for a hot dry sunny position and intermittent rainfall. Min. −10°C.

Geranium palmatum at Trebah, Cornwall

Geranium canariense wild by a stream in NW Tenerife

Geranium maderense Yeo   A huge rosette perennial erupting in a mass of flowers before seeding and dying, native of Madeira where it is frequent in gardens and by roadsides but very rare in the wild, surviving above Levada dos Mouros, growing on moist rocks in full sun at about 1400m, flowering in March–August. Here it is in fog much of the year. Plants to 1.5m in flower, monocarpic, sometimes biennial or flowering after 3–4 years growth; occasionally forming offsets at the base. Main stem of the rosette to 60cm with the old leaf stalks persisting and reflexing to hold the plant steady. Leaves long-stalked, the blade to 60cm across, deeply divided into 5 segments, each segment further divided to the midrib, with the lobes barely overlapping. Inflorescence thickly covered with reddish glandular hairs. Flowers 4–4.4cm across, purplish-pink; petals 13–18mm wide, overlapping, with pale veins and blackish in the centre. Easily grown and free-seeding in well-drained soil. Growing mainly through the winter, drought-tolerant in summer, especially in shade. Min. −3°C. Without doubt the most spectacular of all *Geranium* species, for a conservatory or essentially frost-free climate. It needs a huge pot to reach its full size and flower well.

Geranium palmatum Cav. syn. *G. anemonifolium* L'Hérit.   A very large fleshy short-lived rosette perennial with dark green leaves and glandular-hairy flowering stems,

Erodium hymenodes

Geranium harveyi from Somerset East

native of Madeira, flowering in April–July. Main stem of the rosette very short with branching and spreading inflorescences to 1.2m tall. Leaves long-stalked, the blade to 35cm across, deeply divided into 5 segments, the middle segment stalked and each segment further divided nearly to the midrib, with the lobes not overlapping. Flowers 3.3–4.5cm across, deep pink shading to crimson in the centre; petals 13–18mm wide. Easily grown and free-seeding in moist well-drained soil. Min. −3°C. This species is similar to *G. canariense* in general habit but larger and more striking in flower.

Geranium rubescens Yeo   A small rosette-forming biennial like a large Herb Robert (*Geranium robertianum*), with leaves which colour to a brilliant red in autumn, native of Madeira, flowering in April–July. Rosette with branching and spreading inflorescences to 60cm tall. Leaf stalks shining red; blade to 25cm across, deeply divided into 5 segments, the middle segment stalked, each further divided to the midrib, with the lobes not overlapping. Flowers 2–3.3cm across, bright pink; petals 7–13mm wide, not overlapping. Easily grown and free-seeding in moist well-drained soil in shade. Min. −5°C.

Pelargonium tetragonum

Pelargonium tetragonum with *Crassula argentea* in the Little Karroo in October

Pelargonium longicaule var. *longicaule*

Pelargonium quercetorum at Harry Hay's

Pelargonium rodneyanum in Canberra

Pelargonium australe Willd. (s. *Peristera*)
A leafy perennial with numerous heads of
small flowers, native of Australia from W
Australia to Victoria, NSW, South Australia,
S Queensland and in E Tasmania, growing on
dunes by the sea or on granite outcrops inland,
flowering from September–May. Plants to 1m
across, 30cm tall; leaves rounded, shallowly
toothed, 2–10cm wide. Flowers in umbels of
4–12, upper petals marked with purple and
slightly broader than the lower; little scent.
Easily grown in sandy soil. Min. 0°C. This is
the most widespread of the eight *Pelargonium*
species known in Australia. Another,
P. rodneyanum is described below.

Pelargonium endlicherianum Fenzl
(s. *Jenkinsonia*) A dwarf plant with bright
magenta flowers, native of Turkey near Ankara
and in the Taurus Mountains from Mugla east
to Artvin and in NW Syria, growing on dry
limestone rocks in open woods at up to
1500m, flowering in June–August. Stems thick
and short; leaves soft, rounded, shallowly
lobed and toothed. Flowers in umbels of up to
10; upper petals recurved, about 35mm long,
obovate, lobed, the 3 lower minute. Easily
grown in well-drained poor soil so that the
leaves stay small. Min. −10°C but liable to rot
in wet winters.

Pelargonium longicaule Jacq. var.
longicaule (s. *Myrrhidium*) A delicate
creeping plant with finely divided leaves and
flowers with 2 large petals, native of South
Africa in the SW Cape growing in sandy
places, especially after fires, flowering in
August–January. Stems to 50cm, slender;
leaves deeply bipinnatisect into narrow
segments. Flowers 1–4 in the umbel, the upper
petals obovate, about 25mm long, 12mm
wide, white to pink or mauve with deep red
veins, the lower petals much smaller, 2 or 3,
about 4mm wide; fertile stamens, usually 7.
Easily grown in sandy soil and said to be easy
from stem cuttings. Min. −3°C.
Photographed on Cape Peninsula at Hout Bay.
Var. *angustipetalum* Boucher is a striking plant
with narrower, yellowish upper petals, about
40mm long.

Pelargonium myrrhifolium (L.)
L'Hérit. var. **coriandrifolium** (L.) Harv.
(s. *Myrrhidium*) A delicate scrambling plant
with very finely divided leaves, native of South
Africa in the SW Cape, growing in sandy,
often disturbed places, flowering August–
February. Stems to 40cm; leaves bipinnatisect
with the segments less than 2mm wide.
Flowers 2–5 in the umbel with 2 large upper
petals 20mm long, 10mm wide, obovate, white
to pinkish-purple. Fertile stamens, usually 5.
Easily grown in sandy soils and likely to sow
itself. Min. −3°C. Close to *P. longicaule* but
has fewer stamens and smaller flowers. Var.
myrrhifolium has broader leaf segments and
even smaller flowers, the petals 18mm long.

Pelargonium quercetorum Agnew
(s. *Jenkinsonia*) A large leafy plant with dense
umbels of flowers, native of SE Turkey in the
Zab Gorge and on Beyaz Da, and of NE Iraq
growing in moist rocky clearings in oak scrub
at around 1200m, flowering June–August.
Leaves to 18cm across, glabrous, deeply
7-lobed and toothed; flowers up to 30 in the
umbel, the upper petals 22–28mm long,
oblanceolate, the three lower 3–5mm or
absent. For well-drained soil and tolerant of
partial shade. Min. −10°C. I have seen both
this and *P. endlicherianum* thriving outside in
the Royal Botanic Garden, Edinburgh.

Pelargonium rodneyanum Mitchell
(s. *Ligularia*) A leafy plant with a tuberous
root and small flowers, native of Australia in
South Australia, NSW and Victoria growing in
dry rocky places, in sclerophyll forest,
flowering in November–May. Stems to 40cm.
Leaves mostly basal, 5–7-lobed. Flowers about
3cm across. Easily grown in sun or part shade.
Min. −7°C. Rather similar to the South
African *P. ionidiflorum*.

Pelargonium tetragonum (L. fil.) L'Hérit.
(s. *Jenkinsonia*) A shrubby plant with fleshy
stems and large creamy-white flowers, native
of South Africa in the S Cape from Worcester
to Grahamstown, growing with other shrubby
succulents on dry rocky hills, flowering
September–December. Stems triangular to
square in section, smooth, sprawling or
climbing to 2m; leaves small, fleshy, about
4cm across, lobed and toothed. Flowers in
pairs with four petals, the upper broadly
spathulate, about 3.5cm long, creamy-white,
striped with purple, the lower much smaller,
about 2.3cm. Easy to grow in dry sandy soil,
watered mainly in spring; easy to cultivate
from cuttings. Min. 0°C. Photographed in the
Karroo near Tradowspas in October.

Pelargonium endlicherianum in a garden in W Sussex

Pelargonium australe

Pelargonium myrrhifolium var. *coriandrifolium*

Pelargonium trifidum

Pelargonium alpinum

Pelargonium cotyledonis at Kew

Pelargonium barklyi

Pelargonium alpinum Eckl. & Zeyh.
(s. *Ligularia*)   A suckering and spreading
dwarf up to 15cm, native of South Africa in
the SW Cape growing in mountains around
Ceres and Tulbagh at 900–2000m, in moist or
wet places in fynbos, flowering in November–
January. Stems creeping and scrambling;
leaves softly hairy and glandular, heart-shaped,
toothed and wrinkled, often with a ring of
purple near the margin, 3–5cm long. Flowers
usually in pairs, pinkish or salmon-pink, rarely
white, about 4cm across. Easily grown in moist
peaty soil. Min. −5°C, perhaps less, as it is
regularly snow-covered in the wild.

Pelargonium barklyi Scott Elliott
(s. *Ligularia*)   A winter-growing plant with a

woody tuber and cyclamen-like leaves, native
of South Africa from the Richtersveld to
Kamiesberg in the NW Cape, growing in the
shade of rocks and shrubs at 600–900m,
flowering August–October. Stems short, dying
away in summer; leaves 5–7cm across, heart-
shaped, finely toothed, purple beneath, in a
rosette on the ground. Flowers on long slender
upright stalks, 3–5 in an umbel, creamy-white,
about 2.5cm across. Needs sandy soil, moist in
winter, drier in summer. Min. 0°C. Plant from
Namaqualand.

Pelargonium cotyledonis (L.) L'Hérit.   A
small, succulent shrublet with rugose leaves
and white flowers with equal petals, native of
the island of St Helena, growing on dry cliffs at

200–600m, often bathed in fog and mist,
flowering in September–February. Stems
rarely to 1m, usually around 15cm; leaves 3–
4cm across, on slender stalks. Flowers white or
pale pink, 25–30mm across. Now endangered
in the wild. Very tender. Min. 0°C.

Pelargonium fulgidum (L.) L'Hérit.
(s. *Ligularia*)   A sprawling shrubby succulent,
native of South Africa along the coast of the
W Cape, north to the Orange River, growing
on fixed dunes and rocky hills near the sea,
flowering June–November. Roots tuberous;
stems fleshy, covered with the remains of dead
stipules and leaves, to 2m long if supported by
surrounding vegetation. Leaves deciduous in
summer, softly hairy, acrid, with up to 3 pairs

Pelargonium spinosum

Pelargonium fulgidum

Pink form of *Pelargonium fulgidum* at Fibrex Nurseries

Pelargonium fulgidum on dunes at Lambert's Bay

of deep lobes. Flowers bright scarlet, up to 9 in a stiff flattened umbel, with a wide throat, adapted for pollination by sunbirds. For sandy soil, dry in summer, moist in winter. Min. 0°C. This species, introduced to Holland in the early 18th century, was one parent of the old Uniques. A salmon-pink form is grown in England.

Pelargonium spinosum Willd. (s. *Ligularia*) A low, stiff, spiny succulent shrub, leafless in summer, native of South Africa in the NW Cape in the Richtersveld, and of SW Namibia growing in rocky and sandy places in desert conditions; what rainfall there is in this area falls in winter, but fog is frequent in early

morning. Flowering is usually after rain, mainly in August–October. Stems succulent, much branched with spiny stipules and persistent leaf stalks up to 10cm long. Leaves fleshy, the blades about 2.5cm across, toothed and shallowly lobed. Smaller, totally deciduous leaves are borne in the axils of the large leaves. Flowers 3–10 in an umbel on a short stiff stalk, 5–6cm across, white to pale pink with purple feathering on the upper two petals. Cuttings are said to be difficult to root. Very coarse well-drained soil and full sun are needed for successful flowering. Min. 0°C. Photographed in the Karroo Botanic Garden, Worcester; plants from McKillan's Pass.

Pelargonium trifidum Jacq. syn. *P. fragile* (Andr.) Willd., *P. tripartitum* Willd. (s. *Ligularia*) A small twiggy and shrubby species with persistent fleshy roots, native of the S and E Cape from Worcester to Peddie and in the Swartberg, growing in hot dry, rocky places, often among bushes, flowering September–January. Stems straggling to 1m. Leaves 1.5–4cm across, divided into 3 stalked and toothed lobes. Flowers 3–6 in an umbel, cream with red stripes on the 2 upper petals, about 4cm across. Plants should be kept on the dry side and can be propagated easily by cuttings. Min −3°C, perhaps if dry.

121

Pelargonium triste

Pelargonium triste on the Cape Peninsula

Pelargonium alternans

Pelargonium crithmifolium

Pelargonium alternans Wendl. (s. *Otidia*)
A small shrubby much-branched succulent,
native of South Africa in the SW Cape,
especially in the Karroo semi-desert between
Vanrhyns Pass and Prince Albert, growing in
rock crevices, flowering mainly in autumn and
spring. In this area, what little rain there is falls
in winter, and summers are very hot and dry.
A knobbly shrub to 40cm tall, with thick
woody stems; leaves deciduous in summer,
pinnate, hairy and glandular, 20–60mm long.
Inflorescence simple, with 1–4 flowers in the
umbel; petals white or pale pink, narrow, the
upper pair bent back, slightly larger than the
others. Said to be one of the easiest of the
succulent species to grow, in very open sandy
soil. If watered in summer, the plants remain
green. Min. 0°C.

Pelargonium brevipetalum N. E. Br.
(s. *Otidia*) A low, succulent shrub striking for
its dense umbels of spiky purple seed heads,
native of South Africa in the SW Cape,
described from near Matjesfontein, flowering
September–November. Stems to 20cm, fleshy
and woody, much branched. Leaves fleshy,
pinnate, the lobes incurved on the edges.
Inflorescence much branched, deep purple
with very short pedicels; flowers minute, the
creamy-yellow petals shorter than the sepals,
in dense umbels of 15 or more. We
photographed this strange plant, which is close
to *P. carnosum*, in the Karroo Botanic Garden
at Worcester in flower and fruit in November.
Min. 0°C, perhaps.

Pelargonium caffrum (Eckl. & Zehr.) Harv.
(s. *Polyactium*) A robust plant with deeply cut
leaves and flowers with dissected petals, native
of South Africa from Knysna to the Katberg,
growing in grassland and scrub, flowering
mainly in December–February. Roots
tuberous. Leaves all basal, usually dissected
into linear lobes. Flowers yellowish to purplish,
about 5cm across. Cultivation as for *P. luridum*.
Min. −5°C if dry.

Pelargonium crithmifolium J. E. Sm.
(s. *Otida*) A gnarled shrub with knobby
stems and fleshy leaves, native of S Namibia
and South Africa in the W Cape, growing in
dry rocky places, flowering in May–October.
Shrub to 50cm; leaves 5–12cm long, with
short pinnae, branched at apex. Flowers about
2.2cm across. For dry stony soil. Min. −3°C.

Pelargonium gibbosum (L.) L'Hérit.
(s. *Polyactium*) A sprawling and scrambling
plant with swollen nodes and small green
flowers, native of South Africa in the W Cape
from Hondeklip Bay south to the Cape
Peninsula, growing on dunes and on rocky
places near the sea, flowering November–
April. Stems long-scrambling to 1m or more,
swollen at the nodes, becoming pale brown
and woody; leaves deciduous in summer,
glaucous, thin and fleshy, glabrous, with one
or two pairs of leaflets and a 3-lobed terminal
leaflet. Flowers green to yellowish, opening
and scented at night like cheap soap, 15–
17mm across; the petals rounded, all equal.
Easily grown in sandy soil and easy to root.
Min. −3°C.

Pelargonium luridum (Andr.) Sweet
(s. *Polyactium*) A robust leafy plant with
knobbly tuberous roots and deeply cut leaves,
native of southern Africa from Tanzania and
Zaire south to Angola and the eastern Cape,
growing in rich grassland, flowering
September–April. Stems short, at ground
level; leaves all basal, variable in shape but
usually deeply dissected into linear lobes about
1cm wide. Inflorescence to 1m, topped by an
umbel of 5-60 flowers. Petals about equal,
about 2cm long, white to pink or pale yellow,
sometimes red in Angola and Mozambique.
This species grows in summer and responds to
rich soil, especially if bonfire ash is added; it
should be kept dry in winter. Min. −5°C,
perhaps less.

Pelargonium triste (L.) L'Hérit.
(s. *Polyactium*) A tuberous plant with ferny
leaves and small dull but wonderfully scented
flowers, native of South Africa in the W Cape
from Steinkopf in the north to Riversdale,
growing in sandy soil, flowering August–
February. Roots tuberous and spreading to
form new plants; stems short; leaves mostly
basal, short stalked, 10–45cm long, hairy,
deeply dissected and carrot-like. Inflorescence
to 60cm; flowers in umbels of 6–20, scented in
the evening, 2–2.5cm across, yellowish-green
to brownish, often with purple lines. Easily
grown in sandy soil, kept dry in summer,
moist in winter and spring. This was one of the
earliest of the Cape pelargoniums to be grown
in England, by John Tradescant in 1632.
Min. 0°C. Photographed at Hout Bay in
October.

Pelargonium brevipetalum in the Karroo Botanic garden, Worcester, SW Cape in October

Pelargonium caffrum at Fibrex Nurseries

Pelargonium luridum in Natal, near Nottingham Road

Pelargonium gibbosum on dunes at Lambert's Bay in October

Pelargonium fruticosum on the Groot Swartberge in October

Pelargonium coronopifolium on the Pakhuis pass above Clanwilliam in October

Pelargonium ovale subsp. *hyalinum* on the Franshoek pass, Worcester in October

Pelargonium coronopifolium Jacq. (s. *Campylia*) A dwarf mat-forming shrub, native of South Africa in the Cedarberg, especially near Clanwilliam, growing in dry, sandy and rocky places in the mountains, flowering September–December. Plant suckering and forming mats of short stems to 40cm, usually less. Leaves long-stalked with narrow blades with few scattered teeth, 7–9cm long and 6–7mm wide. Flowers deep pink to purple, 2–3 in the umbel with spathulate petals, the upper pair 10–14mm, the lower 3 about 9–12mm long. In the area where this species grows wild it receives most of its water in the cold winter and survives very hot dry summers. Min. −3°C, perhaps. Photographed on the Pakhuis Pass above Clanwilliam.

Pelargonium fruticosum (Cav.) Willd. syn. *P. divaricatum* (Thunb.) DC. (s. *Glaucophyllum*) A dwarf cushion-forming shrub, native of South Africa in the S Cape between Ladismith and Willowmore, at low altitudes on the coast and up to 1500m in the mountains inland, growing in fynbos and on moist rocky slopes, flowering throughout the year, but particularly September–November. Stems thin and woody when old, forming cushions to 1m high and across; leaves rather fleshy and tough, pinnate and finely divided into narrow pointed lobes. Flowers solitary, rarely 2–4 in an umbel, 23–30mm across, white to pale pink, the upper petals streaked with red. This species is very similar to *P. ternatum* (*see below*) but is found further east; it is reported to be difficult to root from cuttings and to be intolerant of drought as it comes from an area where rainfall is spread throughout the year. Min. −3°C, perhaps less. Photographed on the Swartberg north of Oudtshoorn in October.

Pelargonium ovale (Burm. fil.) L'Hérit. (s. *Campylia*) A dwarf tufted or almost cushion-like shrub, native of South Africa found scattered through the S Cape, from Ceres and Worcester to Swellendam, growing in mountain and coastal fynbos (heathland), flowering throughout the year. Stems creeping and ascending; leaves not scented, long-stalked, with flat ovate to almost round, toothed blades, silvery or grey-green, hairy, strongly ribbed beneath. Flowers 3–5 in the umbel, 3.5–5cm across, pale to deep magenta-pink, the upper petals often much larger than the rest. Three subspecies are recognized: Subsp. **ovale** with ovate leaves has the upper and lower petals the same length; subsp. *veronicifolium* (Eckl. & Zehr.) Hugo, with very narrow leaves and tiny narrow petals is found in the eastern part of the species range; and subsp. **hyalinum** Hugo, found at high altitudes in the SW Cape has almost round leaf blades with long spreading hairs and deep pink flowers, the lower petals quite broad; this last subspecies is photographed here on the Franshoek Pass near Worcester.

Pelargonium ternatum (L. fil.) Jacq. (s. *Glaucophyllum*) A dwarf shrub, native of South Africa in the W Cape in the Langeberg between Montagu and Riversdale, growing in sandy and rocky places, flowering through the year, but mainly in September. Very similar to *P. fruticosum*, but differs in its distribution and in its leaves which are more ternate with wider lobes. The flowers of *P. fruticosum* are formed

Pelargonium ternatum

Pelargonium tricolor on the Robinson pass near Oudtshoorn in October

Pelargonium tricolor from the Swartberge

in the axils of long-petioled leaves, while the flowers of *P. ternatum* are formed in the axils of almost sessile leaves. Reported to be easy to propagate from cuttings and easy in acid sandy soil. Photographed on the Tradowes Pass near Swellendam in late October.

Pelargonium tricolor Curtis syn. *P. violareum* Jacq. (s. *Campylia*)   A dwarf tufted and suckering plant with very striking flowers, native of South Africa in the Swartberge and the Rooiberg near Oudtshoorn and in the Langeberg, growing on dry rocky slopes and mountain fynbos, flowering September–December. A variable species, with thin stems to 30cm, usually around 15cm tall; leaves long-stalked with small deeply toothed narrowly ovate to linear blades, greyish-green or silvery. Flowers opening in the sun, 2–4 in the umbel, 2.5–3.5cm across, glistening white, the upper petals with a large blackish-crimson spot at the base or sometimes all crimson; the lower three petals usually pure white. One of the most charming of all the species, three different forms are shown here: that from the Garcia Pass through the Langeberg has the upper petals all crimson; that from the Robinson Pass near Oudtshoorn has linear leaves and a red spot on the upper petals only; and that from the Swartberg has obovate leaves and red lines on the three lower petals (C. D. & R. 899). Easily grown in sandy peaty soil, kept rather dry in winter. Cuttings sometimes difficult to root. Hardy to −3°C, perhaps less. The name *tricolor* has often been given to the hybrid between *P. tricolor* and *P. ovale* correctly called 'Splendide' (*see p. 131*).

Pelargonium tricolor on the Garcia pass

Pelargonium ovale subsp.*ovale*

125

Pelargonium echinatum in the Huntington gardens, Los Angeles

Pelargonium echinatum 'Miss Stapleton'

Pelargonium longifolium on the Pakhuis pass above Clanwilliam in October

Pelargonium crassicaule L'Hérit.
(s. *Cortusina*)   A shrubby much-branched succulent with thick stems and silky-hairy leaves, native of the southwest coast of Namibia near Luderitz, to the mouth of the Orange River just inside South Africa, growing in rock crevices in desert conditions where what little rain there is falls in winter but early morning mist may occur throughout the year.

Flowering in March–October (autumn–spring) but mainly in August–September. Stems about 1.5–2cm thick, to 20cm high, slow growing; leaves deciduous in summer in the wild, the blades round, wavy, toothed, decurrent into the petiole, to 6cm across, silky hairy. Flowers in umbels of 5–9, about 2–2.5cm across, pale pink or white to pale yellow, unmarked or with spots and lines, sometimes on all the petals.

Easy to grow in well-drained sandy soil; if allowed to become dry the leaves drop but if watered carefully the plant remains leafy and flowers throughout the year. I have found that in warm moist conditions the stems are susceptible to botrytis and care must be taken to keep the leaves dry in winter. Min. 0°C. Specimen from Luderitz.

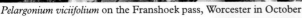
Pelargonium viciifolium on the Franshoek pass, Worcester in October

Pelargonium incrassatum

Pelargonium echinatum Curtis
(s. *Cortusina*)   One of the most attractive
species with little-branched succulent spiny
stems, native of South Africa in the NW Cape,
from the mouth of the Orange River south to
Clanwilliam, growing on dry stony hills,
usually under rocks or bushes, flowering July–
November. Roots tuberous; stems about 1cm
in diameter, covered with the short spiny
remains of stipules; leaves deciduous in
summer, rounded, shallowly 3-, 5- or 7-lobed
and toothed, silky hairy, especially beneath.
Umbels of 3–8 flowers on long stalks; petals
white turning pink or pale pink to purple, the
upper pair brightly spotted with red. Easily
cultivated in well-drained soil, losing its leaves
if allowed to dry out in summer. Cuttings are
easy to root if taken when the plant is growing
actively. Min. −3°C. **'Miss Stapleton'** has
bright magenta-pink flowers.

Pelargonium incrassatum (Andr.) Sims
(s. *Hoarea*)   A small plant with a rosette of
silvery leaves and a succession of bright
pinkish-purple flowers, native of South Africa
in the NW Cape, from near Springbok to near
Clanwilliam, often common on gravelly or
stony plains, with fine displays of annuals,
flowering August–September. Root a short
blackish tuber; leaves all basal, the blade
3–6cm long, with narrow irregular pinnae,
silky hairy, appearing in autumn, dying away in
early summer. Flower stems 15–20cm.
Flowers 20–40 in dense umbels; the upper pair
of petals 18–22mm long, spathulate; the lower
three narrow, 10mm long. Easily grown in
sandy soil; water brings the plant into leaf and
it should be kept dry for several months after
the leaves begin to die away. Propagation is by
seed or division of the tubers. Min. 0°C.

Pelargonium longifolium (Burm. fil.) Jacq.
(s. *Hoarea*)   A small tuberous-rooted plant,
exceptionally variable, native of South Africa
in the SW Cape, growing in rocky or sandy

Pelargonium crassicaule from near Luderitz, Namibia

soil, usually in dry fynbos, flowering mainly
November–January. Tubers small, covered
with the remains of old leaf bases. Leaves all
basal, entire to pinnate and carrot-like.
Flowers on a short (to 25cm) branching
inflorescence, in umbels of 3–5; petals about
12mm long, narrow, white, yellowish or
pinkish, often all with dark markings. For well-
drained sandy soil; should be watered
sparingly, only in winter or when the leaves are
growing. Min. −3°C.

Pelargonium viciifolium DC. (s. *Hoarea*)
A small tuberous-rooted plant, native of South

Africa in the SW Cape, growing in rocky or
sandy soil, usually in fynbos in the mountains,
flowering mainly November–January. Tubers
small, the remains of old leaf bases extending
above the ground. Leaves all basal, pinnate
with narrow lobes; flowers on a short (to
10cm) branching inflorescence, in umbels of
3–5; petals about 12mm long, narrow, usually
pinkish. This is part of the *P. pinnatum* group,
common in the mountains of the SW Cape,
with variably pinnate leaves and white, pale
yellow or orange-pink flowers. These small
plants need sandy peaty soil and water only in
winter. Min. −3°C.

Pelargonium reniforme in the National Botanic garden, Pretoria

Pelargonium reniforme

Pelargonium abrotanifolium on dry hills near Riversdale, S Cape in October

Pelargonium abrotanifolium

Pelargonium exstipulatum in Kirstenbosch Botanic garden, near Cape Town

Pelargonium dichondrifolium

Pelargonium ionidiflorum   *Pelargonium sidoides* near Rhodes

Pelargonium abrotanifolium (L. fil.) Jacq. (s. *Reniformia*) A greyish twiggy shrublet, native of South Africa in Cape Province and the southern Orange Free State, growing in dry rocky places, flowering most of the year. Roots fleshy; stems up to 1m, woody at the base. Leaves finely divided, appressed silky or with long spreading hairs, scented of *Santolina*. Flowers white to pink or purple, 15–20mm across. Easily grown in dry sandy soil and rooted from stem or root cuttings. Min. −5°C. C. D. & R. 862 from near Riversdale.

Pelargonium dichondrifolium DC. syn. *P. reliquifolium* N. E. Br., *P. cradockense* Knuth, *P. burchellii* Knuth, *P. middletonianum* Knuth (s. *Reniformia*) A small tufted plant spreading by underground roots, native of the E Cape in the area between Middleberg and Somerset East, growing in rock crevices on hot dry hills at up to 1700m, flowering January–May. Roots tuberous, far spreading and forming new plants; stems short, covered with the remains of old leaf stalks. Leaf blades almost round, shallowly lobed, 5–23mm across, softly hairy, smelling slightly of hops. Inflorescence repeatedly branching; umbels 2–5-flowered. Petals white, rarely pale pink, the three lower unmarked, obovate, 13mm long, larger than the two upper which are spathulate, feathered and spotted with red. Easily grown in dry poor soil. Min. −5°C, perhaps less if dry.

Pelargonium exstipulatum (Cav.) L'Hérit. (s. *Reniformia*) A small upright very aromatic shrub with sticky silvery leaves, native of South Africa in the Little Karroo, growing in sandy rocky places, flowering June–December. Stems thin and woody to 1m or more in cultivation. Leaves alternate, 5–15mm across, with three shallow lobes; flowers on stiff purplish peduncles, around 6 in an umbel, 15–20mm across, with narrow pinkish petals. Grow in well-drained sandy soil, kept rather dry; cuttings root easily. Min. −3°C.

Pelargonium ionidiflorum (Eckl. & Zeyh.) Steud. (s. *Reniformia*) A dwarf sprawling shrublet with deep green leaves, native of the SE Cape around Cradock, Somerset East and Grahamstown, growing in rocky places among Karroo vegetation, flowering throughout the year. (In this area most rain falls in summer and winters are cold and dry.) Stems up to 50cm, greyish and woody when old; leaves deeply 7-lobed with long glandular hairs; flowers on branched stems, 3–7 in the umbel with narrow pink to dark purple petals, about 28cm across. Said to be easy to grow in well-drained soil and full sun. Min. −5°C, perhaps.

Pelargonium odoratissimum (L.) L'Hérit. (s. *Reniformia*) A sweetly apple- and mint-scented plant with soft leaves and creeping flowering stems, native of South Africa mainly along the coast of the S Cape, but also in the Transvaal, growing in shady places and under trees, flowering April–November. Roots slightly fleshy; main stems short with a rosette of leaves and creeping, branching flowering stems; leaves pale green, softly hairy, round, the blades 3–12cm across, strongly scented. Flowers 3–10 in the umbel, white with small red spots on the upper petals, around 1.5cm across. Easily grown in ordinary good soil but needs regular repotting to remain vigorous. Min. −3°C.

Pelargonium odoratissimum from Olifants' Kop, near Port Elizabeth

Pelargonium reniforme Curtis (s. *Reniformia*) A dwarf perennial with silvery leaves and small bright magenta flowers, native of South Africa in the E Cape, growing in dry grassy veldt, flowering throughout the year. Roots tuberous; stems usually short and upright, covered with the remains of old petioles; leaves soft and silvery, acrid-smelling, finely lobed and toothed, strongly veined beneath. Inflorescence repeatedly branching. Flowers in umbels of 3–12, bright magenta or pinkish, the upper marked with pink and crimson. Two forms are cultivated: one has short stems with very long petioles and magenta flowers; the other has longer flexuous stems, shorter petioles and paler flowers. Both are easily grown in poor dry soil. The tuberous roots help this species survive the fires which are frequent in its native habitat. Min. −3°C.

Photographed in the National Botanic Gardens, Pretoria.

Pelargonium sidoides DC. syn. *P. sidaefolium* (Thunb.) Knuth (s. *Reniformia*) A perennial with silvery leaves and small blackish flowers, native of South Africa from the Transvaal to the SE Cape, and of Lesotho, growing in grassland and among rocks at up to 2600m in the Drakensberg, flowering October–January. Roots tuberous; stems short; leaves in a basal rosette, silvery, the blade irregularly lobed and toothed, around 4cm across. Inflorescence repeatedly branched, the umbels with 5–7 small black flowers, 22–28mm across. Easily grown, but I have lost this species by allowing it to become too wet. Min. −10°C, if dry. Photographed in the NE Cape on Carlyle's Hoek above Rhodes.

'Fragrans Variegatum'

Pelargonium odoratissimum

'Lilian Pottinger'

'Fragrans'

'Old Spice'

Pelargonium odoratissimum

Specimens from Vernon Geranium Nursery, Surrey, May 8th, 1/2 life size

Pelargonium × lawrencianum

Pelargonium 'Splendide'

The majority of this group are small, low, sweetly scented, soft-leaved plants related to *Pelargonium odoratissimum*. Like this species they have small white flowers and smell of apples. 'Blandfordianum' and its variety 'Roseum' are ancient hybrids of uncertain parentage, possibly related to *P. cortusaefolium*. 'Splendide' and *P. × glaucifolium* are also old long-cultivated crosses between wild species.

'Blandfordianum'   A hybrid of unknown parentage raised in 1805 by the then Marquess of Blandford who made a fine and extravagant garden at Whiteknights near Reading. From the leaf this seems to involve *P. graveolens*; the silvery flowers and leaves have some of the qualities of *P. cortusaefolium*; this is the parentage given by Andrews when he described and illustrated the plant in around 1809. One of the *Myrrhidium* section such as *P. candicans* would also provide the right characters. Leaves about 5cm across, scented of rose geranium. Flowers 2cm across, produced all the year. If grown well and staked, it can make a bushy plant to 1m or more in height, its long thin stems also make it suitable for a hanging basket. It is easily grown but the roots are liable to attack by vine weevils. Min. 0°C.

'Blandfordianum Roseum'   Another hybrid of unknown parentage, close to 'Blandfordianum', but more bushy and with smaller leaves and pink flowers.

'Fragrans'   An old hybrid or group of hybrids of uncertain parentage known since 1800. Sweet suggested *P. odoratissimum × P. exstipulatum* but there are many small species which could be involved. Leaves soft and silky-hairy with prominent veins beneath, 3- or 5-lobed, about 3cm across, scented of pine. Easy and shade-tolerant. Min. −3°C.

'Fragrans Variegatum' syn. 'Creamy Nutmeg', 'Snowy Nutmeg'   A form of 'Fragrans' with an irregular margin of cream around the leaf.

P. × glaucifolium   An old hybrid of unknown origin. The bicoloured flowers are sweetly scented and similar to those of *P. lobatum*. Several hybrids of the section *Polyactium* were raised in the early 19th century. This is probably *P. lobatum × P. gibbosum*. *P. × bicolor* is very similar. *P. × ardens*, another old hybrid with slightly more divided leaves and dark reddish flowers is thought to be *P. lobatum × P. fulgidum*.

Pelargonium 'Blandfordianum Roseum

Pelargonium 'Blandfordianum'

'Lilian Pottinger'   Close to 'Fragrans' but with more finely toothed and lobed leaves, their scent described as 'camphor pine'.

P. lanceolatum (Cav.) Kern. syn. *P. glaucum* (L.) L'Hérit. (s. *Glaucophyllum*)   A dwarf species with unusual narrow grey leaves, native of a small area of the Cape around Worcester, growing in sandy and rocky places, flowering through the year. Leaf blades about 6cm long, 1.5cm wide; flowers about 4.5cm across, white to yellow. For dry conditions. Min. −3°C.

P. × lawrencianum Sweet   A hybrid between *P. lobatum* and *P. × ardens*, illustrated by Sweet in 1828. Leaves lobed; flowers dark velvety-purple.

P. odoratissimum (L.) L'Hérit. (*for full text see p.129*)   Two forms are shown here: a small one with dark green leaves which is commonly grown in England; and a larger, paler-leaved form collected inland from Port Elizabeth. Leaves scented of apples.

'Old Spice'   A dwarfer plant than 'Fragrans' with more deeply lobed leaves. Clifford gives the parentage of this as 'Fragrans' × *odoratissimum* and says that it has larger leaves than 'Fragrans'. Raised by Logee in Connecticut before 1970.

'Splendide' syn. *P. violareum* hort. (and sometimes wrongly listed as *P. tricolor*)   A lovely dwarf shrubby plant with grey leaves, the ovate toothed blades about 3cm long. Large flowers, upper petals crimson, faintly stippled with white, the lower petals white. A hybrid *P. tricolor × P. ovale*.

Pelargonium lanceolatum

Pelargonium × glaucifolium

Pelargonium quercifolium

Pelargonium glutinosum

Pelargonium cordifolium on Robinson Pass near George in October

Pelargonium radens

Pelargonium panduriforme

Pelargonium glutinosum

132

Pelargonium quercifolium in the Langkloof near Uniondale

Pelargonium cordifolium (Cav.) Curtis
(s. Pelargonium) A tall upright plant with
unlobed, heart-shaped leaves, native of South
Africa in the S and E Cape, from Bredasdorp
to King Williamstown, growing in moist sandy
heathy areas, in fynbos and in open forest,
flowering June–January but mainly in
September–November. Stems robust, upright,
about 1m, but to 2m in gardens. Leaves apple-
scented, heart-shaped, sometimes slightly
lobed, finely toothed dark green velvety above,
silky-hairy with curled hairs or glabrous
beneath, 6cm long, 12cm wide. Flowers in a
branched inflorescence, in umbels of 4–8;
upper petals 2.5–3cm long, 1cm wide, pink,
veined with purple, recurved; lower petals
white, 2.3cm long, 2mm wide. Easily grown in
sandy soil. Min. −3°C. Glabrous-leaved
plants, said to be commonest in the George
district, are shown here on Robinson Pass.

Pelargonium glutinosum (Jacq.) L'Hérit.
(s. *Pelargonium*) An upright bush with sticky
balm-scented leaves and small flowers, native
of South Africa throughout the S Cape, and in
the Soutpansberg in N Transvaal, growing in
dry rocky places and by streams, flowering
mainly in September–November. Plant bushy,
upright to 1.8m; leaves often dark green,
rough, sticky, balm-scented, almost glabrous,
with 7–9 elongated, acute lobes, 5–13cm long,
6–16cm wide. Flowers in umbels of 1–8, pale
to deep pink, with the upper two petals 12–
25mm long, 3–6mm wide, veined and spotted,
the lower slightly wider. Close to P.

denticulatum but always with less divided leaves
which are never bipinnate. Easy in well-
drained soil, watered sparingly throughout the
year. Min. −3°C, perhaps less.

Pelargonium panduriforme Eckl. & Zeyh.
(s. *Pelargonium*) A tall bushy shrub with
abundant large flowers, native of South Africa
in the SE Cape, especially between
Willowmore and Riebeeck East, growing by
streams in ravines in the foothills, and
receiving rainfall throughout the year,
flowering August–January. Plants to 1m high
and more across; leaves softly hairy, often
woolly beneath, not scabrid, slightly sticky,
balm-scented, with a pair of spreading
rounded basal lobes and 1–3 obtuse terminal
lobes, the margins crenate. Flowers 2–20 in
the umbel, pinkish, the upper petals veined
and spotted with purple, 20–35mm long,
the lower 15–28mm. A fine species, very
striking in flower. L'Heritier's illustration of
P. quercifolium in *Geranicaeae* t.14, is assigned
to this species by van der Walt. Min. −3°C,
perhaps less.

Pelargonium quercifolium (L. fil.) L'Hérit.
(s. *Pelargonium*) An upright shrub with
variably lobed balm-scented leaves, native of
South Africa in the S Cape, around
Oudtshoorn and Willowmore, growing in
fynbos on mountain slopes and on roadsides,
where it is common in parts of the Langkloof,
flowering August–January. Stems to 1.75m;
leaves overall 2–7cm long, 2.5–9cm wide,

rough, with a few long, soft hairs and
numerous glandular hairs, variable, from an
oak-like shape with 9 toothed lobes about
8mm wide with wavy edges, to a fine-leaved
shape with the lobes repeatedly divided into
narrower lobes about 6mm wide. Flowers in
umbels of 2–6, pinkish; upper petals 18–
25mm, obtuse or emarginate, veined and
spotted with red or purple; lower petals about
20mm long. Easy in rather dry sandy soil and
easy from seed or cuttings. The species as
defined by van der Walt is illustrated by
L'Héritier (t. 15) as var. *pinnatifidum*. Those
shown here growing along the road between
George and Uniondale have similarly finely-
divided leaves (C. D. & R. 907) but most of
the old cultivated plants have leaves more like
an oak. Min. −3°C, perhaps less.

Pelargonium radens H. E. Moore syn.
P. radula (Cav.) L'Hérit. (s. *Pelargonium*)
An upright bushy plant with finely-divided
leaves, native of South Africa along the south
of Cape Province and in the Transkei, growing
in mountain scrub and by rocky streams,
flowering mainly in August–December. Plant
shrubby to 1m; leaves sweetly scented of
lemon and rose, rough, deeply divided into
narrow segments, the leaf margins curled
under so that the edge appears thickened, with
blunt teeth, 3–8cm long, 3–11cm across.
Flowers in umbels of 2–6, pale pink with dark
veins on the upper petals, about 3cm across.
Easy in well-drained soil. Min. −5°C, perhaps
less. A source of oil of geranium.

133

'Asperum'

'Joy Lucille'

'Graveolens'

'Graveolens Minor'

'Royal Oak'

Pelargonium denticulatum 'Filicifolium'

Pelargonium capitatum

'Village Hill Oak'

'Radula'

Specimens from Vernon Geranium Nursery, Surrey, May 8th, 1/2 life size

Pelargonium quercifolium 'Fair Ellen'

Pelargonium quercifolium 'Village Hill Oak'

Pelargonium 'Carlton Fern'

Pelargonium capitatum (L.) L'Hérit.
(s. *Pelargonium*) A creeping or sprawling
plant with sweetly scented leaves and tight
heads of flowers (*described in full on p.141*).

Pelargonium denticulatum Jacq.
(s. *Pelargonium*) An upright bushy plant with
sticky finely cut leaves and small flowers,
native of South Africa in S Cape around
Herbertsdale, growing in damp ravines and by
rocky streams in the mountains, flowering
mainly in September–January. Stems shrubby
at base, to 2m; leaves finely divided with
pinnatisect segments, sticky, strongly smelling,
rather stiff, 6–8cm long, 7–9cm wide. Flowers
with upper petals around 16mm, lower 14mm
long, pale pink with dark markings on the
upper petals.
'Filicifolium' syn. 'Fernaefolium'(*shown here*)
This is an old variety, a selection of *P.
denticulatum*. Its very finely cut leaf segments
are very clammy, 2–4mm wide, finely toothed.
Flowers with the upper petals 18mm long,
deeply forked, striped; the lower 1.7cm,
emarginate with a faint red stripe. Illustrated
by Andrews in 1805 as '*Geranium multifidum*'.
This variety is said to be poisonous. It needs
good peaty sandy soil and is less tolerant of
drought than most others. Min. 0°C.

'Asperum' syn. (or close to) 'Viscosissimum',
'Jatrophaefolium', 'Pheasant's Foot'
Intermediate between *P. glutinosum* and *P.
denticulatum*. Leaves balm-scented, rough,
sticky when young, with leaf segments
10–15mm wide; petals pale pink, rounded,
about 15mm long, the upper pair lightly

marked with red. 'Viscosissimum' as
illustrated by Sweet (2:118) in 1822, is
probably a narrow-leaved form of *P.
glutinosum*.

'Carlton Fern' Raised by Or. Arndt in the
USA in 1950, a hybrid between *P. denticulatum*
'Filicifolium' and *P. quercifolium*, with slightly
broader leaves and larger flowers than
'Filicifolium'.

'Graveolens' This is an old cultivar, a
probable cross between *P. capitatum* and
P. radens, commonly grown for its essential oil,
known as oil of geranium, which is used as a
substitute for the very expensive attar of roses.
Several other related hybrids are grown for the
same purpose; that named 'Attar of Roses' (*see
p. 136*) has broader leaves than 'Graveolens'
and is closer to *P. capitatum*.
'Graveolens Minor' is another hybrid close
to 'Graveolens', with deeply divided leaves and
small tight heads of flowers. 'Little Gem' (*not
shown*) is even smaller in all its parts.

'Joy Lucille' Probably a hybrid between
'Graveolens' and *P. tomentosum*, with
peppermint-scented leaves, softly hairy and
greyish-green and very pale pink flowers.
Raised in USA in 1940 but very close to the
old English variety 'Lady Seymour'.

Pelargonium quercifolium (L. fil.) L'Hérit.
(*Described in full on p.132*.) The following
cultivars have broader leaf lobes, usually with
purple veins and may be selections of wild *P.
quercifolium* or possibly of hybrid origin

between *P. quercifolium* and *P. panduriforme*.
'Fair Ellen' Leaves rough, with very few
long soft hairs beneath, with narrow purplish
staining along the main veins, shallowly 3–7-
lobed, cordate at the base, up to 18cm long
and 15cm across, but usually smaller and less
lobed on flowering shoots. The plant shown
here originated on Tresco. It is rather
creeping, free-flowering and the spots on the
lower as well as the upper petals are
characteristic.
'Royal Oak' Leaves softly hairy, irregularly
7–9-lobed, about halfway to the midrib, with a
wider area of purple along the main veins, to
around 8cm long, 7cm wide. Flowers large
with the upper petals about 28mm long. A
similar variety has more narrowly lobed leaves
and flowers with a slight horseshoe-shaped
spot on the lower petals. There is also a
smaller, less free-flowering form, usually sold
as *P. quercifolium*.
'Village Hill Oak' Leaves softly hairy,
divided nearly to the midrib, with purple along
the main veins, to around 6cm long and 5.5cm
wide. Flowers in tight heads, the upper petals
about 23mm long. Named after the garden of
Dorcas Brigham, a great grower of scented
pelargoniums at Village Hill, Williamsburg,
Mass. around 1945.

'Radula' An old cultivar or group close to
'Graveolens'. Often confused with the wild
P. radens but with broader leaf lobes, their
margins recurved but not rolled under.
Flowers small, pinkish-purple, with sterile
anthers. Plant well-scented, of oil of geranium,
similar to 'Attar of Roses' (*see pp. 136–7*).

'Atomic Snowflake'

'Rober's Lemon Rose'

'Attar of Roses'

Pelargonium tomentosum

Pelargonium citronellum 'Mabel Grey'

'Endsleigh'

'Chocolate Peppermint

Specimens from Vernon Geranium Nursery, Surrey, May 8th, 1/2 life size

Pelargonium tomentosum naturalised on Tresco with other southern hemisphere exotics

Pelargonium 'Chocolate Peppermint'

Pelargonium 'Endsleigh' on Tresco

'Atomic Snowflake'   Plant scented of lemon verbena; leaves with a narrow white edge and a white centre if growing slowly.

'Attar of Roses'   This old cultivar is given in Cannell's catalogue of 1900. It is probably of hybrid origin between *P. capitatum* and 'Graveolens'. The plant is small, much-branched and leafy with soft leaves, scented of roses.

'Chocolate Peppermint'   Plant large and creeping with softly hairy leaves up to 15cm across, with a dark central area of chocolate-brown, spreading up the veins. Scent of peppermint mixed with spice. Flowers small, pinkish with dark lines near the base of the petals, showing the influence of *P. tomentosum*. The other parent possibly *P. quercifolium* or one of its hybrids.

Pelargonium citronellum J. J. A. van der Walt (s. *Pelargonium*)   A small rough-leaved shrub smelling strongly of lemon, native of South Africa in the S Cape especially in the northern foothills of the Langeberg north of Riversdale, growing near streams in sandy soil,

flowering mainly in September–October. Stems to 2m; leaves deeply palmately cut with acute lobes and teeth, rough and strongly lemon-scented, deeply 7–9-lobed, the lobes acute with the margins irregularly toothed, 5–7.5cm long and 5.5–10cm wide. Flowers 4–6 in the umbel, about 3.5cm across, the two upper petals bent back, spotted and veined, longer and wider than the lower three. For sandy soil, kept rather dry. Min. 0°C. The clone shown here is generally called **'Mabel Grey'** and was introduced to England from Kenya in 1960. It is easily grown but is susceptible to botrytis in damp stagnant air, especially in winter, so would be happier on a sunny windowsill than in the cold greenhouse.

'Endsleigh' (*Pelargonium capitatum* × *quercifolium*)   This hybrid, of which one clone has been named 'Endsleigh', forms large dense bushy patches. Leaves wavy-edged, hairy, sweetly scented, showing the dark centre derived from cultivated *quercifolium* and *capitatum*-like, dense heads of bright, pinkish-purple flowers. 'Endsleigh' is an old variety, illustrated by Andrews in 1805–9. The plant with paler leaves was photographed at Tresco,

that with darker leaves at Rosemoor in Devon. 'Andersonii' is very similar or possibly the same.

'Rober's Lemon Rose'   A tall plant with irregularly 3–7-lobed, softly hairy, greyish leaves scented of lemon and geranium combined. Flowers small, similar to 'Attar of Roses'.

Pelargonium tomentosum Jacq. (s. *Pelargonium*)   A robust, spreading and clambering plant with very soft, peppermint-scented leaves, native of South Africa in the SW Cape, from Hottentots Holland to Riversdale, growing in sandy soil on the margins of forest along streams. Plant to 2m or more, forming dense spreading patches; leaves covered in soft woolly hairs, 5–7-lobed, cordate at the base, pale green, 4–8cm long and 5–12cm wide. Inflorescence repeatedly branching, the umbels with 4–15 small, pale pink or white flowers. Upper petals about 9mm long, 5mm wide, marked with purplish veins at the base, the lower very narrow, about 11mm long and 1.5mm wide. Easily grown and rooted from cuttings. Min. 0°C.

Pelargonium cucullatum subsp. *tabulare*

Pelargonium cucullatum subsp. *cucullatum* after a fire near Gordon's Bay, SW Cape

Pelargonium cucullatum subsp. *tabulare*

Pelargonium cucullatum (L.) L'Hérit.
(s. *Pelargonium*)   This species is a
conspicuous feature of the sea cliffs and coastal
mountains of the southwestern Cape where the
plants form large shrubs, covered with flowers
in early summer. It was introduced to England
in 1690 and became one of the main parents of
the modern Regal pelargoniums, which now
differ mainly in their smaller growth and larger
flowers. The species is now divided into three
subspecies, by habitat and leaf shape.
Subsp. **cucullatum** syn. *P. angulosum* (Mill.)

L'Hérit.   An erect shrub with bright purplish-
pink flowers, found in the east of the Cape
Peninsula north of Simonstown and around
the coast from Somerset West to Hermanus,
growing on rocky headlands and cliffs,
flowering from September–February. Shrubs
to 2m high, rather less across. Leaves not
scented, with the edges curved upwards, with
obtuse but pointed lobes and sharp teeth,
subcordate to cuneate at the base, 4–7cm
long, 5–9cm wide with long soft hairs and
glandular hairs. Flowers in umbels of 3–6,
bright pinkish-purple to pale pink, the upper
petals veined, about 25mm long, 14mm wide,
obovate, the rest narrower. Easily grown in
sandy soil; robust and free-flowering, needing
water mainly in winter and spring. Min. 0°C.
A pure white form, shown here, is in
cultivation in New Zealand.
Subsp. **strigifolium** Volschenk syn.
P. acerifolium L'Hérit.   This subspecies is less
coastal than the other two and is found from
near Bainskloof south and east to the
Kleinrivier Mountains near Caledon, growing
in fynbos at 300–900m, flowering mainly in
October–November. It differs in its more
deeply cut leaves, with stiff bristly hairs
interspersed with glandular hairs, cuneate at
the base and paler flowers, usually pale pink to
pinkish-mauve, the upper petals 2–3cm long,
1–1.7cm wide. Easily grown in any soil and
said to be more drought-resistant than the
other subspecies.
Subsp. **tabulare** Volschenk   This subspecies
is found along the coast from near Saldanah
north of Cape Town to the Cape Peninsula,
where it is very common, growing in masses
on rocks by the sea and on steep grassy slopes,
flowering mainly in September–December. It
differs from subsp. *cucullatum* in its sweetly
scented leaves, rounded and not lobed, with
blunter teeth and wavy margins, deeply
cordate at the base, to 10cm or more across,
densly covered with long soft hairs and few
glands. Flowers in umbels of 4–10, usually
bright pinkish-purple, with blotches and veins
on the upper petals. Easily grown in sandy soil;
very fast-growing and free-flowering if well
watered. Min. 0°C. The form shown here,
with beautifully veined flowers was selected
from a population of many thousands near
Simonstown on Cape Peninsula.

Pelargonium cucullatum subsp. *tabulare* wild on the cliffs near Simonstown, Cape Peninsula in October

Pelargonium cucullatum white form in New Zealand

P. cucullatum subsp. *strigifolium* wild near Cape Hangklip, SW Cape

Pelargonium betulinum wild near Simonstown, Cape Peninsula in October

Pelargonium hispidum

Pelargonium capitatum wild near Betty's Bay, SW Cape in October

P. betulinum × *cucullatum* subsp. *tabulare* at Kirstenbosch

Pelargonium papilionaceum by a stream on Tradouws Pass

Pelargonium betulinum (L.) L'Hérit.
(s. *Pelargonium*) A spreading and sprawling sub-shrub, native of South Africa in the SW Cape, growing on dunes and sandy places near the sea, flowering mainly in August–October. Plant to 1.3m; stems woody at the base. Leaves in 2 ranks up the stem, ovate, simply toothed, 1–3cm long, 0.7–2.5cm wide, glabrous, stiff, faintly orange- or camphor-scented. Flowers in umbels of 1–6, usually 2–4, about 5cm across if open flat but usually somewhat tubular; petals pink or white, the upper veined with purple, broader than the lower. Easy in sandy soil, growing mainly in winter and spring. Min. 0°C, perhaps less.

Pelargonium betulinum × **cucullatum**
subsp. *tabulare* This hybrid is illustrated in *Pelargoniums of Southern Africa* (vol. 2) and is intermediate between the parents with the relatively large flowers of *P. cucullatum*, bright pink in colour and hairy leaves, larger and more wavy than those of *P. betulinum*. The several-flowered umbel is also distinct from the usual few-flowered umbel of *P. betulinum*. The hybrid has been found wild in several places where the parents grow together and has long been cultivated. A similar plant grows commonly in Madeira (*shown on p. 150*). The plants set seed easily.

Pelargonium betulinum × **cucullatum**
subsp. *cucullatum* This hybrid is also known from the wild, especially around Betty's Bay, where the parents grow together. The specimen shown here was photographed in Kirstenbosch Botanic Garden.

Pelargonium capitatum (L.) L'Hérit.
(s. *Pelargonium*) A creeping or sprawling plant with sweetly scented leaves and tight heads of flowers, native of South Africa around the coast from SW Cape to S Natal, growing on dunes and sandy hills near the sea, flowering most of the year, mainly in September–November. Stems fleshy to 1m; leaves almost convoluted, shallowly to deeply 3–6-lobed, softly hairy, around 5cm long and 6cm wide. Flowers in a dense 8–20-flowered umbel, pale pink to deep pinkish-purple, about 4cm across, the upper petals striped purple-red. Easily grown in sandy soil and easy to root. Min. 0°C. *P. vitifolium* (L.) L'Hérit. (*not shown*) has similar tight heads of pink flowers

P. betulinum × *cucullatum* subsp. *cucullatum*

but has upright, not creeping stems and larger, less hairy and slightly rough leaves.

Pelargonium papilionaceum (L.) L'Hérit.
(s. *Pelargonium*) A tall upright shrub with large leaves and masses of small but striking flowers, native of South Africa in the S Cape, from Stellenbosch east to Grahamstown, growing on the edges of forests and by rocky streams, flowering in September–January. Stems to 2m. Leaves shallowly 3–5-lobed, almost round, about 10cm across. Flowers pinkish, in umbels of 5–12, the upper pair of petals obovate, marked with crimson, with a white blotch about 2cm long, 1cm wide; the three lower very small and narrow, less than 1cm long. Easily grown in good moist soil. Min. −3°C.

Pelargonium hispidum (L.fil.) Willd.
(s. *Pelargonium*) A tall upright shrub with large deeply lobed leaves and small flowers, native of South Africa in the southwestern Cape and in the Swartberg, east to near Oudtshoorn, at 300–1300m, growing in shady ravines, usually by streams, flowering in September–April but mainly in spring. Stems to 2.5 m. Leaves deeply 7–9-lobed, 10–13cm across, the lobes pointed. Flowers pinkish, in umbels of 6–12, the upper pair of petals obovate, marked with crimson near the base, bent back, about 1.2cm long, 7mm wide, the three lower very small and narrow, about 8mm long and 2mm wide. Easily grown in good moist peaty and sandy soil, they need to be watered throughout the year. Min. −3°C.

141

Pelargonium ribifolium on the Swartberge pass

Pelargonium scabrum near Citrusdal in October

Pelargonium scabrum × *englerianum*

Pelargonium greytonense

Pelargonium citronellum J. J. A. van der Walt (s. *Pelargonium*) (*For text see p.136*) This is close to the cultivar 'Mabel Grey' (*p. 136*). It needs sandy soil with water mainly in winter and spring. Min. −3°C.

Pelargonium crispum (Berg) L'Hérit. (s. *Pelargonium*) A stiff upright shrub with very small leaves scented of lemon, native of South Africa in the SW Cape especially in the area of Montagu and Worcester, growing on the dry lower slopes in sandy soil among boulders, in the winter-rainfall area, flowering mainly in September–October. Stems to 75cm, upright. Leaves rough and glandular-hairy, 3-parted, with acute teeth, short-stalked, very small, about 5mm long, 7mm wide. Flowers single or in pairs, rather large, the upper two petals about 18mm long, 10mm wide, purplish to white, spotted and veined with red, sometimes emarginate; the lower three smaller. To keep its character in cultivation this species needs rather dry soil with little water, full sun and air. Min. −3°C, perhaps less.

Pelargonium englerianum Knuth (s. *Pelargonium*) An upright or spreading shrub with small leaves scented of rose and camphor, native of South Africa in the SW Cape, from near Calvinia east to the Swartberg Pass, growing in damp sandy soil among heathers, sedges and boulders in the winter-

rainfall area, flowering mainly in November–January. Stems to 1m, usually upright, often purplish or reddish, with long hairs. Leaves bristly and glandular-hairy, usually 3-parted, with acute teeth, long-stalked, about 15mm long, 20mm wide. Flowers 2–5 in the umbel, rather small, the upper two petals 10–18mm long, 4–8mm wide, pink to purplish, spotted and veined with dark purple; the lower three smaller. For moist sandy soil and sun or partial shade. Min. −3°C, perhaps less.

Pelargonium greytonense J. J. A. van der Walt (s. *Pelargonium*) An upright shrub with small leaves, native of South Africa in the SW Cape especially in the Riviersonderend Mountains, growing in ravines on the southern slopes, flowering mainly in October–November. Stems to 1m, upright. Leaves glandular-hairy, 3-lobed, with blunt teeth, long-stalked, about 35mm long, 40mm wide. Flowers 2–9 in the umbel, the upper two petals about 20mm long, 8mm wide, pinkish to white, spotted and veined with purple, reflexed; the lower three much smaller. For moist sandy soil with ample water in winter and spring. Min. 0°C.

Pelargonium hermanniifolium (Berg) Jacq. (s. *Pelargonium*) A stiff upright shrub with small usually unscented leaves in 2 rows up the stem, native of South Africa in the SW Cape, especially from Worcester east to Caledon and

Pelargonium citronellum

Pelargonium englerianum in marshy ground near Citrusdal

Swellendam, growing in mountain fynbos in sandy soil, in cooler and damper habitats than the related *P. crispum*, flowering mainly in September–October. Stems to 1m, upright. Leaves rough and glandular-hairy, obovate, 3-parted with few teeth, short-stalked, cuneate at the base, very small, about 5mm long, 4mm wide. Flowers single or in pairs, rather large, the upper two petals about 19mm long, 13mm wide, pinkish to white, spotted and veined with red, sometimes emarginate; the lower three narrower. Needs sandy soil and water mainly in winter and spring with full sun and plenty of air. Min. −3°C, perhaps less.

Pelargonium ribifolium Jacq.
(s. *Pelargonium*) A tall upright shrub with aromatic leaves and heads of numerous small white flowers, native of South Africa in the eastern Cape, especially from the Swartberg Pass eastwards to the Katberg and in the coastal mountains, growing in moist ravines and on the edges of forest, often with bracken, flowering mainly in September–November. Stems to 2m, upright, much-branched, woody at the base. Leaves rough and glandular-hairy, 3–5 parted, with 7 lobes, long-stalked, about 5cm long, 6cm wide. Flowers 6–12 in the umbel, rather small, the upper two petals 17mm long, 11mm wide, white, veined with red; the lower three smaller. Needs well-drained sandy peaty soil and a position that is not too hot in summer. Min. −3°C, perhaps less.

Pelargonium scabrum (Burm. fil.) L'Hérit.
(s. *Pelargonium*)   An upright shrub with small leaves scented of lemon and insignificant pink flowers, native of South Africa almost throughout the S and W Cape, growing in dry sandy soil among boulders, in the winter-rainfall area, flowering in May–January. Stems to 2m, upright. Leaves rough and almost glabrous with 3 long narrow lobes and few acute teeth, cuneate at the base, about 4cm long. Flowers 2–6 in the umbel, small, the upper two petals about 15mm long, 5mm wide, purplish to pink or white, blotched or veined with purple, sometimes emarginate; the lower three smaller. Needs sandy soil in full sun. Difficult to grow and to root from cuttings. Min. −3°C, perhaps less.

Pelargonium scabrum × englerianum
Plants intermediate between these two species were found growing with the parents on the east side of the Cedarberg near Citrusdaal.

Pelargonium crispum cultivated form in England

Pelargonium hermanniifolium at Kirstenbosch

143

Pelargoniums and salvias planted in the ground in the greenhouse

'Concolor Lace'

'Prince of Orange'   'Limoneum'

Specimens from Vernon Geranium Nursery, May 8th, 1/3 life size

'Catford Belle'   The forerunner of the modern Angel pelargoniums, the upright growth and small leaves showing the influence of *P. crispum* on the group; the other parents were Regals. Raised by Langley-Smith in 1935.

'Citriodorum' syn. 'Queen of Lemons' Whole plant covered with long soft hairs; leaves 3–4cm across, shallowly 3-lobed and crisped with fine sharp teeth. Flowers silvery mauve, freely produced with good feathering. 'Toronto' is rather similar, but is said to smell of ginger and has pinker flowers.

'Concolor Lace'   Leaves faintly scented with unusual small deep pinkish-red flowers.

Pelargonium crispum (Berg) L'Hérit. (s. *Pelargonium*)   A stiff upright dwarf shrub with very small leaves scented of lemon, native of South Africa in the SW Cape, especially in the area of Montagu and Worcester, growing on the dry lower slopes in sandy soil among boulders, in the winter-rainfall area, flowering mainly in spring. This is an important parent, giving dwarf habit and good scent to many of the dwarf scented pelargoniums shown here (*see also p. 142*).
'Major'   A form of *P. crispum* with larger leaves and broader-petalled flowers. 'Minor' (*not shown*) is a form with especially small leaves.
'Variegatum' syn. 'Variegated Crispum', 'Variegated Prince Rupert'   A form of *P. crispum* with cream-edged leaves and lightly marked flowers, known since 1774. Growth stiffly upright.

'Galway Star'   Close to *P. crispum* 'Variegatum' but more bushy, with slightly larger leaves and brighter well-marked flowers.

'Gemstone'   A scented variety with a small lobed leaf and a sweet fruity scent.

'Lemon Fancy'   This combines the small leaves of *P. crispum* with the rough textured jaggedly lobed leaves, to 4cm across, and bright flowers of *P. citronellum*. An upright shrubby plant of good habit and strong lemon scent but few flowers. Raised by Helen Bowie in 1979. 'Prince of Orange' × 'Mabel Grey'.

'Limoneum'   Flowers pinkish-mauve with good feathering; leaves scented of rose and lime.

'Mrs G. H. Smith'   An Angel, scented of rose-lemon. Flowers white with pink markings; leaves shallowly lobed.

'Prince of Orange'   Plant upright with delicate stems, softly hairy when young. Leaves small, about 3cm wide, deeply 3-lobed, scented of orange. Flowers mauve with purple veins and a blotch. Known since 1880.

'Saint Clement's Bell'   Roger photographed this variety in Auckland Botanic Garden in New Zealand. It is one of the oranges and lemons group, making, in the open, a good rounded bush with deeply cut leaves and well-marked flowers. Close to 'Lemon Fancy'.

'Verdale'   A rare Angel variety, available from Fibrex Nurseries, Worcestershire.

'Galway Star' 'Catford Belle'

'Variegatum'

Pelargonium crispum 'Lemon Fancy' 'Major'

Pelargonium 'Saint Clement's Bell'

Specimens from Vernon Geranium Nursery, May 8th, 1/3 life size

Pelargonium 'Mrs G. H. Smith' at Fibrex nurseries

Pelargonium 'Verdale' at Fibrex nurseries

Pelargonium 'Gemstone'

Pelargonium 'Citriodorum' with 'Village Hill Oak' in Devon

145

Pelargonium 'Scarlet Unique' in an old cottage garden on St Martins, Isles of Scilly

Pelargonium 'Carefree' at Fibrex Nurseries

The Unique pelargoniums are a small group of cultivars, mostly dating from the 19th and early 20th centuries, with small- or medium-sized but showy flowers. Their main characteristics are their very long flowering period and the tendency of the plants to grow into good permanent shrubs in suitable climates. Old shrubs of several different Uniques can be seen in the garden at Tresco and in gardens in a warm Mediterranean climate.

Pelargonium fulgidum (*illustrated on p. 120*) is one of the main ancestors of this group, and its deeply lobed leaves and small scarlet flowers can be seen in 'Scarlet Pet' which is also one of the best for winter flowering. 'Purple Unique' as grown today, is very close to *Pelargonium cucullatum* and the larger-flowered Uniques have this species and probably Regals in their ancestry too.

There is a group of beautiful cultivars closely related to Uniques, but also with affinities to the scented group. 'Clorinda' and 'Sweet Mimosa' are two of these. Some of them make very large free-flowering shrubs and have **Pelargonium quercifolium** (*see p. 132*) and Regals in their ancestry.

'Carefree' A new unique, with intense deep pink flowers, photographed in the National Collection at Fibrex Nurseries, Worcestershire.

'Scarlet Pet' syn. 'Moore's Victory' A Unique. Plant spreading, leaves rather thin with sparse hairs. Upper petals lightly veined, not blotched, flowering over a very long period. Probably a very old variety, known under this name since 1900.

'Crimson Unique' Plant medium or dwarf, all petals marked with black. Raised by Cannell before 1880.

'Jessel's Unique' Plant dwarf and bushy; leaves thin in texture. Flowers reddish-pink. A new name for an old variety, proposed in 1953.

'Rollisson's Unique' Plant medium height, leaves coarse and scented. Petals retuse at apex. Raised by Rollison before 1880.

'Scarlet Unique' Close to 'Scarlet Pet' but with more deeply divided leaves. Raised by Cannell before 1907. This is also very close to 'Colville's Storksbill' (*p. 148*).

'Shrubland Pet' A Unique. Plant dwarf to medium, leaves soft, scented. Flowers pinkish-red. Known since 1912.

'Unique Aurore' Plant tall and upright, leaves softly hairy. Flowers bright red with all petals heavily marked, not opening flat. Raised by Cannell in 1870.

'White Unique' Plant compact, bushy and spreading. The only Unique with white flowers. Known since before 1912.

'Scarlet Pet'

'Jessel's Unique'

'Scarlet Unique'

'Rollisson's Unique'

'White Unique'

'Shrubland Pet'

'Unique Aurore'

'Crimson Unique'

Specimens from Vernon Geranium Nursery, May 8th, 1/2 life size

'Copthorne'

'Clorinda'

'Golden Clorinda'

'Sweet Mimosa'

'Purple Unique'

'Madame Nonin'

Specimens from Vernon Geranium Nursery, May 8th, 1/4 life size

Pelargonium 'Pink Aurore'

Pelargonium 'Brunswick'

Pelargonium 'Purple Unique' at Quinta de Palheiro Ferreiro in Madeira

'Brunswick'   Plant tall; leaves rough, deeply lobed. Flowers close to 'Copthorne' but deeper in colour.

'Claret Rock Unique'   Plant dwarf with dark green leaves. Flowers small, with a paler centre.

'Clorinda'   Plant very large. Leaves scented of cedar; flowers lightly blotched. Probably a hybrid between a Regal and *P. quercifolium*. Raised by Cannell in 1907.

'Colville's Storksbill' or possibly **'Ignescens'**   Plant tall and straggly. Close to 'Scarlet Pet' but with very soft hairy leaves. Flowers small with heavy black feathering sometimes concentrating into a blotch. Raised by Colville in 1819. (Shown by Sweet, 1:69 [1820] and by H.V. P. Wilson, fig. 45.) The plant illustrated is also very close to *P. × ignescens* of Sweet, an early hybrid of *P. fulgidum*.

'Copthorne'   Plant compact and upright. Leaves aromatic, deeply lobed. Flowers freely into winter. Raised by Mrs Popperwell in 1984, from 'Aztec' × *P. quercifolium*.

'Colville's
Storksbill'

'Claret Rock Unique'

'Rollison's Unique'

Specimens from Vernon Geranium Nursery, May 8th, 2/5 life size

'Golden Clorinda'   A sport of 'Clorinda' with pale green leaves, narrowly edged with cream.

'Madame Nonin'   Plant of medium height, freely branching. Leaves finely dissected; flowers with the petals curled and frilled. Raised by M. Nonin in 1870.

'Paton's Unique'   Plant spreading. Leaves deeply and finely dissected, aromatic. Close to 'Madame Nonin' but with single flowers and flat petals. Known since 1870.

'Pink Aurore'   Plant tall, softly hairy. Flowers deep pink, the upper petals darker with black markings. Close to 'Unique Aurore' but that has all the petals clearly marked.

'Purple Unique'   Plant tall, upright. Leaves aromatic. Close to the species *Pelargonium cucullatum* but with more deeply lobed leaves. Known since 1869. Another similar plant with larger rounded leaves is shown here, growing in an old garden in Madeira.

'Rollisson's Unique'   Plant medium height; leaves coarse and scented. Petals retuse at apex. Raised by Rollisson before 1880.

'Sweet Mimosa'   One of the very best for freedom of growth and flowering. The aromatic leaves are possibly derived from the cultivated *P. quercifolium*; flowers pale rose pink, produced non-stop most of the year. Very hardy; min. −5°C.

Pelargonium 'Paton's Unique'

149

Pelargonium an old variety naturalised in Madeira

The first Regal pelargoniums were raised at the Royal gardens at Sandringham in the mid-nineteenth century and were characterized by their ruffled, overlapping petals. The earliest of these varieties were introduced by Cannell's nursery in 1877. The ancestors of the group had been very popular in the early 19th century, when they were generally called 'show geraniums', but had fallen out of favour. The group name *Pelargonium* × *domesticum* is now often applied to Regals and their forerunners and in America they are called 'Martha Washington' or 'Lady Washington' pelargoniums. The wild species which gave rise to the group include *Pelargonium cucullatum*, *P. betulinum* and their hybrid, which is very close to the old cultivar shown here in Madeira, as major parents, and *P. grandiflorum*, *P. cordifolium* and *P. fulgidum*, as lesser parents, the last of which provided red colour.

'All My Love'   Plant tall growing, raised by Outwater in USA in 1955.

'Askham Fringed Aztec' syn. 'Betty Bly' A sport of 'Aztec', found in USA before 1975. Plant compact. An unusual characteristic of this variety is the finely incised petal edge.

'Aztec'   Plant compact and much branched, raised by William E. Schmidt in 1962 in Palo Alto, California. The colour of the flower varies according to the amount of feeding.

'Beau Geste'   Plant bushy, raised by Fred Bode in Australia before 1965.

'Blackcurrant Sundae'   A darker-flowered sport of 'Strawberry Sundae'.

'Cezanne'   Plant compact, raised by Janus in England in 1962.

'Cherie' syn. 'Cheerie'   Plant compact and upright, raised by Howard Kerrigan in USA before 1954 .

'Green Woodpecker'   Plant tall and strong-growing.

Old variety in Madeira   We saw this old variety in several places in Madeira in 1992. It is very close to some of the very early hybrids from which Regal pelargoniums were bred, showing the influence of both *P. cucullatum* and *P. betulinum*.

Old variety in Tresco (possibly *P.* × *macranthon* illustrated by Sweet in 1821) This old-fashioned Regal has survived in the garden at Tresco, on the Isles of Scilly and shows several characteristics which have now been superceded, notably the smaller and rather separate lower petals and the black blotch on the upper petals, shading to red. In spite of recent cold winters which have reduced their numbers, the garden at Tresco is still a rich treasure house of ancient cultivars.

'White Bonanza'   A pure white Regal, raised in 1984.

Pelargonium an old variety on Tresco

Pelargonium 'Green Woodpecker'

'Beau Geste'

'Blackcurrant
Sundae'

'Green Woodpecker'

'Askham
Fringed Aztec'

'Cezanne'

'Aztec'

'White Bonanza'

'All My Love'

'Fringed Aztec'

'Cherie'

'South American Delight'

'Peggy Sue'   'Burgundy'

'Portsmouth'   'Dollar Bute'

'Springfield Black'

'South American Bronze'   'Mercia'

'Rembrandt'

Specimens from Vernon Geranium Nursery, July 3rd, 1/4 life size

Pelargonium 'Lord Bute' used as summer bedding at Wisley

Few old varieties of Regal pelargoniums remain in gardens and most of those that do such as 'Mrs Langtry' and 'Lord Bute' date from around 1900: The old purple variety shown here growing wild on Alcatraz, probably dates from around this time. While most Regals will survive outside unharmed along the coast in southern California and in much of Australia, frosts of −4°C or lower are likely to start to damage the leaves; woody stems and roots will shoot again even after exposure to lower temperatures.

'Black Butterfly' A spindly plant, difficult to make into a good specimen, raised by Brown in 1953. Flowers black with a ruffled edge.

'Black Velvet' A slow-growing plant with thin stems; flowers of the darkest red.

'Burgundy' A good very dark red with a black throat.

'Dollar Bute' Plant tall-growing with a black mark on each petal.

'Dzazem' A variety with rather frilled petals, only the upper marked with deep purple. A doubtful name.

'Hazel Henderson' A strong-growing plant, one of a range of Hazel cultivars raised by Dennis Fielding in England.

'Lavender Grand Slam' A sport from 'Grand Slam' which occurred in 1953. 'Grand Slam' itself was a reddish-pink, raised by William E. Schmidt in 1950.

'Lord Bute' One of the oldest Regals still cultivated; it received an Award of Merit in 1910.

'Mercia' Plant compact. Flowers with the lower three petals veined with pink.

'Peggy Sue' Plant dwarf, with deepest purple upper petals. Raised by B. Pearce.

'Portsmouth' Plant tall-growing; flowers dark red with a white edge and throat.

'Rembrandt' Raised by G. Morf around 1972.

'South American Bronze' Flowers with a narrow white margin to the petals.

'South American Delight' A darker sport of 'South American Bronze'.

'Springfield Black' A good robust plant and one of the darkest-flowered.

'Susan Pearce' Raised by B. Pearce. Free-flowering and compact with markings on all the petals.

Naturalised on Alcatraz An old unnamed variety growing on the former prison island of Alcatraz near San Francisco, probably dating from before 1920.

An old regal *Pelargonium* naturalised on Alcatraz island in San Francisco Bay

Pelargonium Black Velvet'

Pelargonium 'Black Butterfly'

'Lavander Grand Slam'

'Dzazem'

'Susan Pearce'

'Hazel Henderson'

Specimens from Vernon Geranium Nursery, July 3rd, 1/4 life size

153

'Souvenir'

'Cherry Orchard'

'Chorus Girl'

'Harewood Slam'

'Arthings Slam'

'Miss Australia'

'Salmon Slam'

'Sunrise'

'Judith Thorp'

Specimens from Vernon Geranium Nursery, July 3rd, 2\5 life size

'Carisbrooke'

'Love Song'

'Rasberry Sundae'

'Nellie'

'King Edmund'

'Senorita'

Specimens from Vernon Geranium Nursery, July 3rd, 1/4 life size

'**Arthington Slam**'   Plant strong-growing. The lower three petals are veined.

'**Carisbrooke**' syn. 'Ballerina'   Strong bushy growth and still one of the best varieties. Raised by Hodges in England before 1928; a seedling of 'Queen Mary'.

'**Cherry Orchard**'   Plant low-growing and compact. Raised by B. Pearce before 1977.

'**Chorus Girl**'   Plant has an extra-long flowering season and in suitable climates is almost continuously in flower. Raised by Harry and Clara May in Long Beach, Florida in 1957.

'**Dark Venus**'   A rare variety available from Derek Lloyd Dean, South Harrow, Middlesex.

'**Harewood Slam**'   Flowers bright red with reddish-brown markings.

'**Judith Thorp**'   Plant strong-growing. Raised by Thorp in 1975.

'**King Edmund**'   Plant strong growing, with purple flowers shaded maroon.

'**Langley**'   Rather small pink flowers with dark blotches.

'**Love Song**'   Leaves variegated with cream; free-flowering.

'**Miss Australia**'   Variegated leaves and pale pink flowers.

Pelargonium 'Langley'

Pelargonium 'Arthings Slam'

'**Nellie**'   Plant compact. Pretty orange-pink flowers marked only on the upper petals.

'**Rasberry Sundae**'   Flowers well marked with a white throat.

'**Salmon Slam**'   Flowers deep salmon with purplish-red markings on the upper petals and veins on the lower petals.

'**Senorita**'   Plant tall-growing with pale salmon-pink flowers distinctly veined.

'**Souvenir**'   Large ruffled flowers of dark salmon.

'**Sunrise**'   Plant vigorous. Raised by Schmidt in 1967.

Pelargonium 'Dark Venus'

155

'Velvet Duet'

'Sancho Panza'

'Earleana'

'Royal Ascot'

'Beronmünster'

'Tip Top Duet'

Specimens from Vernon Geranium Nursery, July 3rd, 1/4 life size

Pelargonium 'Beronmünster'

Pelargonium 'Moon Maiden'

Pelargonium 'Black Prince'

Pelargonium 'Captain Starlight'

Angel pelargoniums are related both to the large-flowered Regals and to the small-leaved *Pelargonium crispum* and possibly other wild species. One of the earliest cultivars of this type was 'Angeline', known in the 1820s; related cultivars were grown under the name *Pelargonium × dumosum*. A recent group of the same parentage was raised by Langley-Smith from 1914 onwards and 'Catford Belle' (*illustrated on p. 144*) survives; it was introduced by Langley-Smith in 1935. Miniature Regals are included here; they are very similar but tend to make larger coarser plants. They were popular in the early years of the 20th century and in 1900 Cannell's of Swanley in Kent offered 17 varieties, including 'Mrs Langtry' which is still available.

So-called decorative varieties are similar to small Regals but have flowers in which all the petals are marked or strongly veined. Similar varieties are called 'Pansy Geranium' in America. An old variety called 'Madame Layal', raised in France in 1870, is still widely grown.

Angel pelargoniums need the same treatment as Regals and flower in flushes throughout the warmer months. Some are upright in habit, others spreading or trailing and suitable for hanging baskets or rockeries. With careful pruning they will build into attractive shrubs.

'Beronmünster'   A miniature Regal; plant rather tall.
'Black Prince'   A miniature Regal.
'Captain Starlight'   An Angel; plant spreading.
'Earleana'   A decorative known since before 1939.
'Fairy Orchid'   An Angel.
'Kettle Baston'   An Angel; plant upright and bushy. Raised by R. Bidwell in 1983.
'Mairi'   An Angel.
'Moon Maiden'   An Angel; plant spreading.
'Mrs Dumbrill'   An Angel; raised by Langley-Smith in 1940.
'Mrs G. H. Smith'   An Angel; plant compact.
'Needham Market'   An Angel; raised by R. Bidwell in 1983.
'Roller's Echo'   An Angel; raised by C. Roller in the USA.
'Royal Ascot'   Miniature Regal, a sport from 'Beronmünster'; plant rather tall.
'Sancho Panza'   A decorative miniature

Regal, one of the first of this group; introduced by Telston Nurseries.
'Spring Park'   An Angel; plant very free-flowering.
'Swedish Angel'   An Angel; plant dwarf and slow growing.
'Swilland'   An Angel raised by R. Bidwell in 1983.
'Tip Top Duet' syn. 'Lord de Ramsey' An Angel; raised by Jan Taylor in 1979.
'Velvet Duet'   An Angel; plant spreading, suitable for a hanging basket or similar position. Raised by Jan Taylor in 1982.
'Wayward Angel'   An Angel; plant spreading or hanging. Raised by Jan Taylor in 1977.
'Wattisham'   A miniature Regal.

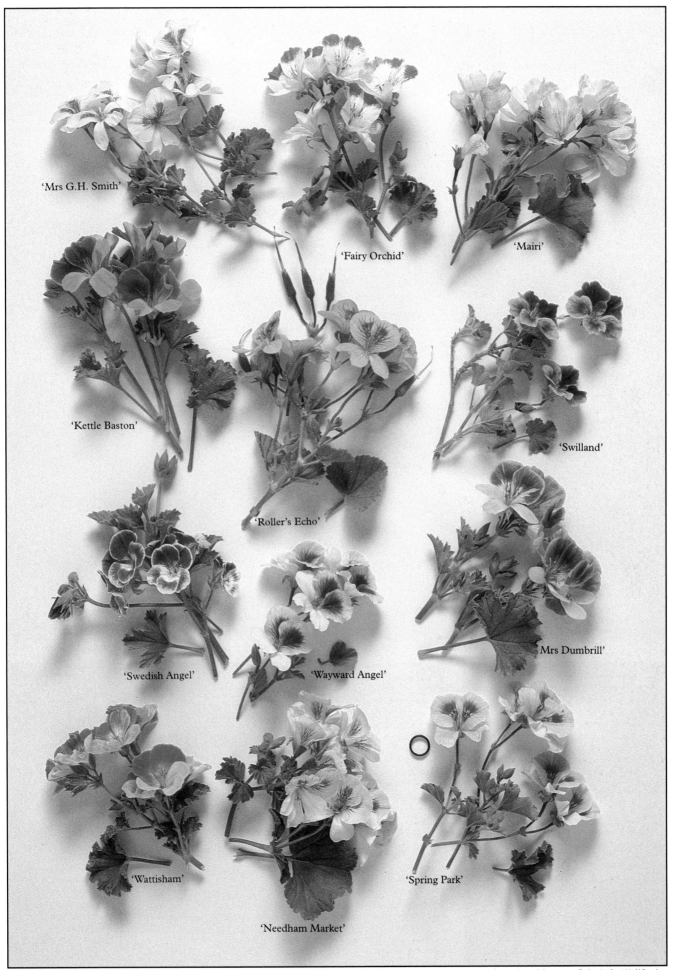

'Mrs G.H. Smith'

'Fairy Orchid'

'Mairi'

'Kettle Baston'

'Swilland'

'Roller's Echo'

'Swedish Angel'

'Wayward Angel'

Mrs Dumbrill'

'Wattisham'

'Spring Park'

'Needham Market'

Specimens from Vernon Geranium Nursery, July 3rd, 1/2 life size

Pelargonium inquinans at Kirstenbosch with part of Table Mountain behind

Pelargonium inquinans in Madeira

Pelargonium transvaalense from Fibrex Nurseries

Pelargonium frutetorum at Kirstenbosch

Pelargonium zonale wild on Robinson pass

Pelargonium alchemilloides (L.) L'Hérit.
(s. *Ciconium*) A small low spreading plant,
native of Africa from the Cape Peninsula north
to Kenya, Ethiopia and Somalia, growing on
grassy slopes, in waste places and bare ground
after fires, flowering throughout the year.
Roots tuberous or suckering; plant around
20cm tall and wider; leaves very variable, silky,
deeply 5-lobed and toothed, on hairy petioles,
the blade 2–7cm across. Flowers usually 3–6,
but up to 15 in an umbel, pinkish to white or
cream, 2–2.5cm across. The very similar
P. elongatum from the SW Cape has narrow
stipules and glandular hairs on the stem and
leaves. Easily grown in sandy soil. Forms from
high altitudes in the Drakensberg where it is
common at up to 2400m, should be hardy to
−10°C.

Pelargonium alchemilloides

Pelargonium zonale

Pelargonium inquinans (L.) L'Hérit.
(s. *Ciconium*) A succulent and somewhat
shrubby plant, native of the E Cape from
Patensie east to Umtata, growing in scrub and
bush, often near the sea, flowering almost
throughout the year. Stems up to 2m,
succulent when young, woody later; leaves
softly hairy, sweet-smelling with a suggestion
of cedar, unmarked, almost round, 4–8cm
across, shallowly 5–7-lobed. Flowers 3–4cm
across, 5–30 in an umbel, the petals almost
equal, bright scarlet, rarely pale pink or white.
This species was cultivated in England by
Bishop Compton at Fulham Palace in 1714
and became one of the most important parents
of the Zonal cultivars. I have seen it
naturalized on sea cliffs in Madeira.

Pelargonium frutetorum Dyer (s. *Ciconium*)
A sprawling shrub with heads of rather small
salmon-pink flowers, native of South Africa in
E Cape Province, near Bathhurst, growing in
scrub near the coast, flowering mainly in
November–January. Stems to 1m, spreading
and ascending; leaves marked with a clear dark
ring near the centre, shallowly 5-lobed, about

6cm across. Flowers up to 15 in an umbel,
salmon-pink, about 3.5cm across. Petals
obovate, 2cm long and 1cm wide, the upper
pair lightly veined, smaller than the lower
three. This wild species is close to the familiar
cultivar 'The Boar' (*see p. 60*). The wild
species, shown here, has slightly wider petals
and less deeply lobed leaves.

Pelargonium transvaalense (L.) L'Hérit.
(s. *Ciconium*) A bushy shrub with thick
tuberous branches, well-marked leaves and
rather spidery flowers, native of South Africa
in E Transvaal above Barberton and with one
old record in NE Natal at Mid-Illovo, growing
in shady wooded ravines at 600–1400m,
flowering in late summer. Annual stems to
30cm or more in the shade. Leaves soft, with
glandular hairs on both sides, with a dark
zone. Stalks slender, with 3–10 flowers in the
umbel. Petals 20–25mm long, 6–7mm wide,

notched, reflexed. Easily grown, but needs
water in summer and a rather dry winter. Best
in partial shade in hot weather. Min. 0°C.

Pelargonium zonale (L.) L'Hérit.
(s. *Ciconium*) A tall much-branched shrub
with masses of small flowers, native of South
Africa from the SW Cape to the NE Cape and
on Bamboo Mountain in the Natal
Drakensberg, growing in dry rocky hills, stony
slopes and on the edges of forests, flowering
almost throughout the year. Stems usually
around 1m, but up to 3m tall. Leaves smooth
or with scattered glands and short hairs, with
little scent, almost circular with shallow lobes
and rounded teeth, usually marked with an
irregular purple ring, 5–15cm across. Flowers
5–70 in an umbel, red to white but usually pale
pink, around 4cm across, with narrow petals.
An easily-grown species for dry sunny slopes
or well-drained soil. Min. 0°C, perhaps less.

'Highfield's Appleblossom'

'Bold Apple Blossom'

'Winford Festival'

'Mr Wren'

'Princess Pink'

'New Life'

'Dryden'

'Princess Margaretha'

Specimens from Vernon Geranium Nursery, July 3rd, 1/2 life size

Pelargonium 'Frank Headley' *Pelargonium* 'The Boar'

'**Bold Apple Blossom**' Plant compact. There were two or more 'Apple Blossoms' around in the 1900s, usually pale pink with a darker or paler eye. Raised by J. Gibbons in 1985.

'**Dryden**' syn. 'Lady Dryden', 'Santa Monica' Very free-flowering with a medium or slender stem. Especially good for growing in large pots. A cyclops or painted lady geranium, raised by Pearson before 1899.

'**Frank Headley**' Plant slender, slightly trailing and free-flowering, with elegant thin flowering stems and small clearly variegated leaves. Raised by Headley in 1957.

'**Highfield's Appleblossom**' Plant compact. Leaves with a clear dark zone. Raised by K. Gamble in 1969.

'**Kewense**' syn. *P.* × *kewense* Dyer, 'Scarlet Kewense' A small plant with dark red flowers found at Kew and named in 1934. It is probably a hybrid between a red cultivar and *P. zonale*.

'**Mr Wren**' Plant tall, with few branches. Flowering stems tall, rather slender. Found by Conn of California in the garden of a Mr Wren. Sometimes reverts to a plain red.

'**Pink Kewense**' A taller plant than 'Kewense' with large umbels of narrow-petalled flowers, closer to the wild *P. zonale* (*see p. 159*). Probably a sport of the original *P.* × *kewense* or a cross back to *P. zonale*.

'**Princess Margaretha**' Plant compact and free-flowering; raised by K. Gamble in 1980.

'**Princess Pink**' Plant with well-marked leaves. Raised by D. Magson.

'**New Life**' syn. 'Single New Life', 'L'Avenir', 'Peppermint Stick' Plant tall and rather spindly with unstable flowers sometimes sporting to pale pink with a dark centre or to red. Raised by Henderson in 1869. A sport of 'Vesuvius'.

'**Skelly's Pride**' syn. 'Salmon Fringed', 'Jeanne' An erect plant with unusual fringed petals. A sport from 'Pride' and often reverting. There are also darker red and pinkish sports of 'Skelly's' with fringed petals.

'**The Boar**' A long trailing or clambering plant to 2m or more, with well-marked small leaves and profuse but rather small flowers on slender stems. This is close to the wild species *P. frutetorum*, which is also the parent of a race of slender hybrid zonals.

'**Winford Festival**' A stout strong-growing plant with a large truss of beautifully veined flowers. Raised by R. Newberry in 1989.

'**White Boar**' A taller-growing white form of 'The Boar' with slightly broader petals.

Specimens from Vernon Geranium Nursery, July 3rd, 1/4 life size

161

'A Happy Thought'

'Lady Dorothy Nevill'

'Monarch'

'Distinction'

'Freak of Nature'

'Miss Burdett Coutts'

'Flower of Spring'

'Madame Salleron'

'Lady Cullum'

'Lass O'Gowrie'

'Mr Henry Cox'

Specimens from Vernon Geranium Nursery, July 3rd, 2/5 life size

'Mrs J.C. Mappin'

'Platinum'

'Little Margaret'

'Merry Go Round'

'Contrast'

'Crystal Palace Gem'

Specimens from Vernon Geranium Nursery, July 3rd, 1/4 life size

Pelargonium 'A Happy Thought'

A good plant of Pelargonium 'Mr Henry Cox'

'A Happy Thought' Plant erect with a slender stem, raised by Lynes in 1877. Often reverts.

'Contrast' Yellow, scarlet and brown leaves with red flowers, raised in 1968.

'Crystal Palace Gem' Plant dwarf and spreading. Raised by Henderson in 1869.

'Freak of Nature' A very unstable variegation, producing all white, all green or leaves with a large cream patch in the centre. Plant dwarf and slow-growing. Raised by Gray in 1880.

'Distinction' Plant dwarf and slender. Raised by Henderson before 1880.

'Lady Cullum' A short plant with dark multicoloured leaves and very poor flowers. Raised by Henderson before 1858.

'Flower of Spring' Stems of medium height. Raised by Turner before 1860.

'Lady Dorothy Nevill' A doubtful name, close to 'Lass O'Gowrie'.

'Lass O'Gowrie' syn. 'Carse O'Gowrie' A short bushy plant with slender flowering stems, easily grown and free-flowering. Raised by Henderson in 1860.

'Little Margaret' Raised by D. Storey in 1971.

'Madame Salleron' Plant with bushy growth, useful as a foil or edging plant. Flowers rarely produced, small with narrow petals. Of unknown parentage, raised by Lémoine in 1840–50.

'Merry Go Round' A dwarf plant, leaves with a broad cream margin, raised by D. Storey in about 1970.

'Miss Burdett Coutts' A slow-growing plant, dwarf and upright, raised by Henderson in 1860.

'Monarch' Tall-growing but upright, with delicate pink flowers, raised by Shady Hill Gardens in America.

'Mr Henry Cox' syn. 'Mrs Henry Cox' Plant of medium height, listed by Cannell's catalogue in 1879 when it was given a First Class Certificate by the RHS in 1879. Still one of the best of this group and will do outdoors in summer in northern climates.

'Mrs J. C. Mappin' Plant tall and upright, flowers white with a red eye, reverting to all red; raised by Townsend before 1880.

'Platinum' Plant upright, leaves with a very narrow cream border. A sport of 'Frank Headley', raised by Heidgen.

Pelargonium 'Caroline Schmidt' by the old graveyard at Wisley

Pelargonium 'Titan'

Pelargonium 'Wantirna'

'Bette Shellard' Plant compact. A very good new variety, with large heads of flowers and well-coloured leaves, raised by A. Shellard in 1991.

'Caroline Schmidt' syn. 'Wilhelm Languth', 'Deutscher Sieger' A dull scarlet double-flowered variegated-leaved Zonal. This variety has long been popular for bedding as well as for growing in pots, and is valuable both for its good, though not large, flowers as well as leaves with a white edge. Robust and upright-growing. An old variety, raised in Germany before 1900. 'Mrs Parker' (*illustrated below*) is a pink-flowered sport and it may also produce a variety with a red flower but green leaf.

'Cherie Maid' Silvery leaves with a narrow white edge and attractive silvery-pink flowers.

'Chocolate Blotch' An upright plant with golden, purple-blotched leaves and striking coral-pink flowers; raised by Jan Taylor in 1976.

'Frank Headley' Plant slender, slightly trailing and free-flowering, with elegant thin flowering stems and small clearly variegated leaves. Raised by Headley in 1957.

'Greetings' A slender plant related to hybrids such as 'The Boar'; raised by C. Miller in Los Altos, California in 1964.

'Hills of Snow' syn. 'Foster's Seedling', 'Mary Anderson' A slender plant with pale mauve flowers and cream-edged silvery leaves. An old variety listed by Cannell's in 1900 but said to date from about 1855.

'Magic Lantern' Plant prostrate, free-flowering and very suitable for steep banks or hanging baskets. Well-marked leaves and good heads of flowers freely produced, like an improved version of 'The Boar'. Raised by T. Both in Adelaide.

'Miller's Valentine' A slow-growing dwarf; raised by C. Miller in Los Altos in about 1964.

'Mont Blanc' Small slow-growing silvery-leaved variety with pure white flowers.

'Petals' Close to 'Hills of Snow' but with a more irregular leaf and deeper pinkish-mauve flower.

'Titan' A strong plant combining a well-coloured leaf and good red flowers.

'Wantirna' An unusual variety raised in USA in which the leaf has golden veins. A similar variegation is found in the trailing ivy-leaved 'Crocodile'.

'Miller's Valentine'

'Magic Lantern'

'Frank Headley'

'Chocolate Blotch'

'Mont Blanc'

'Cherie Maid'

'Petals'

'Hills of Snow'

'Bette Shellard'

'Greetings'

Specimens from Vernon Geranium Nursery, July 3rd, 2/5 life size

'Turkish Delight'

'Katie'

'Blazonry'

'Red Magic Lantern'

'Dainty Lassie'

'Solent Sunrise'

'Falklands Hero'

'Don's Silva Perle'

Specimens from Vernon Geranium Nursery, July 3rd, 1/4 life size

'Blazonry' A slow-growing but tall plant; flowers bright red, single. Raised by Miller in California in 1961.

'Dainty Lassie' A dwarf variegated Zonal.

'Don's Silva Perle' A dwarf variegated Zonal.

'Falklands Hero' A variegated Zonal.

'Golden Butterfly' A green and gold sport of the old gold-leaved variety 'Robert Fish'; raised by Turner in 1871.

'Golden Harry Hieover' An old variety given a First Class Certificate in the RHS trial in 1873 and much used by the Victorians for bedding. Plant dwarf and spreading, suitable for a large pot.

'Katie' Plant upright with very dark leaves and large heads of flowers.

'Little Fi-Fine' Plant dwarf, bushy and free-flowering.

'Lively Lady' A dwarf, coloured-foliage variety.

'Maréchal MacMahon' syn. 'The Czar', 'King George V', 'Jubilee' An old dwarf variety given a First Class Certificate in the RHS trial in 1872 and listed by Cannell in 1880. Still a good plant for pots and summer bedding.

'Medallion' A coloured-leaf Zonal.

'Mrs Quilter' A dwarf slender-stemmed plant; flowers rather small. Raised by Laing in 1880.

'Pink Golden Harry Hieover' A sport of the red-flowered 'Golden Harry Hieover', with pink flowers but the same golden leaves.

'Red Magic Lantern' A red sport of 'Magic Lantern'; plant less creeping than its parent. Raised by K. Gamble in 1985.

'Solent Sunrise' Leaf with a very dark zone and deep red flowers; raised by N. J. West in 1989.

'Turkish Delight' Plant dwarf; raised by Ian Gillam.

'Verona' syn. 'Pink Cloth of Gold' Stem slender, of medium height, free-flowering; listed by Cannell in 1900.

Pelargonium 'Blazonry'

Pelargonium 'Mrs Quilter'

'Lively Lady'

'Little Fi-Fine'

'Golden Butterfly'

'Verona'

'Mrs Quilter'

'Maréchal MacMahon'

'Golden Harry Hieover'

'Pink Golden Harry Hieover'

'Medallion'

Specimens from Vernon Geranium Nursery, July 3rd, 2/5 life size

'Anna'   'Friesdorf'

'Dresden Pink'

'Cindy'

'Bath Beauty'

'Claydon'

'Occold Lagoon'

'Angelique'

'Brenda Hyatt'   'Edith Steane'

Specimens from Vernon Geranium Nursery, July 3rd, 2/5 life size

Zonal pelargoniums trained on the greenhouse wall at Crathes

Pelargonium 'Patricia Andrea' (1/4 life size)

'Angelique' A dwarf Zonal with double flowers; raised by Maudsley in 1987.

'Anna' A dwarf Zonal; the inflorescence often forms a second umbel above the original one. Raised by Holborow in 1987.

'Bath Beauty' A dwarf Zonal with very dark purplish leaves and contrasting salmon-pink flowers. Raised by M. Bennett in 1972.

'Ben Franklyn' A double-flowered Zonal with silvery cream-edged leaves, introduced in 1988.

'Brenda Hyatt' A dwarf Zonal with dark green leaves and double flowers; raised by H. F. Parrett in 1972.

'Cherry Sundae' A double-flowered Zonal with well-coloured leaves with a broad pale margin.

'Cindy' A dwarf Zonal with white flowers flushed with pink.

'Claydon' A dwarf double Zonal; easily grown into a good plant. Raised by R. Bidwell in 1970.

'Dresden Pink' A dwarf narrow-petalled Zonal with dark leaves, introduced in 1979.

'Edith Steane' A dwarf Zonal with dark leaves and bright red flowers; raised by F. Steane in 1982.

'Friesdorf' syn. 'Oxford' A miniature Zonal with erect habit, dark green leaves and narrow-petalled red flowers.

'Ivory Snow' A double Zonal with greeny-white double flowers and cream-edged leaves; raised by Shady Hill Gardens, USA.

'Mrs Parker' A double-flowered pink sport of 'Caroline Schmidt'; raised by Parker in 1880.

'Mrs Strang' A double-flowered Zonal with a multi coloured leaf; raised by Williams before 1882.

'Occold Lagoon' A dwarf Zonal with pale pink petals with a deeper edge; raised by the Revd S. Stringer in 1985.

'Patricia Andrea' In this and a small group of other Zonals, the narrow-petalled flowers never open fully; they are known as 'tulip-flowered'. Raised in USA.

'Princess Alexandra' A double-flowered Zonal with greyish leaves that have a silver edge.

'Retah's Crystal' A pale pink double-flowered Zonal with leaves that have a clear white edge.

'Sussex Beauty' A dwarf Zonal with leaves heavily marked with cream; raised by the Revd S. Stringer.

'Turtle's Surprise' A double dwarf Zonal. A sport of 'F. V. Raspail', listed by Cannell's in 1880.

'Ben Franklyn'

'Mrs Parker'

'Turtle's Surprise'

'Retah's Crystal'

'Cherry Sundae'

'Mrs Strang'

'Princess Alexandra'

'Ivory Snow'

'Sussex Beauty'

Specimens from Vernon Geranium Nursery, July 3rd, 1/2 life size

'Doris Moore'

'Duchess of Devonshire'

'Feuerreise'

'Paul Crampel'

'Highfield's Comet'

'Crampel's Master'

'Osna'

'Highfield's Paramount'

Specimens from Vernon Geranium Nursery, July 4th, 1/2 life size

'Cardinal'

'Highfield's Supreme'

'Emma Louise'

'Velvet'

'Highfield's Pride'

'Highfield's Fashion'

Specimens from Vernon Geranium Nursery, July 4th, 1/2 life size

'Cardinal' Plant bushy and compact; raised in USA.

'Crampel's Master' Plant and flowers very large, free-flowering, of better habit than 'Paul Crampel'.

'Doris Moore' syn. 'Zelia' Plant medium-size, free-flowering; raised by Clifton of Chichester. An old favourite for outdoor planting, possibly a sport from 'Charles Blair'.

'Duchess of Devonshire' Plant robust with good rain-resistant flowers. Raised by K. Gamble in 1982.

'Emma Louise' Plant compact, with white-centred flowers. Raised by K. Gamble in 1980.

'Feuerreise' Plant medium-size; flowers of unusual deep scarlet colour.

'Highfield's Comet' Quick-growing and easy from cuttings. Bred for bedding; raised by K. Gamble in 1970.

'Highfield's Fashion' A good grower with pale foliage and flowers with a pale eye; raised by K. Gamble in 1984.

'Highfield's Paramount' Raised by K. Gamble in 1973.

'Highfield's Pride' Another good variety

for bedding. Raised by K. Gamble in 1973.

'Highfield's Supreme' Very free-flowering, flowers with a white eye; raised by K. Gamble in 1977.

'Osna' Very dark leaves and a large head of long-stalked flowers.

'Paul Crampel' syn. 'Meteor' Plant free-flowering, of medium height; raised by Lémoine of Nancy in 1893. This is one of the classic red Zonals, both for greenhouse and for bedding, doing well outdoors in cool climates.

'Velvet' Flowers purplish-crimson in a large head.

171

'Rose Startel'

'Mrs Pat'

'Golden Staph'

'Stellar Ragtime'

'Stellar Grenadier'

Specimens from Vernon Geranium Nursery, July 4th, 3/5 life size

The first Stellar Zonals were raised by Ted Both of Adelaide in about 1965 from crosses between 'Chinese Cactus', a sport from 'Fire Dragon' an early cactus-flowered Zonal (*see p. 176*), and a range of Zonals. All are dainty small plants with heads of serrated petals on slender stems.

'Golden Staph'   A Stellar with golden leaves and small but numerous flowers; raised by Ted Both in 1986. The name 'Staph' is derived from the hybrid *Pelargonium × staphisagiroides* which was once thought to be an ancestor of this group.

'Mrs Pat'   A Stellar which is a pink-flowered

sport of 'Golden Ears'; raised by Ian Gillam.

'Red Devil'   A Stellar with bright red flowers and a well-marked leaf.

'Rose Startel'   Pink flowers and well-zoned leaves.

'Snowflake'   A miniature Stellar with palest pink flowers and a pale leaf.

'Stellar Arctic Star'   A Stellar with relatively large white flowers; raised by Ted Both before 1970.

'Stellar Dawn Star'   A Stellar raised by Ted

Both before 1970.

'Stellar Grenadier'   A Stellar raised by Ted Both before 1970.

'Stellar Ragtime'   A tall plant with well-marked leaves and double flowers; raised by Hartsook.

'Stellar Telstar'   Well-marked leaves and a rather tight head of very narrow-petalled flowers.

'Vancouver Centennial'   A Stellar with very dark crowded leaves and small single flowers; raised by Ian Gillam in 1986.

172

'Stellar Arctic Star'

'Stellar Telstar'

'Vancouver Centennial'

'Red Devil'

'Snowflake'

'Stellar Dawn Star'

Specimens from Vernon Geranium Nursery, July 4th, 1/2 life size

'Francis Parrett'

'Garnet Rosebud'

'Royal Norfolk'

'Rigal'

'Red Black
Vesuvius'

'Altair'

'Kyra'

'Pink Splendour'

'Frills'

'Memento'

Specimens from Vernon Geranium Nursery, July 4th, 4/5 life size

'Altair'　A miniature Zonal; fast-growing with double flowers, bright salmon. Raised by the Revd S. Stringer before 1962.

'Francis Parrett'　A miniature Zonal with double lavender flowers and dark green leaves. Raised by H. F. Parrett in 1965.

'Frills'　A miniature Zonal with double bright pink flowers with narrow petals; raised by Holmes Miller in Los Altos, California in 1966.

'Garnet Rosebud'　A miniature Zonal with double compact rosette flowers of deep red. Raised by Millerin 1970.

'Golden Ears'　A dwarf and bushy Stellar, leaves golden with a bronze zone; raised by Ian Gillam in 1982.

'Golden Staph'　A Stellar with golden leaves that have a rather pale zone; raised by Ted Both in 1986.

'Kyra'　A miniature Zonal with double white flowers that have a pink base; raised by H. F. Parrett in 1965.

'Memento'　A miniature Zonal with dark green leaves and contrasting pale salmon double flowers.

'PELFI Rio'　An F1 seed-raised strain of miniature Zonals, with marks on each petal. PELFI is a registered trade mark of Fischer Pelargoniums in Germany.

'Pink Golden Ears'　A Stellar with very heavily marked leaves and pink flowers.

'Pink Splendour'　A miniature Zonal with semi-double salmon-pink flowers.

'Red Black Vesuvius'　A miniature Zonal listed by Cannell's in 1890. Leaves nearly black, free-flowering with large bright red flowers.

'Rigal'　A miniature Zonal with dark green leaves and scarlet double flowers; raised by the Revd S. Stringer in 1965.

'Royal Norfolk'　A miniature Zonal with dark green leaves and rich purple double flowers; raised by the Revd S. Stringer.

'Vancouver Centennial'　A Stellar with very dark, crowded leaves and small single flowers, raised by Ian Gillam in 1986.

'Red Black Vesuvius' in a mixed display

'Golden Ears'

'Pink Golden Ears'

'Golden Staph'

'Vancouver Centennial'

Specimens from Vernon Geranium Nursery, July 4th, 2/5 life size

'PELFI Rio' (1/5 life size)

175

'Ruth Bessley'

'Bicoloured
Startel'

'Red Startel'

'Stellar Bird Dancer'

'Stellar Cathay'

'Salmon Startel'

'Stellar Apricot'

'Supernova'

'Pogoda'

'Prim'

Specimens from Vernon Geranium Nursery, July 4th, 2/5 life size

'Fire Dragon'

'Coronia'

'Spitfire'

'Els'

Specimens from Vernon Geranium Nursery, July 4th, 1/2 life size

'Bicoloured Startel'   A Stellar Zonal with single red flowers that have a white streak on each petal.
'Coronia'   A cactus-flowered Zonal with long quilled mid-pink petals.
'Els'   A Stellar Zonal with finger-like leaves and narrow slightly deformed petals; raised in USA.
'Fire Dragon'   A cactus-flowered Zonal with scarlet flowers which are unstable and often sport to broader-petalled forms. An old dwarf and free-flowering variety known since 1899.
'Pogoda'   A Stellar Zonal with double pink and white flowers raised by Duren.
'Prim'   A Stellar Zonal with double white flowers.
'Red Startel'   A Stellar Zonal with single scarlet flowers.

'Ruth Bessley'   A Stellar Zonal with large white flowers on a neat plant.
'Salmon Startel'   A Stellar Zonal with well-marked leaves and good salmon-pink flowers.
'Spitfire'   A cactus-flowered Zonal with variegated leaves and orange-red flowers.
'Stellar Apricot'   A Stellar Zonal with very dainty well-marked leaves and slender umbels of apricot flowers.
'Stellar Bird Dancer'   A Stellar Zonal with well-marked leaves and spidery pale pink flowers.
'Stellar Cathay'   A Stellar Zonal with well-marked leaves and a compact head of small flowers.
'Supernova'   A Stellar Zonal with double narrow-petalled lilac-pink petals.

'Stellar Apricot' at Warminghurst

177

Pelargonium peltatum wild with aloes on dry rocky banks on Olifant's Kop, near Paterson, E Cape in October

Pelargonium tongaense at Wisley

Pelargonium peltatum 'Lateripes' at Kirstenbosch

Pelargonium × salmoneum at M. Pellizaro's, near Grasse

Pelargonium acetosum on dry rocks near Cradock, E Cape

Pelargonium peltatum

Pelargonium acetosum

Pelargonium peltatum (L.) L'Hérit.
(s. *Ciconium*) A creeping or hanging plant
with thin stems and ivy-like leaves, native of
South Africa in the Cape, from Worcester east
to Port Elizabeth, growing in scrub along the
coast or on dry rocky hillsides, flowering
mainly in September–November. Stems
trailing or climbing to 2m or more. Leaves
rather fleshy, with 5 untoothed lobes, peltate,
often with a purple ring near the centre, acid
and lemony to taste. Flowers 2–9 in the umbel,
mauve to pale pink or white, 4–5cm across, the
upper petals veined or spotted with red. This
species was introduced to Holland in 1700 and
is the parent of the important ivy-leaved
cultivars (*p. 180–1*). Photographed in October
in the E Cape at Olifants Kop near Paterson.
'Lateripes' This is a clone or hybrid of

P. peltatum in which the leaf is not peltate, but
has a deep sinus where the stalk is attached.
The plant is more upright and the flowers are
larger than *P. peltatum* and have infertile
anthers. However, plants with similar leaves
are found in the wild and one such is shown
here, photographed in the National Botanic
Gardens at Kirstenbosch.

Pelargonium acetosum (L.) L'Hérit.
(s. *Ciconium*) A glaucous succulent sub-
shrub with thin stems, native of South Africa
in the SE Cape, with isolated localities near
Uitenhage and in the Orange Free State,
growing on dry cliffs and rocky slopes,
flowering throughout the year. Plant to 60cm
tall and wide; leaves smooth, fleshy, irregularly
lobed, 1–6cm long, when crushed the smell
and taste is acidic, like sorrel (*Rumex acetosa*).
Flowers around 5cm across, in umbels of 2–6,
on long stiff stems; petals salmon-pink to
nearly white, narrowly spathulate, the upper
with reddish lines. Easily grown in sandy soil,
kept rather dry, especially in winter.
Photographed near Cradock, C. D. & R. 955.

P. × salmoneum Dyer Probably a hybrid
between *P. acetosum* and *P. zonale* or
P. frutetorum, found in a neglected shrub
border in a park in Port Elizabeth in 1929.
Derek Clifford says that this is the same as
P. hybridum (L. fil.) L'Hérit. which was grown
by James Sherard at Eltham in 1732. The
leaves are fleshy, bristly hairy, with rounded
teeth, cuneate at the base and with a fan of
raised veins beneath.

Pelargonium tongaense Vorster (s. *Ciconium*)
A low-growing plant with striking pale scarlet

flowers, native of South Africa in NE Natal,
near Makane's Pont in Tongaland, growing in
loose sandy soil under low trees, flowering
throughout the summer. Stems thin and
sprawling; leaves with one large terminal lobe
and four smaller side lobes, all pointed from a
broad base, with few shallow irregular teeth,
pale green, stiffly hairy on the upper surface,
4–8cm wide. Umbels of 3–8 flowers held well
above the leaves, on a stalk 20cm long. Petals
bright, pale scarlet, oblanceolate, rounded at
the apex, 1.5cm long. This species was
described as recently as 1983 and is very rare
in the wild. It is easily cultivated, is tolerant of
some shade and should be watered in summer,
kept rather dry in winter when the plants die
back. Min. 0°C. Photographed at Wisley
(Burtt 6848).

Pelargonium peltatum overhanging an azulejos, tiled wall in Madeira

Pelargonium peltatum

Pelargonium peltatum 'L'Elégante' showing coloured leaves

Ivy-leaved pelargoniums are derived mainly from the wild species *Pelargonium peltatum* (*see p. 179*). Cascades are generally smaller, less creeping plants with single narrow-petalled flowers and are especially good for hanging baskets, the edges of large pots or for planting on banks and walls. They are possibly crosses with *Pelargonium acetosum* (*see p. 179*). The Decora group is similar to the cascades but has larger flowers and slightly broader petals. In growth they are a little more trailing and have lightly marked leaves.

'Decora Impérial' Flowers scarlet; introduced around 1990. Raised by Bury in 1973.

'Decora Lavender' Flowers pinkish-mauve. Raised by Bury in 1979.

'Decora Rose' syn. 'Sophie' Flowers rose pink. Raised by Bury in 1971.

'Fiesta' A single-flowered *peltatum* cultivar with large, almost white, flowers and veins on the upper petals. 'Jeanne d'Arc' is similar but has pale pinkish-mauve upper petals.

'L'Elégante' A form of *P. peltatum* with variegated leaves, white, pink and mauve-edged when growing slowly in good light. Flowers white with reddish-purple veins. Listed by Cannell's in 1868.

Pelargonium peltatum (*see p. 179 for full text*) In the wild, flowers of this species vary in the width of the petals and in colour from

‘Decora Lavender’ at Versailles

‘Decora Rose’ at Vaux le Vicomte

Pelargonium ‘Decora Rose’

Pelargonium ‘Fiesta’ with two heads of ‘Rouletta’ behind

almost white to quite a good pink, and from unmarked to having the upper petals blotched or veined.

‘Magaluf’   This variety was found by N. Watkins on a rubbish tip in Spain in 1982. It is striking with large crimson spots on the upper petals.

‘Red Mini Cascade’   Raised by Fischer in Germany; date not recorded, but after 1970.

‘Rose Mini Cascade’   Raised by Fischer in Germany.

‘Rose Silver Cascade’   Leaves silvery, variegated; flowers rose-pink. Sometimes wrongly called ‘Duke of Edinburgh’, an older variety which has small double flowers.

‘Rouletta’ syn. ‘Mexicanerin’   This striking cultivar has semi-double flowers of white petals with a cerise edge. A sport from ‘Mexican Beauty’ found by Bill Schmidt in a Mexican village.

‘Rose Mini Cascade’

‘Magaluf’

‘Red Mini Cascade’

‘Rose Silver Cascade’

‘Decora Lavender’

‘Decora Impérial’

Specimens from Vernon Geranium Nursery, July 3rd, 2/5 life size

Impatiens sodenii in the temperate conservatory at Wisley

Impatiens sodenii

Impatiens tinctoria subsp. tinctoria outdoors in Trengwainton, Cornwall

usually very shady forests, sometimes as an epiphyte, at 370–2400m, flowering throughout the year. Stems fleshy to 1m. Leaves alternate, long-stalked, the blade broadly ovate, elliptic or lanceolate, crenate, 5–22cm long. Flowers on short stalks in the leaf axils with small greenish petals and a large swollen red sepal 19–28mm long, ending in a short up-curved spur. The clone commonly cultivated is known as 'Congo Cockatoo'. It can be easily grown in warm humid conditions in peaty soil. Min. 10°C.

Impatiens quisqualis Launert   An upright or decumbent perennial with pale yellow, white or pale pink flowers among the leaves, native of Malawi on the plateau of Mt Mlanje, growing in cloud forest and along mountain streams, at 1800–2130m, flowering in January–May. Roots tuberous, thin. Stems to 1m, pubescent. Leaves alternate, stalked, the blade 4–14cm long, pubescent, especially beneath. Flowers in groups of 2–3. Lower sepal with a spur 5–8mm long. Lower petal 20–35mm long with a yellow or orange spot towards the base. For cool moist conditions. Min. 0°C. The very similar I. shirensis Bak. fil., also from Mt Mlanje, is glabrous, with taller stems to 3m, almost shrubby below.

Impatiens sodenii Engl. & Warb. ex Engl. syn. I. oliveri C. H. Wright ex W. Wats. A tall, robust, almost shrubby perennial with whorls of leaves and flat pale pink or white flowers, native of Kenya, N and E Tanzania, growing in rainforest, by streams, on cliff ledges and among boulders, often of granite, at 1000–2700m, flowering throughout the year. Stems to 3m, succulent. Leaves in dense whorls of 6–10 at the top of the stem, not stalked, 5–18cm long, oblanceolate. Flowers

Impatiens assurgens Baker (*Balsaminaceae*) A very variable creeping perennial with opposite leaves and white, pale pink or mauve flowers, native of central Africa from Tanzania to S Malawi and east to Zaire and Angola, growing in wet open grassy or shady places at 840–2600m, flowering from October–June. Roots fleshy. Stems to 60cm. Leaves opposite, usually sessile, glabrous to pubescent, suborbicular, to ovate or lanceolate. Flowers with the longest petal 15–28mm long, often

with a yellow spot near the base. An attractive low-growing plant for a wet place; does not need shade. Min. 0°C, perhaps less when dormant.

Impatiens niamniamensis Gilg syn. *I. bicolor* Hook. fil.   A very variable upright, often gaunt perennial with green and red flowers, native of tropical Africa from Cameroon south to Angola and east to SW Kenya and NW Tanzania, growing in moist,

Impatiens assurgens on Mlanje

Impatiens zombensis on wet rocks on Zomba mountain, Malawi

usually solitary, 4–6cm across. Lower sepal with a spur 6–9.8cm long. Lower petal 30–37mm long, often with red veins towards the base. Easily grown in good soil in full light, though C. Grey-Wilson in *Impatiens of Africa* says that it is shy-flowering until a large plant has developed. Min. 0°C. Easily recognized by its whorls of oblanceolate leaves.

Impatiens tinctoria A. Rich. subsp. **tinctoria** A tall fleshy long-lived perennial forming huge clumps with large white scented flowers, native of E Zaire, S Sudan, Ethiopia and N Uganda, growing in mountain rainforest and by shady streams, at 750–3000m, flowering in April–January. Roots fleshy and tuberous. Stems to 2m, succulent. Leaves alternate, shortly stalked; the blade 9.5–19.5cm long, narrowly ovate, elliptic or lanceolate. Flowers 2–8 in a group, 4–6cm across. Lower sepal with a spur 8–12cm long. Lower petal 30–55mm long, often with red streaks towards the base. Easily grown in good moist soil in shade and shelter. Min. −3°C, for the top growth; the roots will survive the winter if deeply mulched to keep away frost. Otherwise they can be lifted and potted up to be kept out of frost. Cuttings root easily in summer.
C. Grey-Wilson recognizes 5 subspecies as follows: Subsp. *tinctoria* (*described above*) has the longest spurs, 8–12cm long. Subsp. *latifolia* Grey-Wilson, from S Tanzania and N Malawi has spurs 6–9.5cm long, but broadly ovate leaves. Subsp. *elegantissima* (Gilg) Grey-Wilson, from Mount Elgon and C and S Kenya, at up to 3630m, has leaves like subsp. *tinctoria* but shorter spurs 3.8–6.5cm long and flowers 3–5cm across, usually streaked in the throat. David Mabberley records that he saw the Eastern Double-collared and the Tacazze

Impatiens niamniamensis

Impatiens quisqualis on Mlanje

Sunbirds visiting the flowers. Subsp. *abyssinica* (Hook. fil.) Grey-Wilson, from C Ethiopia near Ankober, has pure white flowers less than 2.5cm across, with spurs 3.1–4.5cm long. Subsp. *songeana* Grey-Wilson from SE Tanzania, has broad leaves but short spurs of 4.8–5.3cm long, on flowers less than 3cm across.

Impatiens zombensis Bak. fil. A bushy spreading perennial with alternate leaves and starry pale pink flowers, native of S Malawi and Mozambique, growing in forest, by streams and on wet cliffs, at 870–2250m, flowering most of the year. Stems to 75cm, soft and fleshy. Leaves alternate, stalked, glabrous or with scattered hairs, the blade 3–9cm long, ovate, to ovate-lanceolate or elliptic, cuneate at the base, acuminate. Flowers usually solitary, 1.5–2cm across, the lower petals longest. Lower sepal with a spur 16–32mm long. For cool, moist conditions. Min. 0°C.

'Celeria'

'Mirage'

'Dewas'

'Argus'

'Duniya'

'Isopa'

'Thecla'

'Veronica'

'Anaca'

'Cethosia'

'Isis'

'Aurore'

'Phoebis'

'Celsia'

'Sesia'

'Vulcane'

'Flambee'

'Jasins'

Specimens from the Royal Horticultural Society's Garden, Wisley, August 5th, 1/2 life size

New Guinea hybrid *Impatiens* by the pond in the temperate conservatory at Wisley

***Impatiens* New Guinea hybrids**   This race of spectacular hybrids was begun between 1960 and 1970 by crossing *I. hawkeri* with its large brick-red flowers, with *I. linearifolia* in which the leaves usually have a white centre. More recently, other species from the Celebes and Java have been used in the strain. *I. hawkeri* Bull. from New Guinea and the Sunda Islands was introduced to cultivation in 1886, but it was not until an expedition made by Dr A. B. Graf (author of *Exotica* and *Tropica*) to the Chimbu Valley in the Finisterre Mountains in the central highlands of New Guinea in 1960 that *I. linearifolia* and a form of *I. hawkeri* with exceptionally highly coloured leaves were introduced, to become the primary parents of the new hybrids. The modern hybrids are suitable for summer bedding outside in warm climates in cool shady positions and make excellent pot plants for the greenhouse, conservatory or windowsill. Leaves are 8–15cm long and flowers 3–7cm across. We have illustrated the following varieties.
Anaca, Argus, Aurore, Celeria, Celsia, Cethosia, Dewas, Duniya, Eclipse raised by Mikkel in USA, **Flambee, Isis, Isopa, Jasius, Mirage, Phoebis, Sesia, Thecla, Veronica, Vulcane.**

Impatiens 'Eclipse'

Impatiens acaulis by wet rocks in the Cardamom Hills, Kerala in October

Impatiens acaulis in Kerala

Impatiens verticillata from Kerala

Impatiens subecalcarata

Impatiens acaulis Hooker (*Balsaminaceae*)
A dwarf tuberous perennial with a single leaf
and pink flowers, native of SE India in Kerala,
growing on wet rock faces in forest and gullies,
flowering in October–December at the end of
the monsoon. Tuber around 3cm across,
dormant in winter. Leaf blade ovate, 6–9cm
across. Inflorescence leafless, umbellate, to
10cm tall. Flowers 3cm across. Petals with
wide-spreading lobes. As far as I know this
species has not been cultivated for many years,
but the three species from Kerala, shown here,
provide a taste of the great richness of the
genus in the hills of southern India. Over a
hundred species have been described, from
dwarfs such as *I. acaulis* to shrubby species in
the grasslands at high altitudes. Seed should be
kept slightly moist after collection until
planting, as it tends to die if dried out
completely.

Impatiens arguta Hook. fil. & Thoms.
A dwarf perennial with blue to pink or rarely
white flowers, native of SW China in Yunnan,
growing in damp shady places and in small
streams at 1500–2000m, flowering in June–
October. Stems to 40cm, rooting at the nodes.
Flowers 2–3cm across. for moist but well-
drained soil. Min. −5°C.

Impatiens balsamina L.   A bushy annual,
native of E Asia, but now found throughout
the tropics, usually growing in waste places in
villages, flowering much of the year. Stems to
50cm, crowded with leaves; flowers in the leaf
axils, close to the stem, red, pink or white,
often double, especially in 'Camelliaeflora'.
Seed pods white-hairy. Easily grown in warm,
moist conditions. Min. 5°C.

Impatiens marianae Rchb. fil. ex Hook. fil.
A sprawling perennial that has striking leaves
with white veins and small purplish flowers,
native of Assam, growing in forests, flowering
in summer. Stems to 20cm long. Leaf blade
around 6cm long. Flowers 2–3cm across. For a
humid, shady position. Min. 0°C.

Impatiens parasitica Bedd.   A small
annual with a slender stem and red flowers
with curved spurs, native of S India in the
Cardamom Hills in Kerala, growing in shady
leafy places in the forested gullies, flowering in
October–November. Stems about 20cm;
flowers 4–5cm across. For a cool shady
position. Min. 0°C. Close to *I. jerdoniae* Wight,
which has red and green flowers.

Impatiens recurvicornis Maxim.
A creeping and rooting perennial, native of W
China in SW Sichuan, growing in ditches and
moist places among the tea gardens at about
1500m, flowering in September–November.
Stems creeping and ascending to 20cm.
Leaves about 7cm long; flowers about 2cm
across, the spur extending horizontally from
the flower, with a recurved point. Min. 0°C.

Impatiens subecalcarata (Hand.-Mazz.)
Y. L. Chen   A delicate annual, native of W
Yunnan, growing in woods among damp
rocks, at 2500–3000m, flowering in August–
November. Stems to 30cm. Leaves long-
stalked, crenate. Flowers about 2.5cm across.
For a cool moist position. Min. 0°C, although
the seed presumably survives frost.

Impatiens verticillata Wight   A low bushy
perennial with narrow leaves and orange-
scarlet flowers, native of S India in the
Cardamom Hills in Kerala, growing in stony
streams in the forest, flowering in October–
December. Stems to 70cm or more. Leaves in
whorls, narrowly lanceolate, the blade about
7cm long. Flowers 2.5cm across, the spur to
4.5cm long. Easily grown in moist well-
drained soil in a warm shady position.
Min. 5°C.

Impatiens marianae at Wisley

Impatiens parasitica in Kerala

Impatiens recurvicornis with *Iris confusa*, near Ya-an, SW Sichuan

Impatiens balsamina cultivated in Yunnan

Impatiens arguta by the Zhongdian river, NW Yunnan

Oxalis pes-caprae with Lobularia maritima, naturalised in S Spain in March

Oxalis pes-caprae

Oxalis megalorhiza on Tresco

Oxalis bowiei Lindl. (*Oxalidaceae*)
A perennial with elongated bulbs, only basal
leaves and bright pink flowers, native of South
Africa in the E Cape, flowering in March–May
(late summer). A robust plant with leaflets to
5cm long; flowering stems 10–25cm with an
umbel of 3–12 flowers, each 3–4cm across.
An easily grown plant, dormant in winter.
O. articulata Savigny, with slightly smaller
bright magenta flowers is often seen in cottage
gardens in warm parts of the British Isles.
Min. −10°C for short periods if the bulb is
protected.

Oxalis gigantea Barnéoud   An upright
succulent shrub with almost spiny stems,
thickly covered in spring with very small fleshy
deciduous leaves and yellow flowers, native of
Chile, growing on rocky hills in the south of
the Atacama Desert near Caldera, flowering in
spring. Stems several, little-branched, to 2.5m
but usually around 1m. Leaflets about 3.5mm
long, hairy beneath. Flowers 1–2cm across,
solitary or in groups of 3–6. For very dry well-
drained soil. Min. −3°C for short periods.
Photographed in Berkeley Botanic Garden.

Oxalis hirta L.   A bulbous plant with
upright leafy stems and mauve, magenta, white
or rarely yellow flowers, native of South Africa
along the W coast of the Cape and in S
Namaqualand, flowering in April–June
(autumn). Stems to 30cm, hairy, branching,
floppy when mature. Leaves sessile, leaflets
linear to narrowly oblanceolate, about 1cm
long. Flowers about 2.5cm across. Named
varieties include: 'Gothenburg', flowers deep
pink; var. *fulgida* (Lindl.) Knuth, flowers
purple. Easily grown in well-drained rich soil.
Min. −3°C.

Oxalis megalorhiza Jacq. syn. *O. carnosa*
auct.   A dwarf perennial with fleshy leaves
and bright yellow flowers, native of Chile, the
Galapagos Islands and Bolivia, and naturalized
on the Isles of Scilly, growing on stony banks
and in cracks in old walls, flowering in
summer–autumn. Plant with short stems to

Oxalis pes-caprae double form in Madeira

Oxalis gigantea in Berkeley Botanic Garden

Oxalis hirta in Devon in October

Oxalis triangularis

Oxalis ortgiesii

30cm, usually almost stemless; leaflets 10–18mm long with crystalline papillae beneath. Flowers to 2.5cm across. Easily grown and self-seeding. Min. −3°C.

Oxalis ortgiesii Regel   An upright perennial with deeply divided leaflets, brownish-green above, purple beneath and small yellow flowers, native of the Peruvian Andes, flowering most of the year. Stems to 45cm. Inflorescence with branching and curling cymes. Leaflets 6cm long. Flowers to 2.5cm across, pale yellow with dark veins. Often grown as a pot plant in shade. Min. −3°C.

Oxalis pes-caprae L. Bermuda Buttercup A bulbous perennial with basal leaves and heads of beautiful lemon yellow flowers, native of South Africa in the SW Cape and naturalized in SW England, the Mediterranean, California and Australia, growing in fields and waste places, flowering in winter–spring. Plant producing numerous bulbils, hence its success as a weed. Leaflets rather fleshy, obcordate, 1.6–2cm long. Stems to 18cm. Flowers to 2.5cm across. Easily grown and likely to become a weed in frost-free Mediterranean climates. Min. −3°C. The double-flowered form shown here is naturalized in Madeira.

Oxalis smithiana Ecklon & Zeyher   A very variable bulbous perennial with deeply bi-lobed leaflets and large lilac or white flowers with a crimson centre, native of South Africa from the SE Cape to the Natal midlands, at up to 2650m in the Drakensberg, growing in bare dry places, in open grassland and rarely on rocks in the forest, flowering in autumn or spring. Plant with chesnut-like bulbs, producing numerous bulbils. All leaves basal. Leaflets divided to the middle or to the base, into very narrow lobes, to 6.5cm long and 3mm wide. Stems 9–20cm. Flowers solitary, to 3.5cm across, usually lilac with a white and greenish throat. Easily grown with a dry dormant period and flowering soon after coming into growth. Min. −3°C, for Cape plants as shown here, C. D. & R. 938, from Olifant's Kop near Port Elizabeth. Montane forms should be hardier.

Oxalis triangularis A St. Hil.   A small perennial with striking purple leaves, native of Brazil, around Rio de Janiero, growing among rocks by streams at 600m, flowering in October. Stems to 15cm; leaflets 2cm, deeply forked. Good for a dry shady corner. Min. −3°C.

Oxalis smithiana from Olifant's Kop, near Paterson, E Cape in September in Devon

Oxalis bowiei in a cold greenhouse at Harry Hay's

Tropaeolum tricolorum in a cold greenhouse at Harry Hay's

Tropaeolum ciliatum on a warm wall in Kent

Tropaeolum azureum with *Puya alpestris* in the greenhouse in Devon

Tropaeolum azureum Miers (*Tropaeolaceae*) A delicate climber with rounded bright purplish-blue flowers, native of Chile, growing on hot dry hills, scrambling through bushes, flowering in spring, dormant in summer. Tubers rounded, to 6cm across. Stems to 2m or more, climbing by the leaf stalks. Leaves with 5 free obovate lobes, to 2cm across. Flowers 1–2cm across. Petals blue with a white base. Sepals short, green; spur short, about 5mm, green. Fruits hard and dry. Easily grown from seed, forming hazelnut-sized tubers in the first year. These are often difficult to get into growth again, but if they do begin to grow they put out a delicate, very thin brown shoot in late summer. This must not be damaged or the tuber will not produce another that year, if it survives at all. Repotting should therefore be done in midsummer and the tubers watched for the emergence of the thread-like shoot before watering begins. The plant needs very sandy soil and little water in winter, until the leaves are fully developed. Feeding is beneficial to build up a good tuber. After flowering the plants should be kept dry. Min. 0°C. Source: Reg. Metro., Chacabuco, near Polpaico, 500m, Pern & Watson 6055.

Tropaeolum ciliatum Ruiz & Pavon   A delicate but rampant climber spreading from thin white roots, native of Chile, around Conception and Valparaiso, from 38°N to 33°S, growing in shady places and by streams, flowering in October–January (summer). Stems usually annual, to 3m climbing by the leaf stalks. Leaves with the middle lobe 4cm long; flowers 4cm across. For any moist soil. Min. −5°C, or less with the roots protected.

Tropaeolum incisum (Spreng.) Sparre A sprawling or scrambling perennial with deeply cut bluish-green leaves and yellow-orange flowers, native of W Argentina, growing on steep banks in gravelly or sandy clay at 1000–1200m, flowering in January–February

Tropaeolum sessilifolium

Tropaeolum incisum in a cold greenhouse

Tropaeolum pentaphyllum in the Jardin exotique du Val Rameh, Menton, S France in April

Tropaeolum pentaphyllum fruit

Tropaeolum tuberosum subsp *sylvestre*

(late spring in cultivation). Stems to 1m; leaves 5-lobed, each lobe deeply dissected. Flowers about 3cm across; calyx red-tipped; petals yellow, orange or apricot; spur slender, green. For deep well-drained soil, moist in winter and spring, dryish in summer. Min. −5°C. Shown here J. C. Archibald 12452, collected in Argentina, Neuquen, Lacar, NE of Lago Lolog to Lago Cunnuhue, 1200m.

Tropaeolum pentaphyllum Lam.
A delicate but rampant climber with green and red spotted flowers, native of Chile, flowering in spring, dormant in summer. Tubers elongated, to 10cm across, becoming woody with age. Stems to 6m or more, climbing by the leaf stalks. Leaves with 5 ovate-lanceolate lobes, to 4cm across. Flowers 2–3cm across with persistant green, red-streaked sepals and small red petals. Spur pink to red, about 2cm long, slightly saccate at the base. Fruits blue-black, juicy. An easily grown climber, dormant in summer. Tubers should be handled with care as they are likely to rot if damaged. This species grows well outside in warm parts of the Mediterranean, climbing into cypress hedges. Min. −2°C, perhaps.

Tropaeolum sessilifolium Poepp. & Endl.
A dwarf perennial with upright or sprawling stems and white or pale lavender flowers, native of Chile, growing on open stony slopes and in sandy gullies near snow patches, flowering in spring. Stems to 20cm. Leaves short-stalked with 3 or 5 obovate lobes. Flowers about 3cm across with cordate, stalked petals, the upper streaked with grey; sepals green, yellow at the base with a thin yellow spur. This should be a cold-tolerant species, adapted to a dry summer after brief spring rain and snowmelt. Source: Reg. Metro., Lagunillas, 2200m.

Tropaeolum tricolorum Sw.
A delicate climber with bright red, yellow and black or blue flowers, native of Chile and Bolivia, flowering in spring, dormant in summer.

Tubers rounded, to 6cm across. Stems to 2m or more, climbing by the leaf stalks. Leaves with 5–7 obovate to linear lobes, to 3cm across. Flowers 1–2cm across. Spur short, about 15–23mm, red or yellow with the tip green or blue. Fruits not seen. This is one of the hardier species, surviving well in a cold greenhouse, growing through the winter. It needs cool well–drained soil, dry in summer. Min. −3°C for short periods only.

Tropaeolum tuberosum Ruiz. & Pav. var. lineamaculatum Cardenas 'Ken Aslet'
A tall climber with tuberous roots, peltate leaves and orange flowers, native of Peru, Colombia, Ecuador and Bolivia. In the high Andes it is grown as a vegetable, called *anu*, often in the same fields as primitive potatoes. Tubers knobbly, replaced each year, to 10cm long and 5cm thick, yellowish, streaked red. Stems climbing to 3m or more. Leaves peltate, 5-lobed to around half, the lobes indented. Flowers about 2cm across with deep yellow petals and red sepals and spur to 2cm long. The variety **'Ken Aslet'** has the advantage of flowering from midsummer onwards as it is not affected by day length. Most clones do not begin to form buds until the long nights of autumn. In frosty climates this plant can be treated like a potato and lifted in autumn, kept indoors and planted out again when danger of hard frost has passed.

Tropaeolum tuberosum Ruiz. & Pav. subsp. sylvestre Sparre
A rampant climber with peltate leaves and bright red flowers, native of the Andes from Colombia to Argentina, growing in scrub at 2400–3950m, flowering in February–July (in summer and autumn in cultivation). Stems climbing to 4m. Roots thin, white, fleshy. Leaves peltate, with 5 rounded lobes. Flowers about 1.5cm across with red petals, sepals and spur about 2cm long. A beautiful climber for a cool position, dormant in winter. Min. −5°C, provided that the roots are well covered.

T. tuberosum var. *lineamaculatum* 'Ken Aslet'

Polygala virgata on Prince Alfred's Pass, above Knysna

Polygala virgata

Polygala arillata

Polygala arillata in the temperate rain forest near Moxi, SW Sichuan

Polygala fruticosa at Stormsrivier

Polygala myrtifolia

Comesperma confertum

Polygala myrtifolia var. *grandiflora*

Polygala × *dalmaisiana*

Comesperma confertum Labill.
(*Polygalaceae*)   A small upright shrub with
dense racemes of lilac-pink flowers, native of
SW Western Australia, growing in sandy
heathland, flowering in September–December.
Stems to 1m. Leaves narrowly linear, about
2.5cm long, thick and fleshy. Flowers in
racemes 5–10cm long. For well-drained soil
and light shade. Min. −3°C, perhaps.
C. ericinum DC., with pink or purple flowers
and shorter leaves is the most commonly
cultivated species in Australia.

Polygala arillata Buch.-Ham. ex D. Don
(*Polygalaceae*)   A low, shade-tolerant shrub
with leathery leaves and racemes of yellow
flowers, native of the Himalayas from C Nepal
to W China, south to India and SE Asia,
growing in forests and shady cliffs at 1500–
2700m, flowering in May–October. Stems to
2m, exceptionally to 5m. Leaves 5–15cm,
lanceolate to oblong-elliptic, stalked. Flowers
yellow fading to orange; petals often with red
tips, about 1.5cm long. Capsules to 2cm long,
becoming dark red and fleshy. For moist peaty
soil. Min. −5°C if sheltered.

Polygala × dalmaisiana hort.
This spreading shrub, to 3m tall, with purple
flowers like small butterflies, is an old garden
hybrid, probably between *P. myrtifolia* and
P. fruticosa, (*described below*). It is close to
P. myrtifolia but has leaves broad at the base,
both opposite and alternate on the same
branch. Flowers throughout the year. Tolerant
of summer drought. Min. −5°C.

Polygala myrtifolia L.   An upright shrub or
small tree with small evergreen leaves and
purplish flowers, native of South Africa from
the SW Cape to the Karroo and Natal,
growing on mountain slopes, (var. *cluytioides*
Burch. Harv. reaches 2000m in the
Drakensberg), flowering all year, but best in
spring. Stems to 3m, usually about 1.5m.
Leaves alternate, oblong to obovate, tapering
at the base into a short stalk, to 1.8–3cm long.

Flowers purple with green shading, about
1.5cm long with the standards spreading.
Var. **grandiflora** Hook.   An old garden
selection with large, rich purple flowers.
The Plant Finder 1995/96 considers this
synonymous with *P.* × *dalmaisiana*.

Polygala fruticosa Bergius syn. *P. oppositifolia*
L.   A spreading shrub with small evergreen
opposite leaves and purple flowers, native of
South Africa from the S Cape to the Karroo
and Natal, growing on mountain slopes and
coastal hills, flowering most of the year, but
usually best in spring. Shrub to 2m. Leaves
variable, cordate, mucronate, about 2cm long,
often acute, sessile and bluish-grey. Flowers
purple, about 1.5cm long, with the standards
pointing upwards. For well-drained soil,
watered sparingly throughout the year. Min.
−3°C.

Polygala virgata Thunb.   An upright or
arching broom-like shrub with green
cylindrical branches and racemes of purple
flowers, native of South Africa from the SW
Cape to Natal, reaching 2000m in the
Drakensberg and on high ground to Tanzania,
growing in stony places, abandoned fields and
on the edges of forest, flowering most of the
year, but mainly in spring after a dry winter
rest. Stems to 3m. Leaves linear, tapering from
near the apex, soon dropping, to 3cm long.
Flowers to 2.5cm across, nodding, in erect
racemes, reddish-purple; wings upright,
slightly concave. Easily grown in good well-
drained soil. Grows well in coastal California
and is good in a large pot if pruned in winter
before the new growth begins; the flowers
appear from buds in the lower leaf axils of the
previous year's shoots. Min. −5°C, perhaps if
from high altitude. A very large-flowered
unnamed species close to this or to
P. macrostigma Chod., is illustrated in *Wild
Flowers of Malawi* by Audrey Moriarty. It has
lanceolate leaves and several racemes to 30cm
long. Found on the Vipya and Nyika
escarpments, flowering in May–July.

Citrus limon 'Menton' in the Jardin exotique du Val Rameh, Menton, S France in April

Most citrus species and cultivars will flower and fruit in the greenhouse, provided that they are given a minimum temperature of 5°C at night and a little more by day. They need plenty of light and do not like sudden changes in temperature and humidity. Careful watering is required: either too much or too little will result in yellow, sickly looking foliage. A compost made up of half loam and half leaf-mould plus a little charcoal should produce good results; do not add manure, which citruses dislike. The trees can either be planted out in a bed in the conservatory or grown in large pots or tubs so that they can be moved outside in warmer weather. If grown in containers, they will need potting on every two to three years, and a top-dressing of the compost described above should be applied every year. Beware of scale insects.

Citrus limon (L.) Burm. (*Rutaceae*) Common Lemon   This lemon is of unknown origin but was introduced to the Mediterranean by the Arabs some time before 1200AD. It is widely cultivated in warm temperate and subtropical areas and has many named varieties, some of which are listed below. A spiny small tree, to 7m. Leaves elongate-ovate, acute at the apex, pale green, flushed red when young; petiole narrowly winged. Flowers white above, tinged purple below, well scented. Fruit to 15cm long, 7cm wide, oval, yellow when ripe. Named varieties (*not shown*) of *C. limon* include 'Imperial', with large fruits; 'Ponderosa', dwarf habit, large fruit and flowers; 'Sungold', medium-sized, oblong with tricoloured skin and leaves; and 'Villa Franca', medium to large fruit on almost thornless bushes. Min. −5°C for short periods.

Citrus limon **'Menton'**   Another variety, photographed here in the botanic garden in Menton, S France.

Citrus limon **'Variegata'**   Variegated green and cream leaves; medium-sized fruits striped green and yellow, becoming completely yellow when fully ripe. Min. −5°C for short periods.

Citrus* × *paradisi Macfad. in Hook. Grapefruit   Origin unknown but thought to be a cross between the Shaddock (*C. maxima*) and the Orange (*C. sinensis*). It makes a large tree with a rounded crown and dense foliage. Leaves ovate, blunt at apex, broadly rounded at base, glabrous. Flowers large, solitary or in small clusters in flower axils, scented. Calyx 5-lobed; petals larger than sweet orange. Fruit globose, large, yellow or slightly orange, very juicy, with white seeds. Grown commercially in Israel, Turkey, hot areas of the USA and elsewhere. Cultivars (*not illustrated*) include 'Foster's', 'Red Blush', 'Ruby' (needs hot conditions) and 'Star Ruby' (all these are pink-fleshed); 'Golden Special', a large golden-yellow variety; 'Marsh', seedless with large light yellow fruit (common in western USA); 'Oro Blanco', large light yellow sweeter fruit. Min. −2°C for short periods.

Citrus limon 'Variegata'

Potted lemons in the Villa Gamberaia near Florence

Lemons at Palm Springs

Citrus × paradisi, the Grapefruit, in Los Angeles

Citrus aurantium var. *myrtifolia*

Citrus medica at Wisley

Citrus aurantium var. *myrtifolia* in the Jardin exotique du Val Rameh, Menton, S France

Citrus auriantium, the Seville Orange, in the garden of the Villa Gamberaia, Florence

Citrus medica L. **'Ethrog'** Citron   This species is also of unknown origin and is thought to be the first citrus introduced to the Mediterranean region, reputedly by the returning armies of Alexander the Great in 300BC. Today it is cultivated there (especially in Corsica) and in the East Indies; the large fruit (which can weigh up to 2.5 kg) is prized for making crystallized peel. Shrub or small tree to 5m. Leaves to 18cm long, elliptic-ovate, serrate. Flowers white, 5-petalled, flushed pink without, scented. Fruit large, to 30cm long and 15cm wide, ovoid or oblong, fragrant, lemon yellow when ripe; rind thick and rough. Min. −5°C for short periods.

Citrus aurantium L. (*Rutaceae*) Seville or Bitter Orange   A small tree, native of SE Asia and cultivated in Spain for its sour fruit, used in marmalade-making. In the USA it is grown as a specimen tree or used as a hedging plant,

while in Britain it is admired for its showy flowers. Tree to 10m. Leaves to 10cm, ovate, bluntly pointed at the apex. Flowers solitary or clustered, large, white, fragrant. Fruit subglobose, depressed at ends, 5–8 cm in diameter, orange-red with thick peel and numerous seeds. Min. −3°C for short periods.

C. aurantium var. ***myrtifolia*** **'Chinotto'**
As the name suggests, a variety with myrtle-like leaves.

C. limon (*See previous page for full text.*)

Citrus limon **'Lisbon Panachée'**
A medium-sized lemon, this striped form of 'Lisbon' is almost as hardy as 'Meye's' (*see p. 198*). Min. −3°C for short periods.

Citrus sinensis (L.) Osbeck Sweet Orange
A tree of unknown origin but probably native

of S China and Vietnam, introduced into the Mediterranean area by sailors in about 1500 AD. It is cultivated for its fruit throughout the warmer areas of the world and is important as a commercial crop; it is also prized for its ornamental qualities and for the delicious scent of the flowers. Tree to 13m. Leaves medium-sized, acute at apex, rounded at base. Flowers very fragrant, solitary or in small groups in leaf axils. Fruit oval or slightly flattened globose, orange when ripe. There are many varieties (*not illustrated*) including: 'Jaffa', an old variety and the largest of the sweet oranges; 'Moro Blood', an early ripening Italian variety with orange skin flushed with red and red flesh; 'Ruby Blood', also a blood orange; 'Shamouti', a sweet-smelling, almost seedless large fruit from Israel; 'Washington Navel', a juicy sweet variety commonly grown in California. Min. −5 °C for short periods.

C. sinensis **'Malta Blood'**   A delicious large thin-skinned fruit with deep red flesh.

C. sinensis **'Valencia'**   A rather acid late-fruiting variety; keeps well.

Citrus sinensis 'Malta Blood'

Citrus limon
'Lisbon Panachée'

Citrus medica 'Ethrog'

Citrus sinensis 'Valencia'

Seville Orange

Citrus reticulata
'Satsuma'

Citrus × tangelo 'Minneola'

x *Citrofortunella microcarpa*

Citrus limon 'Quatre Saisons'

x *Citrofortunella microcarpa*
'Tiger'

Citrus meyeri 'Meyer's Lemon'

Fortunella japonica 'Fucushii'

Specimens from Read's Nursery, 15th April, 2\5 life size

Citrus × limonia 'Rangpur'

Fortunella japonica at the Huntington garden, California

× **Citrofortunella microcarpa** (Bunge) D. O. Wijnands syn. *Citrus mitis* (Blanco) J. Ingram & H. E. Moore Calamondin Orange Probably a natural hybrid between a Kumquat and a sour orange, bearing small fruits suitable for cooking. A decorative small bush which is often sold commercially at Christmas time as a miniature potted orange. Min. −6 °C for short periods.

× **Citrofortunella microcarpa 'Tiger'** Another variety with leaves edged and striped with white.

Citrus × limonia Osbeck '**Rangpur**' The Rangpur Lime is not actually a true lime (*C. aurantifolia*) and does not really look like one either, having as it does orange fruits, but it is a very attractive small- to medium-sized bush, native of China and now naturalized in Australia. Leaves oblong to elliptic, dull green. Flowers flushed purple, fragrant. Min. − 5°C for short periods.

Citrus limon 'Quatre Saisons' Also known as the 'Eureka' Lemon, this variety bears good crops of fruit throughout the year, as its name suggests. Popular in the Mediterranean. Min. −5°C for short periods.

Citrus meyeri Tan. '**Meyer**' Meyer's Lemon (Possibly a hybrid between *C. limon* and *C. sinensis.*) This compact variety is very similar to *C. limon*, except that the fruit is smoother and rather more rounded. It was discovered in China in the early 1900s by Frank N. Meyer, an American who journeyed across Asia in search of economically useful plants for the US Dept of Agriculture. Min. −5°C for short periods. Grown commercially in Florida, Texas, South Africa and New Zealand, principally for local markets and for processing as the fruit bruises easily. It was grown by the Chinese as a houseplant and does well in pots; it is also the hardiest of all lemons and can survive outside in warm parts of Britain if grown against a warm wall. It flowers fairly freely throughout the year and produces

fragrant, medium-sized, juicy rounded fruits. Easily propagated from cuttings. 'Improved Meyer' (*not illustrated*) is a virus-free selection of Meyer's Lemon.

Citrus reticulata Blanco '**Satsuma**' In fact a Japanese tangerine, this compact bush with a weeping habit produces deliciously sweet fruit. This is the variety grown by the famous Rivers' Nursery of Hertfordshire, England, which stocked a great variety of fruit trees and successfully exported citrus trees to Florida and California during the mid-19th century. Min. −5°C for short periods.

Citrus × tangelo J. Ingram & H. E. Moore. Tangelo or Ugli Fruit. This variable hybrid of *C. paradisi* and *C. reticulata* arose in the USA earlier this century. It usually has bright orange, aromatic fruits. There are several cultivars including 'Orlando' and '**Minneola**' (*shown here*). Min. − 3°C for short periods.

Fortunella japonica (Thunb.) Swingle (*Rutaceae*) Kumquat, Round or Marumi Kumquat A dense tree with small ovoid fruit, native of S China. Bushy, spiny tree to 4m. Leaves lanceolate, small, light green. Flowers white, fragrant. Fruit ovoid, yellowish-orange, about 4cm long. Min. −5°C for short periods. The genus *Fortunella*, with about 5 species, is named after Robert Fortune (1812–80) plant collector for the Royal Horticultural Society and important as the introducer of tea to India.

Fortunella japonica 'Fucushii' A bushy weeping variety of Kumquat, which bears large oval fruits.

Fortunella margarita (Lour.) Swingle '**Nagami**' Sometimes known as the Oval Kumquat, this small tree grows up to 4m. Leaves lanceolate, obtuse at apex, to 3cm long, dark glossy green above, paler beneath. Few fragrant flowers. Fruit small, oblong, bright orange. Min. −6°C for short periods.

Fortunella margarita 'Nagami'

Orange pots concealed in clipped box

Correa baeurlinii in a cold house at Marwood Hill Gardens, Devon

Correa reflexa

Correa alba at Coleton Fishacre, S Devon in October

Correas are small evergreen shrubs, with tubular flowers in shades of green, pink or red, particularly valuable for flowering mainly in winter. There are around 11 species found in SE Australia and Tasmania and several varieties and garden hybrids are cultivated. All do best in well-drained, rather poor soil with some limestone added. They tolerate frost to around −5°C. Propagation by cuttings is generally easy; seed is often formed when two species are grown together, but is difficult to germinate. Leaching with water or a short burst of fire might help them to grow.

Correa alba Andr. (*Rutaceae*) A bushy shrub with white upright flowers, native of New South Wales, Victoria, Tasmania and South Australia, growing in sandy and rocky places near the sea, flowering in November–May (summer–autumn). Shrub to 2m tall and wide. Leaves green above, white beneath. Flowers to 1.3cm, usually upright, white or pink, split nearly to the base. *C. backhousiana*, from Victoria and Tasmania, flowers in winter-spring; it has pale green or creamy-brown flowers to 2.5cm long, hanging, sometimes with reflexed lobes. Both are good shrubs in seaside gardens, tolerant of wind and salt.

Correa baeurlinii F. Muell. A low spreading shrub with soft lanceolate leaves and green tubular flowers with a strange calyx like a chef's hat, native of New South Wales, growing in sclerophyll forest, near the SE coast, flowering in March–August, (winter-spring). Shrub to 2m tall and 3m wide. Leaves to 7cm long, 2cm wide, glandular. Flowers 2–3cm long. Will grow in deep shade and is less tolerant of exposure than other species. Prefers leafy soil.

Correa 'Dusky Bells' syn. 'Carmine Bells', 'Pink Bells' Likely to be a hybrid between *C. pulchella* and *C. reflexa*. A spreading shrub to 1m tall and 4m wide; leaves pale to medium green, to 3.5cm long, 2cm wide. Flowers pink, to 4cm long, mainly produced in March–September in Australia (autumn–spring). An old cultivar, known for at least 50 years.

Correa schlectendalii at Kew

Correa 'Marian's Marvel'

Correa 'Ivory Bells'

Correa pulchella

Correa lawrenciana at Coleton Fishacre

Correa 'Dusky Bells'

Correa 'Mannii'

Correa 'Ivory Bells' A hybrid between
C. alba and *C. backhousiana*. A spreading
shrub to 2m tall and 3m wide; leaves dark
green above, hairy and pale brownish below, to
3cm long, 2cm wide. Flowers white to creamy-
brown, about 2cm long, divided to half, with
recurved lobes, mainly produced in spring–
early summer (June–December in Australia).
Many plants sold in England under the names
C. alba and *C. backhousiana* appear to be this
hybrid.

Correa lawrenciana Hook. A shrub or
small tree with reddish, greenish or cream
hanging flowers, native of Queensland, New
South Wales, Victoria and Tasmania, flowering
in March–November (autumn–winter). Tree
to 9m tall and 5m wide. Leaves ovate to
cordate, 2–8cm long, 1–4cm wide. Flowers to
3cm long, variable in colour or bicoloured
lime yellow and red. Calyx large, cup-shaped,
sometimes lobed. The red-flowered form
shown here with narrow elliptic leaves is
similar to var. **rosea** Paul G. Wilson, which
originates in the Snowy Mountains and should
be one of the largest and hardiest species.
Min. −5°C.

Correa 'Mannii' syn. 'Harrisii' Likely to be
a hybrid between *C. pulchella* and *C. reflexa*. A
spreading shrub to 2.5m tall and 3m wide with
brittle branches. Leaves shining green above,
paler below, to 3.5cm long and 2cm wide.
Flowers red outside, pink inside, about 4cm
long, mainly produced in autumn–spring
(March–September in Australia). An old
cultivar, known since about 1840, but still one
of the showiest.

Correa 'Marian's Marvel' Likely to be a
hybrid between *C. backhousiana* and *C. reflexa*.
An upright shrub to 2m tall and 1.5m wide;
leaves cordate, dark green above, paler beneath
with rusty stellate hairs beneath, especially on
the edge and midrib, to 2.5cm long and wide.
Flowers green and pale pink, tubular, tips
reflexed, 2.5–3cm long, with exserted stamens,
produced from autumn–spring. 'Poorinda
Mary' has tubular flowers, pink with yellowish-

green tips, to 3.5cm long, lobes not reflexed. It
is sometimes sold in England under the name
Correa speciosa, which is a synonym of *C.
reflexa*.

Correa pulchella Mackay ex Sweet A low
spreading or prostrate shrub with small leaves
and horizontal or hanging tubular orange, red
or pink flowers, native of South Australia,
flowering in April–September (winter). Shrub
to 1.5m tall and 3m across. Leaves narrowly
ovate, smooth, green, to 3.5cm long and 1cm
wide. Flowers 1.5–2.5cm long. Prostrate forms
may be used as ground-cover. Tolerant of
drought and limestone soils.

Correa reflexa (Labill.) Vent. syn. *C. speciosa*
A very variable prostrate to upright shrub with
dark green leaves and hanging tubular green to
red or bicoloured flowers, usually with green
tips, native from Queensland to Victoria,
Tasmania and Western Australia, growing in
heathy scrub and open forest, flowering in
March–September. Shrub to 3m tall and wide.

Leaves lanceolate to ovate, sometimes cordate,
smooth to hairy above, pale beneath, to 5cm
long and 3cm wide. Calyx not lobed. Flowers
2–4cm long, tips green, reflexed. Forms with
small rounded leaves and short squat bells are
commonest near the coast; they belong to var.
nummularifolia (Hook. fil.) P. G. Wilson. All
are easily grown in well-drained soils and
drought-tolerant when established.

Correa schlectendalii Behr syn. *C. turnbullii*
Ashby An upright shrub with thin elliptic
leaves and hanging tubular red and green
flowers with exserted stamens, native of South
Australia, growing in mallee sand scrub,
flowering in November–April (usually late
summer and autumn in cultivation). Shrub to
2.5m tall and 2m wide. Leaves broadly elliptic,
dull green above, paler beneath with scattered
stellate hairs, to 4.5cm long and 1.5cm wide.
Flowers pink to red with green lobes or
whitish, to 2.5cm long. An easy species to
grow, tolerant of full sun, drought and high
pH. Can be clipped or pruned to shape.

Phebalium nudum

x *Citroncirus*, the Citrumelo

Choisya 'Aztec Pearl'

Adenandra uniflora near the Dido road

Adenandra uniflora (L.) Willd. (*Rutaceae*)
A small heath-like shrub with white flowers,
striped red in the throat, native of South Africa
in the SW Cape mainly around Cape Town,
growing on rocky slopes, flowering in July–
November (spring). Stems sprawling, to 40cm.
Leaves ovate, appressed to the stem with
conspicuous glands beneath. Flowers white or
pink, solitary or few at the ends of the
branches, about 2cm across. For sandy peaty
soil. Min. −3°C, perhaps.

× Citroncirus (*Rutaceae*) Citrumelo   This is
the hybrid between the grapefruit (*Citrus ×
paradisi*) and *Ponciris trifoliata*. It forms a large
twiggy bush with rather small leaves and
upright scented flowers with spoon-shaped
petals. It is shown here growing in the botanic
garden at Menton, but as far as I know has not
been tried outdoors in frosty climates. The
cross between *Ponciris* and the orange, the
Citrange, × *Citronocirus webberi* is said to
tolerate around −10°C and is hardy in
southern England, so the Citrumelo should be
almost as hardy, but will require more summer
heat to grow well. 'Zehnder' is a clone of
similar parentage.

Calodendron capense (L. fil.) Thunb. Cape
Chestnut (*Rutaceae*)   A large spreading tree
with smooth, pale brown bark and large
clusters of pale pink flowers, native of South
Africa from the coast in the SE Cape near
George, north to Natal, growing in sheltered
patches of forest, flowering in summer,
between September–February in the wild. A
rounded evergreen or briefly deciduous tree to
20m, with opposite, obovate leaves, about
10cm long. The narrow petals are about 6cm
long, marked with red at the base and
accompanied by 5 white purple-spotted
staminodes. Requires shelter and moist soil.
Does well in coastal California. May be
grown from cuttings of half-ripened shoots.
Min. −5°C.

Coleonema album (Thunb.) Bartling &
Wendl. (*Rutaceae*)   A fragrant, soft-stemmed
heath-like shrub with small white flowers,
native of South Africa in the SW Cape,
growing on rocky hillsides, flowering in May–
November. Stems upright to 2m; leaves linear;
flowers about 3mm across. For any open soil.
Min. −3°C. *Coleonema pulchrum* Hook., from
mountain slopes near Swellendam, is also
grown in Europe and California for its fragrant
foliage and small pinkish flowers. It is possibly
hardier, to −5°C.

Crowea exalata F. Muell. (*Rutaceae*)   A
shrub with leaves that smell of aniseed when
crushed, native of Australia in New South
Wales and Victoria, growing in dry forests,
flowering mainly in October–June. Stems to
2m; leaves 1.5–5cm long, linear-lanceolate,
flat. Flowers about 2cm across, usually pink,
rarely white. For well-drained but moist sandy,
peaty soil; easily grown and valuable for its
long flowering season. Several named forms
are in commerce in Australia. Min. −5°C.
Many species of the genus *Boronia* are rather
similar in habit but have four petals and often
pinnate leaves. *B. megastigma* Nees, the Brown
Boronia, is grown for its scented flowers in
various shades of maroon or yellow-brown.

Choisya dumosa (Torr.) A. Gray (*Rutaceae*)
A dense, much-branched shrub with leaves
divided into 7–13 leaflets and small white
flowers, native of Arizona (var. *arizonica* L.
Benson), Texas, New Mexico and NW
Mexico, growing in semi-deserts in rocky
places on limestone with cacti, at 1000–
1500m, flowering in April–July. Shrub to 2m
tall; leaves with linear leaflets to 2.5cm long,
revolute on the margins. Flowers in loose
clusters, about 1.5cm across. For dry heavy
soil. Min. −5°C.
'Aztec Pearl' raised by Peter Moore of
Hillier's Nurseries in 1989 is a hybrid between
var. *arizonica* and *C. ternata*.

Murraya paniculata (L.) Jack. syn. *M. exotica*
L. (*Rutaceae*) Orange Jessamine   A dark
evergreen shrub with white jasmine-scented
flowers and clusters of orange to red fruit,
native of S China and India south to N
Australia, flowering at intervals through the
year. Shrub or small tree to 7.5m. Leaves
pinnate with 3–7 obovate leaflets. Flowers
citrus-like, 2–4cm across with recurved petals.
Fruit oblong, about 12mm long. For good
well-drained soil in partial shade; liable to
attack by whitefly under glass, but good as a
hedge in S California and Australia. Min.
−1°C. Herklots records that the wonderful
scent of the flowers is carried a great distance
through the air; according to its Chinese
name, for nine *leis* (about 5km).

Phebalium nudum Hook. (*Rutaceae*)
A spreading aromatic evergreen shrub with
scented white flowers, native of New Zealand
on North Island, growing on the margins of
forests, flowering in October–December.
Shrub to 3m tall. Leaves to 4.5cm long,
oblong-lanceolate, brownish-green. Flowers
8–10mm across. For a cool position in good
soil. Min. −3°C. This is the only species of
Phebalium found in New Zealand but there are
around 45 species in Australia.

Choisya dumosa from Mexico

Crowea exalata

Choisya dumosa with Yuccas and pines near San Rafael, NE Mexico

Calodendron capense in California

Murraya paniculata in California

Coleonema album the Dido road

Ilex purpurea on Victoria Peak, Hong Kong in May

Euonymus grandiflorus in the wild garden at Wisley

Ilex pubescens on Victoria Peak, Hong Kong in May

Euonymus grandiflorus

Rhus ovata in California

Rhus integrifolia in California

Ilex latifolia Thunb. (*Aquifoliaceae*)
An evergreen tree with spineless or few-spined leaves, native of S Japan and SE China, growing in forests and commonly planted near temples, flowering in May. Tree to 20m tall, usually less in gardens. Leaves 12–20cm long and 4–8cm wide, oblong, with very short spiny teeth. Flowers yellow-green in masses in the leaf axils. Berries red, about 8mm across. Min. −5°C. This is one of the parents of the hardier, large-leaved *Ilex × koehneana* 'Chestnut Leaf'.

Ilex perado Ait. subsp. **perado** A large shrub or small tree with spineless or few-spined leaves, native of Madeira, growing in forests, hedges and scrub, flowering in May, with the berries often lasting until the following spring. Leaves 6–10cm long, obovate to rounded, the few spines usually near the apex. Min. −5°C. This species may be one of the parents of the hardy very popular large-

Ilex perado subsp. *perado* in Madeira

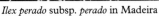

Ilex latifolia on Victoria Peak, Hong Kong in May

leaved *Ilex* × *altaclerensis*, to which belongs the commonly planted female variegated holly 'Golden King'.

Ilex pubescens Hook. & Arn.   An evergreen shrub with elliptic or obovate elliptic leaves and small bright red berries, native of S China including Hong Kong and Taiwan, growing in openings in the forest, flowering in May, fruiting in December. Shrub to 3.5m tall; leaves 2–5cm long and 1–2.5cm wide, untoothed or serrate towards the apex. The flowers are purplish-pink, with 6–8 petals. Berries 4mm across on rather short stalks. Min. −3°C.

Ilex purpurea Hassk. syn. *I. chinensis* Sims, *I. oldhamii* Miq.   An evergreen or briefly deciduous tree with acuminate, oblong-elliptic leaves and bright red berries, native of S Japan from C Honshu southwards and S China including Hong Kong and Taiwan, growing in

openings in the forest, flowering in May–June, fruiting in September–December. Tree to 12m tall; leaves 7–12cm long and 2.5–5cm wide, crenate, thin textured, not spiny. Flowers purplish or reddish, with 4–5 petals. Berries 6–8mm across on long stalks. Min. −3°C. We saw this handsome species in fruit on Yakusima but the seedlings proved to be very tender.

Euonymus grandiflorus Wall. ex Roxb. (*Celastraceae*)   A large evergreen shrub or tree with large pale green flowers, native of the Himalayas from Uttar Pradesh and Nepal to Yunnan, growing at 1500–1800m, flowering in May–June. Tree to 5m tall; leaves obovate to elliptic or linear-lanceolate in f. *salicifolius* Stapf & F. Ballard. Flowers about 2.5cm across. Fruits 4-sided, 15mm across, pink with a bright red aril. Min. −5°C, or less if sheltered.

Rhus integrifolia (Nutt.) Benth. & Hook. (*Anacardiaceae*) Lemonade Berry   A rounded aromatic evergreen shrub with leathery, sometimes spiny and holly-like leaves, native of California and Baja California, mainly along the coast, from Santa Barbara Co. southwards, growing in low scrub and chaparral at up to 800m, flowering in February–May. Shrub to 3m tall. Leaves 2.5–5cm long and 2–3cm wide, elliptic-oblong. Flowers white to pink. Berries pubescent, red, about 10mm across. Min. −5°C.

Rhus ovata Wats. Sugar Bush   An aromatic evergreen shrub with leathery ovate leaves, curving upwards from the midrib, native of California and Baja California, usually inland, from Santa Barbara Co. southwards and east to Arizona, growing in oak woodland and chaparral at up to 800m, flowering in January–May. Shrub to 4m. Leaves 4–8cm long, acute. Flowers pink. Berries glandular, red, about 7–8mm across. Min. −5°C.

Greyia radlkoferi at Kirstenbosch in October

Melianthus major flowering in California in March

Dodonea angustifolia L. fil. syn. *D. viscosa* Jacq. (*Sapindaceae*)   A very variable evergreen shrub with narrow leaves and yellowish or pinkish papery winged fruits. Found widely in subtropical and tropical areas of America, South Africa, Asia and Australia, usually on coasts though often in dry sandy areas inland (Arizona, for example), flowering in spring. Usually a spreading shrub to 3m tall, but up to 6m in some forms; leaves rather sticky, linear to lanceolate, elliptic or triangular, smooth. Flowers small and green, male and female usually on separate plants. Fruits conspicuous, with 2–3 wings, about 2.8cm across. Good in sandy soil and tolerant of wind and drought. Min. −5°C . 'Purpurea', with purple leaves is commonly cultivated and needs to be grown in sun to keep its colour. About 68 species are known, 59 of which are endemic to Australia.

Greyia radlkoferi Syzsyzl. (*Greyiaceae*) A stiff shrub or small tree with leaves greyish when young and heads of scarlet flowers, native of South Africa in N Natal, E Traansvaal, Zululand and Swaziland, growing in the mist belt on the mountains, flowering in September–December, often before the leaves. Tree 3–4.6m tall; leaves to 13cm long, densely felted beneath; petals 2.5cm long, narrowed at the base. Min. −5°C.

Greyia sutherlandii Hook. & Harv. A gnarled shrub or small tree with shining green rounded, toothed leaves and heads of scarlet flowers, native of South Africa in the

Greyia radlkoferi

Drakensberg south to the Loteni Valley, at up to 2000m, growing on cliff edges and in rocky grassland, flowering in November–December. Tree to 4m tall; leaves to 7cm across. Flower heads to 10cm across. Flowers filled with copious nectar. An exciting small specimen tree for well-drained soil, dry in winter. This has grown for many years outside at Tresco on the Scilly Isles. Min. −5°C.
A third species, *G. flanaganii* H. Bolus, from grassy rocky slopes in E Cape Province, has few pendulous flowers.

Koelreuteria bipinnata Franch. syn. *K. integrifolia* Merrill (*Sapindaceae*)   A large tree with bipinnate leaves, small yellow flowers in large branched inflorescences and inflated

fruits, native of SW China in Yunnan, flowering from July–September. Tree to 10m tall. Leaves to 50cm, with 7–12 pinnae, the secondary pinnae 5–7cm long, leathery, finely toothed or entire. Flowers with a red spot at the base of the petal. A striking tree with huge clusters of reddish fruit in autumn. Min. −5°C. This tree thrives along the Mediterranean, but does not survive outside in Britain. It needs hot summers to do well as does the hardier *K. paniculata* Laxm.

Melianthus major L. (*Melianthaceae*)   A soft sappy shrub with bold, jagged blue-grey leaves and upright spikes of chocolate-brown flowers, native of South Africa from the NW to the SE Cape, growing in damp sandy areas, flowering in August–September (late spring). Stems to 1.5m; leaves to 40cm long, pinnate. Flowers about 6cm; fruits inflated. The ample nectar is sought by sunbirds in Africa and attracts hummingbirds in America. The plant is adapted to fire and sprouts up vigorously after being burnt; hence it survives in frosty climates if planted deep, though flowering only after mild winters. Min. −5°C.

Melianthus comosus Vahl.   A leggy, upright shrub with green leaves and red or purple flowers, native of South Africa in the E Cape and Karroo eastwards, growing by rivers, at 1000–2000m, flowering in August–October. Stems to 2m. Leaves 10–15cm long, with a winged rhachis. Flowers 2–3cm long. Fruits inflated. Min. −5°C.

Koelreuteria bipinnata flowering and fruiting in the Hanbury Botanic garden at La Mortola in September

Dodonea angustifolia

Dodonea angustifolia fruit

Koelreuteria bipinnata flowers

Melianthus comosus

Greyia sutherlandii; an old tree in the Abbey Gardens, Tresco

207

Ceanothus spinosus March in the San Jacinto Mountains, California

Ceanothus arboreus wild form, in Eccleston Square

Ceanothus 'Concha'

Ceanothus maritimus

Ceanothus arboreus

Ceanothus arboreus Greene (*Rhamnaceae*) A large evergreen shrub or small tree with broadly ovate leaves and masses of pale blue flowers, native of California on Santa Cruz, Santa Rosa and Santa Catalina islands, growing in chaparral scrub, flowering in February–May. Tree to 7m tall; twigs not spiny, terete; leaves 3–8cm long with 3 veins from the base, tomentose beneath. Flower clusters 5–12cm long. A fine early-flowering species needing shelter from freezing wind. Min. −5°C. 'Trewithen Blue', the clone usually grown in Europe, is a little hardier.

Ceanothus 'Concha' One of the best and most tolerant varieties for different conditions, both in Europe and California, with deep blue flowers in March–May. Leaves narrowly oval. A spreading bush to 3m across. Tolerant of clay soils and water in summer. Min. −10°C.

Ceanothus 'Everett's Choice' A mound-forming shrub with narrowly lanceolate leaves and short-stalked rounded clusters of flowers. Min. −5°C.

Ceanothus griseus (Trel.) McMinn. A large shrub with broadly ovate leaves, greyish tomentose beneath and short dense heads of violet-blue flowers, native of California in Sonoma and Mendocino Cos. and from Santa Barbara to Monterey Cos., growing in scrub and open pine forest, flowering in March–May. Shrub to 3m tall; leaves to 5cm long. Var. *horizontalis* McMinn. is a creeping form from Yankee Point in Monterey Co. 'Yankee Point' is a fast-growing, deep blue flowered clone.
'**Kurt Zadnik**' (*shown here*) is a particularly dark blue bushy clone from Horseshoe Cove in Sonoma Co. Min. −5°C.

Ceanothus maritimus Hoov. A mat-forming shrub with small hard leaves and pale to deep blue flowers, native of California in San Luis Obispo Co., growing on coastal bluffs, flowering in January–March. Stems to 1.5m, prostrate. Leaves glossy above, whitish beneath, truncate, emarginate or obcordate, with 1–3 teeth on each side, 8–20mm long. Flowers small, in rounded clusters. Good for ground-cover in maritime conditions. Min. −5°C.

Ceanothus papillosus Torr. & Gray   A tall dense shrub with finely hairy shoots, glandular toothed leaves and deep blue flowers, native of California from San Mateo to San Luis Obispo Co., growing in Redwood forests and chaparral in the Coast Ranges, below 1000m, flowering in April–May. Stems 1–5m. Leaves oblong-elliptical, rounded at apex, 1-veined, glandular-hairy above with fine glandular teeth, 1.5–5cm long and 1–2cm wide. Flowers small, in stalked elongated clusters to 5cm long. For a sheltered position, cool in summer. Min. −5°C. Var. *roweanus* McMinn., from dryer hills south to Orange Co., has narrow leaves to 1cm wide, with a blunt apex.

Ceanothus 'Sky Blue'   A large spreading shrub with large branching clusters of light blue flowers and broadly lanceolate leaves, a hybrid between *C. arboreus* and *C. griseus*. One of the taller and less hardy hybrids, grown in the collection in Santa Barbara Botanic Garden Min. −5°C. 'Sierra Blue' is similar but makes a smaller and more spreading shrub.

Ceanothus spinosus Nutt. in Torr. & Gray A tall open, stiff shrub becoming tree-like, with smooth green bark, elliptic to oblong leaves and pale blue to almost white flowers, native of California from San Luis Obispo Co. to Baja California, growing on dry rocky hills below 1000m, flowering in February–May. Stems 2–6m. Leaves elliptic to oblong, rounded to emarginate at apex, usually without teeth, 1.5–3 cm long. Flowers small, in branched clusters to 15cm long. This species should tolerate heat and drought well and is lovely in flower, though less attractive in leaf than many others. Min. −10°C.

Ceanothus 'Wheeler Canyon'   A dense spreading shrub to 1.5m with long-stalked narrow flower clusters and narrowly lanceolate, pinnately-veined leaves. Flowers a good blue from pinkish buds, named after Wheeler Canyon, Santa Barbara. Min. −5°C.

Phylicia pubescens Ait. (*Rhamnaceae*) A low shrub with feathery, yellow bracts and small white flowers, native of South Africa in the SW Cape, growing in fynbos, flowering in May–August (winter). Stems to 1.5m; leaves linear. There are around 150 species of *Phylica*, of which 132 are found in the Cape area. Most have feathery and fluffy heads of whitish flowers.

Colletia armata Miers **'Rosea'** (*Rhamnaceae*)   A very spiny upright shrub with green stems, very small leaves and scented pink flowers, native of Chile in Valdivia and Llanquihue, flowering in autumn. Shrub to 3m; leaves deciduous, to 12mm long, usually toothed. Spines to 4cm long. Flowers waxy, white or pinkish especially in bud in 'Rosea'. Easily grown. Min. −5°C. *Colletia cruciata* Gillies & Hook. from Uruguay, with winged stems, flattened spines and white flowers in autumn is sometimes cultivated. *C. infausta* N. E. Br. is more like *C. armata*, but flowers in spring.

Ceanothus griseus 'Kurt Zadnik'

Ceanothus 'Wheeler Canyon'

Ceanothus papillosus

Ceanothus 'Sky Blue' at Santa Barbara

Phylicia pubescens

Colletia armata 'Rosea' at Marwood Hill

'Everett's Choice' in Santa Barbara BG

Ficus benjamina 'Starlight'

Ficus benjamina var nuda

Ficus barteri

Ficus benjamina 'Pandora'

Ficus microcarpa

Ficus elastica 'Black Prince'

Ficus pumila 'Bellus'

Ficus elastica 'Robusta'

Specimens from the conservatory at Wisley, 1/3 life size

Ficus lyrata in Mexico

Ficus auriculata Lour. syn. *F. roxburghii*
Wall. ex Miq. (*Moraceae*) A briefly deciduous
tree with handsome large leaves and reddish
edible fruit on thick branches, native of the
foothills of the Himalayas from Pakistan to
Thailand and SW China, growing in forests at
up to 1600m and commonly planted in
villages; the fruit ripens in April–June. Tree to
18m tall and wide; leaves bright reddish-brown
when young, broadly ovate, cordate, to 30cm
long. Fruit clustered, to 5cm long and 7.5cm
across. Oleg Polunin records that the leaves are
cut for fodder in Nepal. Min. −5°C, perhaps
less for short periods.

Ficus barteri Sprague syn. *F. longifolia* hort.
A large shrub or small tree starting as an
epiphytic strangler, native of tropical Africa.
An upright evergreen shrub when pot-grown.
Leaves about 10–30cm long and 1.5–7cm
wide, linear with a long acuminate tip and
pinnate veins. There is also a variegated
cultivar.

Ficus benghalensis L. Banyan tree A very
large tree, eventually covering several acres
with its aerial roots which form extra trunks,
and leathery broadly ovate leaves, native of
India and Ceylon, but widely planted in the
tropics and in the foothills of the Himalayas to
1400m, the barely edible scarlet fruit ripening
in autumn–spring. Tree to about 30m tall.
Leaves to 25cm long with a blunt or short tip.
Fruit small, to 2cm across. This tree is
commonly planted for shade; the leaves are
edible and are used as plates. *Ficus religiosa*
L. the Pipal tree, is recognized by its leaves
which have a long pointed tip. It is a strangler,
smothering other trees in the forest and
covering old buildings. Both are damaged by
any frost but will recover from −3°C for short
periods, such as might be had in Palm Springs,
California.

Ficus benjamina L. var **nuda** (Miq.) Barrett
syn. var. *comosa* (Roxb.) Kurz. Weeping
Banyan A large evergreen tree with simple
leathery narrowly ovate leaves, native of the
Phillipines (var. *benjamina* is native of India
and Malaysia south to Queensland), growing
in rocky places by streams in rainforest and on
exposed rocks. Tree to 30m tall, but usually
about 15m, weeping when young; leaves
5–12cm long and 2–4cm wide. Var. *nuda*, with
narrower leaves crowded towards the ends of
zigzag branches, is commonly planted in S
Florida. Not suitable for planting near
buildings because of its invasive root system.
Min. −5°C, perhaps less for short periods.
'Pandora' is a small-leaved form, grown as a
houseplant. **'Starlight'** has leaves with a
variable white margin.

Ficus carica L. **'White Marseilles'**
The edible fig is a spreading deciduous tree to
10m, with rough lobed leaves, native of Turkey
and the Middle East where it has been
cultivated for over 5000 years. Wild forms have
dry inedible fruit and often more deeply lobed
leaves. Subsp. *rupestris* (Hausskn.) Browicz,
from SE Turkey, Iraq and Iran has smaller
unlobed leaves. There are numerous named
varieties cultivated for their fruit which varies
in colour from pale green ('White Marseilles')
to red ('Rouge de Bordeaux'), brownish
purple ('Brown Turkey') and black ('Black
Ischia'), and in shape from almost round to
long pear-shaped. Figs grow well in pots in a
cold greenhouse and in cool climates such as
England will produce two crops of fruit, in
June or July and in August–November. They
need good heavy but well-drained soil and
careful watering to produce good crops under
glass. Pinch back the new shoots when they
have about 6 leaves to encourage production of
the second crop of fruit. Outside the fig tree
will survive about −10°C. In colder climates it
needs wall protection against winter cold and
to hasten ripening in summer.

Ficus elastica Roxb. ex Hornem. India
Rubber Plant A giant strangling tree with
both aerial and buttress roots and smooth
ovate evergreen leaves, native from NE India
to SW China, the N Malay peninsula and to
Java and Sumatra, growing in forests. Tree to
60m tall, finally with several secondary trunks,
but more familiar as a pot plant. Leaves to
30cm long and 15cm wide; figs born in pairs,
yellow when ripe, to 1.1cm long. Easily grown
as a small plant indoors, kept rather dry, and
exceptionally tolerant of poor light. Min.
−3°C overnight, but will often recover from
below ground if cut down by frost.
'Robusta' is a large-leaved clone, similar to

Ficus lyrata in a courtyard in Guadeljara, Mexico

Ficus auriculata at Serra de la Madonne, Menton

Ficus carica 'White Marseilles'

Ficus pumila climbing on an ancient pot

Ficus pumila juvenile leaves

'Decora Tricolor' with leaves variegated pink, cream and pale green.
'Black Prince' is a fine dark-leaved cultivar.

Ficus lyrata Warb.   A small evergreen tree with very fine dark green leathery leaves and small green figs, native of W and C Africa, growing in forests. Tree to 12m tall. Leaves to 45cm long and 30cm wide, obovate, cordate, with strong veins. Figs globose, to 3cm. Min. 0°C. This will grow outdoors in only the warmest parts of California and is one of the most striking small trees for a large courtyard.

Ficus microcarpa L. fil., syn. *F. retusa* auct. non L., *F. nitida* auct. Indian Laurel   A small dense evergreen tree with elliptic to obovate

leaves, pale pink or green when young and very small pink or red fruit, native of the Yakushima and Tanegashima, the Ryuku islands and from S China to Queensland and the W Pacific, growing in coastal forest and along tidal rivers. Tree to 18m tall, usually less, about 10m, with a pale grey trunk. Leaves 4–10cm long and 2–7cm wide. Two forms of this tree are commonly cultivated as street trees: that usually called 'Retusa' has a slightly weeping habit and makes a good specimen; the variety 'Nitida' has an upright bushy habit and narrower leaves, is good as a large hedge and can be clipped or pruned to shape. In California the leaves are often damaged by thrips, but a variety 'Green Gem' is said to be resistant. Min. −5°C.

Ficus pumila Thunb. syn. *F. repens* auct. non Willd.   An evergreen ivy-like climber with very small, appressed leaves when in the young climbing state and, like ivy, larger spreading leaves in the mature, arborescent state, with large blue figs, native of Japan from C Honshu southwards and to China and Vietnam, growing on trees and rocks. Plant climbing to 12m tall and powerful enough to cover a whole building. Juvenile leaves ovate-cordate, thin, about 2cm long; mature leaves oblong, leathery, 5–10cm long. One of the hardiest figs, to −5°C, it will sprout again if cut to the ground; often used to cover unsightly walls and best planted in the shade in sunny areas. 'Sonny' and **'Bellus'** (*shown here*) are varieties with a white edge.

Ficus benghalensis in the Fairchild Botanic Garden, Florida *(For text see previous page)*

Ficus macrophylla an old tree in the Bermuda Botanical Garden

Ficus aspera 'Parcellii' in California

Debregeasia salicifolia (D. Don) Rendle (*Urticaceae*) An evergreen shrub with narrow leaves, white beneath and clusters of yellow or orange fruit, native of Ethiopia and W Asia to the W Himalayas, fruiting in autumn. Stems to 5m; leaves narrowly lanceolate to 15cm long. Male and female flowers on separate plants. Min. −5°C. The very similar *D. longifolia* (Burm. fil.) Wedd., is found from the E Himalayas to China and SE Asia. It has broader leaves and flowers in short-stalked clusters.

Ficus aspera Forst. fil. **'Parcellii'** (*Moraceae*) Usually grown as a shrub, but eventually a large tree with slightly rough deciduous or evergreen leaves, variegated and speckled white, pale and dark green with variegated

Tetrastigma voinierianum in Menton

Debregeasia salicifolia in fruit

Myoporum parvifolium

Macropiper excelsum on Tresco

Pilea 'Moon Valley' at Wisley

Pilea peperomioides in Yunnan

fruits, native of Vanuatu. Branches hairy; leaves asymmetric, ovate, hairy beneath, to 32cm long. Fruit ripening red, pink or purple, 2.5cm across. For any good soil and tolerant of shade. Min. 0°C.

Ficus macrophylla Desf. Moreton Bay Fig
A large spreading evergreen tree with blunt oblong to ovate leaves, native of W Australia in Queensland and NSW, growing in rainforest, but commonly planted in gardens. Tree to 35m tall and 25m wide, without aerial roots. Leaves 15–25cm long and 8–15cm wide. Figs purple with white dots when ripe. Needs plenty of water. Good for planting near the sea. Min. −3°C.

Macropiper excelsum (Forst. fil.) Miq. (*Piperaceae*)   An evergreen shrub or small tree with shiny, broadly heart-shaped leaves and spikes of yellow to orange fruits, native of New Zealand on North and N South Island, growing in lowland forest, fruiting throughout the year. Eventually to 6m tall, though usually about 2m as a shrub. Leaves 5–10cm long, 6–12cm wide with 5–7 nerves. Fruits 2–3mm across, dense on the upright spikes 2–8cm long. An attractive shade-tolerant shrub. Min. −3°C, perhaps less. Var. *majus* (Cheesem.) Allan, from the islands off the NE coast of North Island, has larger leaves and flower spikes about 15cm long. It is less hardy.

Myoporum parvifolium R. Br. (*Myoporaceae*)   A spreading ground-covering shrub with small shiny leaves and white flowers, native of Australia in Victoria, South Australia and West Australia, flowering in spring–summer. Plant to 2m across. Leaves linear, to 2.5cm long and 1cm wide, often widest towards apex. Flowers scented, 12mm across. Requires good drainage and is best on a bank. Min. −3°C. *Myoporum laetum* is an evergreen shrub or small tree with fleshy, lanceolate to obovate leaves, dotted with oil glands, about 8cm long and small white purple-spotted flowers. It is native of New Zealand and commonly planted near the sea, in cool areas like N California and Cornwall.

Pilea 'Moon Valley' (*Urticaceae*)
A perennial, like a bullate-leaved Coleus, with bright green and brown leaves, native of Costa Rica at 1500m, collected by Maurice Mason. Stems square, to 12cm. Leaves obovate to ovate, about 6cm long. Now considered a form of *P. involucrata* (Sims) Urban. Min. 0°C.

Pilea peperomioides Diels   A fleshy perennial with a short upright stem, broadly ovate, peltate leaves and tiny green flowers, native of SW China in Yunnan, growing on shady limestone rocks, at 2100–2700m, flowering in April–May. Leaves 4–9cm long and wide, on stalks 12cm long. Male and female flowers on separate inflorescences. Min. 0°C. The unusual history of this plant is described in the *Kew Magazine*. It has been grown in Europe for many years but its identity and origin were for a long time unknown, though it acheived some popularity as a houseplant. It was assumed to be a species of *Peperomia* which it resembles in leaf, and was not identified as a *Pilea* until a flowering specimen was sent by a lady from Northolt to the herbarium at Kew in 1978 and was recognized as a species collected by George Forrest in 1906. It was subsequently found to have been introduced in Europe by a Norwegian missionary in 1946. Seen here in the rock garden in Xiaguan near Dali in 1989.

Tetrastigma voinierianum (Pierre ex Nichols. & Mottet) Gangep. (*Vitaceae*)
A rampant vine with reddish-brown velvety hairy shoots and 3–5-parted leaves, native of Laos. Stems to 10m or more. Leaves evergreen, dark glossy green, the leaflets 10–20cm long, toothed. Related to *Vitis* and *Cissus*. For any good very well-drained soil and tolerant of deep shade. Min. −3°C. Other species of *Tetrastigma* are found from the Himalayas and W China to N Australia. The roots of some are the host of *Rafflesia arnoldii*, the largest known flower.

Carpobrotus acinaciformis wild at the Cape of Good Hope

MESEMBRYANTHEMUMS

The family *Mesembryanthemaceae* is concentrated in southern Africa, especially in the Cape where there are 61 genera and around 660 species. Many are 'stone plants', such as *Lithops* which are specialized succulents from dry desert areas and are thus outside the scope of this book, but others grow in cooler, damper areas such as on the Cape Peninsula and do well in cold greenhouses and outside in areas such as the Mediterranean, coastal California and the Canary Islands. Several are even naturalized on the Scilly Isles and the southern coasts of England, growing on dunes or out of old walls and rocks by the sea.

Carpobrotus acinaciformis (L.) Bolus
A trailing mat-forming succulent with large pinkish-purple flowers, native of South Africa in the Cape, from the Peninsula to Natal and widely naturalized in other parts of the world, growing in sandy and rocky places near the sea, flowering in August–October (spring–early summer). Stems to 1.5m; leaves triangular in section, broadest at or above the middle, to 9cm long and 1.5–2cm wide, glaucous. Flowers about 12cm across. Min. −3°C.

Carpobrotus edulis (L.) Bolus Hottentot fig
A trailing mat-forming succulent with large pale yellow flowers becoming pinkish as they fade, native of South Africa in the Cape and widely naturalized in other parts of the world such as California, growing in sandy and rocky places near the sea, flowering in August–October (spring–early summer). Stems to 1m; leaves triangular in section, broadest at the base, to 12cm long and 8–17mm wide, not glaucous. Flowers about 8.5cm across. Min. −3°C.

Lampranthus aureus (L.) N. E. Br.
A small spreading shrub with orange flowers, native of South Africa in the western Cape, flowering in August–November (spring). Stems to 40cm; leaves with a greyish bloom, about 5cm long. Flowers about 6cm across, on stalks about 6cm long. For sandy well-drained soil, dry in summer. Min. −3°C.

Lampranthus glaucus (L.) N. E. Br.
A small spreading shrub with yellow, to white or orange flowers, native of South Africa in the Cape from the Gifberg to Bredasdorp, flowering in August–November (spring). Stems to 20cm; leaves with a greyish bloom, 1.5–3cm long; flowers 4–5cm across. For sandy well-drained soil, dry in summer. Min. −3°C.

Lampranthus haworthii (G. Don) N. E. Br.
An upright or spreading shrub with thin greyish leaves and magenta to pale silvery purple flowers, native of South Africa in the Cape from Clanwilliam to Worcester and the Little Karroo, growing on dry hills and in semi-desert scrub, flowering in August–October (spring). Stems to 1.2m; leaves with greyish-green bloom, 2.5–4cm long; flowers about 7cm across. For sandy well-drained soil, dry in summer. Min. −5°C.

Lampranthus multiradiatus (Jacq.) N. E. Br. A small spreading shrub with pink to magenta flowers, native of South Africa in the Cape from the Cape Peninsula to Worcester and Namaqualand, flowering in August–November (spring). Stems to 25cm; leaves with a greyish bloom; flowers 4–5cm across. For sandy, well-drained soil, dry in summer. Min. −3°C.

Lampranthus spectabilis (Haw.) N. E. Br.
A prostrate shrub with yellow to white to bright purple flowers, native of South Africa in the Cape from Clanwilliam southwards and east to Natal, flowering throughout the year, but mainly in late spring. Stems to 30cm; leaves 4.5–6cm long, red-tipped with a greyish-green bloom; flowers 5–7cm across, on stalks 8–15cm long. For sandy, well-drained soil, dry in summer. Min. −3°C.

Lampranthus haworthii on Tresco

Lampranthus spectabilis

Carpobrotus edulis in California

Lampranthus multiradiatus

Lampranthus glaucus

Lampranthus aureus

215

Conicosia pugioniformis wild in sandy fields near Clanwilliam, W Cape

Conicosia pugioniformis

Disphyma crassifolium in an old wall on Tresco

Erepsia inclaudens in the Cape

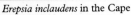

Drosanthemum speciosum

Drosanthemum floribundum

Oscularia caulescens on Tresco

Drosanthemum candens

Conicosia pugioniformis (L.) N. E. Br.
(*Mesembryanthemaceae*)   A large tufted
biennial or perennial with narrow grey-green
leaves and yellow flowers, native of South
Africa in the Cape from Clanwilliam and
Bellville to S Namaqualand (and naturalized
on the Pacific coast near San Francisco),
growing on flat sandy fields, flowering in
August–October (spring in S Africa). Plant to
60cm across and 20cm tall; leaves 15–20cm
long, 3-angled; flowers 7cm across. Easily
grown in areas with a warm wet winter and dry
summer. Min. −5°C.

Drosanthemum candens (Haw.) Schwant.
(*Mesembryanthemaceae*)   A small shrubby
succulent forming mats of glistening, papillose
leaves with pale pink or white flowers, native of
South Africa in the Cape from the Peninsula
east to near Bredasdorp, growing on rocks by
the sea, flowering in October–January
(summer). Stems to 10cm. Leaves to 10mm
long; flowers about 15mm across. Suitable for
crevices in coastal rocks, walls or other sunny
places. Min. 0°C.

Drosanthemum floribundum (Haw.)
Schwant.   A small shrubby succulent forming
mats of glistening, papillose leaves with pale or
deep pink flowers, native of South Africa from

the E Cape to Namaqualand, growing on
rocks, flowering in September–December
(summer). Stems to 50cm. Leaves cylindric,
to 12–14mm long; flowers to18mm across.
Suitable for walls or sunny ledges where the
stems can hang down. Min. 0°C.

Erepsia inclaudens (Haw.) Schwant.
(*Mesembryanthemaceae*)   A low or prostrate
shrublet with succulent leaves and bright
mauve flowers, native of South Africa in the
S Cape, growing in the mountains and in
rocky places along the coast between Paarl and
Caledon, flowering in October–December.
Stems to 20cm; leaves spathulate, often
reddish; flowers 2.5cm across with distinctive
linear-lanceolate or oblanceolate petals. For
any good well-drained soil. Min. −5°C.

Oscularia caulescens (Mill.) Schwant.
(*Mesembryanthemaceae*)   A small spreading
succulent shrub with grey-green leaves and
masses of pale pink flowers, native of South
Africa in the SW Cape, growing in rocky
places, flowering in September–December.
Plants to 20cm across; leaves incurved, keeled
on the back, about 2cm long, usually without
teeth. Flowers 1.2cm across in groups of 3.
For a rock crevice or well-drained position.
Min. −5°C, perhaps less.

Disphyma crassifolium (L.) L. Bolus
(*Mesembryanthemaceae*)   A low succulent,
woody at the base, forming mats of leaves with
pink, white or magenta flowers, native of the
coasts of South Africa from near Clanwilliam
to Port Elizabeth and to most of Australia and
Tasmania; also naturalized in California,
growing on rocks close to the sea and on saline
rocks inland in Australia, flowering in July–
October (spring). Stems to 2m; leaves flat
above, rounded or angular beneath; flowers
2.5cm across, with 5 stigmas. Easily grown in
open sandy soil. Min. −3°C.

Drosanthemum speciosum (Haw.)
Schwant.   A spreading bushy succulent with
stiff, wiry stems, short leaves and large bright
orange-red flowers, native of South Africa in
the Cape around Worcester and Robertson, in
the Little Karroo, growing in dry rocky places,
clambering through shrubs, flowering in May–
October (winter–early summer). Stems to
60cm; leaves round in section, covered in
round, transparent cells, to 18mm long and
2–3mm wide, glaucous. Flowers about 12cm
across. A showy and easily grown shrublet for
a dry sunny position. Min. −3°C.

217

BOUGAINVILLEAS

Bougainvilleas in the Villa Garzoni in Tuscany

Bougainvillea 'Barbara Karst'

The genus *Bougainvillea*, first described in Rio de Janeiro by the French botanist Philibert Commerson, was named after the French Admiral Louis Antoine, Comte de Bougainville (1729–1811), on whose ship *Bordeuse*, Commerson travelled to the Pacific. It is native of tropical South and Central America and consists of about 18 species of deciduous shrubby climbing and creeping plants and small trees; these are grown for their brilliantly coloured bracts which surround the insignificant flowers. There are many beautiful hybrids, cultivars and mutations, with single or double bracts, of which a selection is illustrated here; due to the instability of the flower colours as a result of fading and the plants' propensity for producing 'sports', it is often difficult to identify cultivars confidently.

Bougainvilleas make good conservatory plants when grown in pots in a mixture of loam and peat-based compost, but need plenty of light, adequate water and regular feeding with a high nitrogen fertilizer during the growing season. When repotting plants, treat the roots extremely carefully as they are easily damaged, and do not press the compost down firmly when replanting; watering will settle the roots satisfactorily. In their native habitat Bougainvilleas climb up through trees and other shrubs, attaching themselves by thorns, so in the greenhouse they should be provided with a trellis or wires up which they can scramble.

During cold weather watering should be reduced to a minimum; the plant will often drop its leaves and become semi-dormant. After the winter rest, dead shoots and straggly stems should be removed and side shoots can be cut well back to encourage new growth in the spring. Very large plants can be reduced in size by heavy pruning in the autumn, if required, with no ill effects, and small shrubby specimens can be given frequent clipping to promote new growth and improve flowering. Bougainvilleas are flexible plants; once they have become established they can survive temperatures as low as $-7°C$, but can also be grown outside in containers and brought in for the colder months. When grown under glass, Bougainvilleas are unfortunately susceptible to mealybug, red spider mite and scale insect.

Bougainvillea glabra Choisy in DC. (*Nyctaginaceae*) A vigorous climbing shrub which scrambles by means of curved thorns situated in its leaf axils. It grows to about 2.5m when confined to a pot and up to about 8m outside or planted in a greenhouse border. Panicles of brilliantly coloured bracts in variable shades of reddish-purple surround the insignificant white flowers. The mid-green leaves are ovate, paler beneath and usually have sparse short hairs on both surfaces. A native of Brazil where it flowers almost continuously, it was first described in 1849 and brought to Europe in the late1850s. According to Herklots, the first recorded form cultivated in Europe flowered at Holkham in Norfolk in 1860. A striking shrub for containers in the conservatory or for smothering fences and walls in warmer climates. Min $-7°C$ or cooler for short periods once the plants have become established.

'Harrissii' syn. 'Variegata' A variety of *B. glabra*, with variegated grey-green and cream foliage and small purple bracts.

'Barbara Karst' syn. 'Crimson Jewel' A medium-sized free-flowering cultivar with

Bougainvillea glabra covering a huge tree

Bougainvilleas in a monastery courtyard in Oaxaca, Mexico, now the hotel Camino Real, Mexico

Bougainvillea 'James Walker'

Bougainvilleas from the nursery of Peter Greensmith in Nairobi; top row (left to right) 'Poultonii', 'Rosenka', 'Gwyneth Portland'; middle row 'Harrissii', 'Elizabeth Angus', 'Double Pink'; bottom row 'Camerillo Fiesta', 'Orange King', 'Betty Lavers'

deep red bracts surrounding conspicuous white flowers. It has dark green broadly ovate leaves.

'Betty Lavers' A medium-sized cultivar with ruffled bracts, crisped at the margins and pointed at the tip. The bracts which surround conspicuous cream flowers are gold to begin with, fading eventually to pale pink. The leaves are ovate, pointed at the apex.

'Camerillo Fiesta' syn. 'Coral' A vigorous cultivar with large rounded bracts opening dark orange, fading to orange-red.

'Double Pink' As its name suggests, a double pink cultivar; unfortunately we have no further details of this elegant little variety. Photographed in Nairobi at Peter Greensmith's nursery.

'Elizabeth Angus' A vigorous cultivar of *B. glabra* with large purple bracts surrounding conspicuous large creamy-yellow flowers. The leaves are dark green and glossy.

'Gwyneth Portland' A relatively compact shrubby cultivar with medium-sized broadly

ovate bracts with golden yellow flowers. The medium-sized leaves, borne on short petioles, are ovate and glossy with a copper tinge at first.

'James Walker' syn. 'Ambience' A vigorous free-flowering cultivar with large bright purple-red bracts. The large leaves have wavy margins. The conspicuous flowers are creamy-white.

'Orange King' syn. 'Louis Wathen' Thought to be a sport from either 'Mrs Butt' or 'Scarlet Queen'. The rounded bronze-coloured bracts deepen in colour to bright reddish-pink.

'Poultonii' syn. 'Ooh La La' A small bushy variety with ovate bracts opening copper-red and becoming purple. The conspicuous flowers are cream. The leaves are broadly ovate with pointed apex, often tinged with copper when young.

'Rosenka' A free-flowering bud-sport of 'Poultonii', this is another compact variety with medium-sized bracts which open orange, deepening to dark rose pink. The flowers are cream and conspicuous. The broadly ovate leaves are rather leathery.

219

A wilderness of Bougainvillea and Wisteria in Madeira in March

Bougainvillea 'Donyo'

***Bougainvillea* 'Alison Davey'**
A free-flowering medium- to large-sized plant.
The large rounded bracts open orange-red
becoming deep magenta later. The creamy-
white flowers are conspicuous. The leaves are
flat and pointed, bronze when young.
'Brazilian' A variety with purple bracts
surrounding conspicuous cream-coloured
flowers.
'Daphne Mason' A free-flowering
moderately vigorous bud-sport of 'Killie
Campbell'. The large bracts open orange-pink
and change to violet-purple later. The creamy-
white flowers are conspicuous and quite large.
The leaves are long and pointed and are borne
on a long petiole.
'Donyo' A vigorous bud-sport from 'James
Walker', with large dark pink bracts
surrounding conspicuous creamy-white
flowers. The large pale green leaves have wavy
margins.
'Jennifer Fernie' syn. 'Beryl Lemmer',
'Mudanna' A moderately vigorous cultivar of
B. glabra with beautiful pure white bracts.

Bougainvilleas from the nursery of Peter Greensmith in Nairobi; top row (left to right) 'Daphne Mason', 'Alison Davey', 'Jennifer Fernie', 'Brazilian'; bottom row 'Mary Palmer's Enchantment', 'Mary Palmer', 'Ralph Sander'

Bougainvilleas in Nairobi

Bougainvillea 'Mary Palmer' and Mary Palmer's Enchantment'

'Mary Palmer' A bi coloured bud sport from 'Mrs H. C. Buck' which arose in the garden of a Mrs Palmer in Alipore, India. It was propagated by layering and named after her by S. Percy-Lancaster who noted that when this plant grows strongly most of the bracts are white, but when it is weakened, they are predominantly purple. Under normal conditions some of the bracts are soft pink, becoming white, while the others are purple, as in our picture.

'Mary Palmer's Enchantment' syn. 'Penelope', 'Shubra' A white-bracted sport of 'Mary Palmer', to which it is very similar although it has lighter green leaves that are copper-coloured when they first appear.

'Ralph Sander' A very attractive white-bracted cultivar with green veining.

Mirabilis multiflora (Torr.) A. Gray (*Nyctaginaceae*) This tuberous herbaceous perennial has much-branched stems (giving it the appearance of a shrub), grows up to 1m and is commonly found growing on rocky hillsides from Colorado and Utah to N Mexico. The large magenta-purple flowers are set off to advantage by the greyish-green ovate leaves. Min. −10°C. *M. jalapa* (*not illustrated*), with convolvulus-like flowers in a wide variety of colours, is a common weed throughout subtropical areas of the world. Flowers from spring–autumn.

Mirabilis multiflora in Arizona

Bougainvilleas from the nursery of Peter Greensmith in Nairobi; top row (left to right) 'Gillian Greensmith', 'Texas Dawn', 'Orchid Pink', 'Sanderiana'; second row 'Sunrise', 'Roseville's Delight', 'Killie Cambell'; on left 'Golden Glow'; third row 'President', 'Mahara Double Red', 'Lady Mary Maxwell'; bottom row 'Greensmith Spot', 'Rhodamine' (with flower). 'Ralph Sander's Spot'

Malpighia glabra

***Bougainvillea* cultivars** The following hybrids were photographed at the late Peter Greensmith's nursery in Nairobi, Kenya.

'Golden Glow' syn. 'Millarii', 'Gold Queen', 'Hawaiian Gold' A very free-flowering cultivar of *B. × buttiana*. Its bright yellow sport is called 'Lady Mary Baring' syn. 'Hawaiian Yellow'.
'Gillian Greensmith' Red, slightly paler than 'Isobel Greensmith', with pointed bracts. Raised by Peter Greensmith.
'Greensmith Spot' Single white with splashes of purplish-pink mainly on the backs of the bracts.
'Killie Campbell' A hybrid with reddish-purple bracts and large white flowers; habit climbing, becoming pendulous. Raised by William Poulton in Durban.
'Lady Mary Maxwell' Single pale purple.
'Mahara Double Red' syn. 'Carmencita', 'Manila Magic Red', 'Klong Fire' An old double bracted cultivar with bracts deep purplish-red. A sport of *C. × buttiana*.
'Orchid Pink' Single, purple bracts.
'President' Pale pinkish-purple, double bracted.
'Ralph Sander's Spot' Bracts pale-geenish pink.
'Rhodamine' Bracts purplish-red.
'Roseville's Delight' syn. 'Doubloon', 'Golden Doubloon', 'Mahara Orange', 'Thai Gold', 'Tahitan Gold', 'Golden Glory' A sport from 'Mahara', a brownish-orange sometimes fading to pink.
'Sanderiana' An old cultivar of *B. glabra* with purple green-veined bracts.
'Sunrise' Single pinkish-russet.
'Texas Dawn' syn. 'Purple King' A sport from Mrs Butt. Flowers light purple-pink.

***Melia azederach* L.** (*Meliaceae*) A deciduous tree with large twice pinnate leaves and branched heads of scented purplish flowers, native of N India and S China, and commonly planted elsewhere in subtropical climates, flowering in March–May. Tree to 15m; leaves to 80cm long, the secondary pinnae with 5 leaflets c. 5cm long. Flowers

Bougainvillea 'Golden Glow' in Nairobi

Melia azederach in California

Malpighia coccigera

Tristellateia australasiaca in Hong Kong

Galphimia glauca in Malawi

7–9cm long; the stamens united into a tube. Easily grown in frost-free climates; min −5°C. The fruits are often used as beads. Var. *umbraculiformis* Berckmans is the Texas Umbrella tree, a spreading small tree with drooping leaves, often grown in southern U.S.A. The family *Meliaceae* includes *Swietenia*, the Mahogany, native of central America.

Galphimia glauca Cav. syn. *Thryallis glauca* (*Malphigiaceae*)   A large evergreen shrub with narrowly ovate leaves with two small teeth near the base and yellow flowers, native of Central America from Mexico to Panama, flowering in summer. For any good soil with rain in summer. Min. −3°C.

Malpighia coccigera L. (*Malphigiaceae*) A dwarf holly-like shrub with broad leathery prickly leaves and pale pink flowers, native of the West Indies. Shrub to 1m; leaves 0.6–2.5cm long, opposite. Flowers solitary or paired. Fruit subglobose, red, 5–15mm across. For any good soil. Can be used as a hedge and may be clipped to shape. Min. 0°C.

Malpighia glabra L. Barbados Cherry A shrub with dark green lanceolate leaves and red or pink flowers in umbels, native of Texas, the West Indies and northern South America. Shrub to 3m; leaves about 8cm long, opposite. Flowers in umbels of 3–5. Fruit globose, red 5–10mm across. For any good soil. The fruits are a very rich source of vitamin C. Min. 0°C.

Tristellateia australasiaca A. Rich. (*Malphigiaceae*)   A twining shrub with smooth leaves and yellow flowers with smooth-margined petals and filaments becoming red in older flowers, native from Taiwan to Malaysia, Queensland and New Caledonia, growing in mangrove swamps, flowering most of the year. Climber to 4m or more. Leaves 5–8cm long; flowers 18–30 in a terminal raceme; the petals about 1.2cm long with red stalks. Fruit starry, adapted to dispersal by sea. Geoffrey Herklots in *Flowering Tropical Climbers* mentions that this is commonly cultivated in Singapore and Malaysia, as well as in Ghana and Trinidad. Min. 0°C.

Iresine herbstii

Clipped shapes of *Muehlenbeckia complexa* at Quinta de Palheiro Ferreiro in Madeira

Silene laciniata in Mexico

Homalocladium platycladum in Menton

Antigonon leptopus Hook. & Arn.
(*Polygonaceae*) Coral Vine   A rampant climber
with bright crimson-pink flowers, native of
Mexico on the coastal plain, climbing into
trees, flowering in summer–autumn. Stems to
12m, from tuberous roots. Leaves thin,
smooth heart-shaped. Flowers about 1cm long
in racemes that end in branched tendrils.
There are also deep red ('Baja Red'), white
and double-flowered varieties in cultivation.
For a hot position with ample water in
summer; good in desert climates where it may
become summer-dormant if dry. Min. 0°C,
but lower if the tuber is protected from frost.

Coccoloba uvifera (L.) L. (*Polygonaceae*)
An evergreen tree with almost round leathery
leaves and purplish edible grape-like fruit,
native of Bermuda, the West Indies and
tropical America, growing on sand dunes and
rocks by the sea, flowering in spring and
summer. Tree to 10m with grey bark. Leaves
about 20cm across, cordate at the base, with
red veins. Flowers scented, greenish. Berries
1.5–2cm across. For sandy soil and tolerant of
salty wind. Min. 0°C.

Dianthus caryophyllus L. (*Caryophyllaceae*)
Malmaison carnations are like old roses, the
few survivors of cultivars popular in the 19th
century, renowned for their scent.
'Souvenir de Malmaison'   Named after the
Bourbon rose and was raised by M. Laisne in
1857. It is also called 'Old Blush'. Most other
varieties are sports of this including the
salmon-pink 'Princess of Wales' (1875), which
appeard in Musselburgh, near Edinburgh.
'Tayside Red'   Another old Scottish variety
which has survived. Malmaison carnations
need cool conditions in summer and a dry
atmosphere in winter; cuttings should be taken
in winter. Min. −3°C.

Homalocladium platycladum (Muell.)
Bailey (*Polygonaceae*)   A strange shrub with
green flat branches, irregular leaves and
purplish red fruit, native of the Solomon
Islands, flowering in spring. Shrub to 3m.
Stems 1–2cm wide; leaves 1.5–6cm long.
Flowers greenish-white, the 5 sepals becoming
fleshy in fruit. For any soil. Min. −5°C.

Coccoloba uvifera unripe fruit

Ptilotus macrocephalus

Iresine herbstii Hook. (*Amaranthaceae*)
A dwarf shrubby perennial with decorative
leaves, native of Brazil. Stems to 50cm; leaves
2–7cm long, usually reddish, but in 'Aureo-
reticulata' green with yellow veins. Can be
grown as a pot plant or planted outside in
warm seasons, grown from cuttings. Min. 0°C.

Muehlenbeckia complexa (Cunn.) Meissner
(*Polygonaceae*)   A scrambling twining shrub
with thin wiry stems and tiny leaves, native of
New Zealand, growing on rocks near the coast
and in lowland forest, flowering from
November–March (summer) and fruiting from
December onwards. Plants to several metres
across; leaves round, 5–25mm; flowers
greenish in short spikes followed by fleshy 5-
lobed, white berries surrounding a black seed.
This unusual shrub responds well to clipping
and training and can be used as a substitute for
box. It is naturalized on the cool coasts of
California. Min. −5°C.

Polygonum capitatum Buch.-Ham. syn.
Persicaria capitata (Buch.-Ham.) Gross
(*Polygonaceae*)   A trailing rooting perennial
with ovate leaves and spherical heads of pink
flowers, native of the Himalayas from Pakistan
to SW China, growing on damp shady banks
and by paddy fields at 600–2400m, flowering
from March–November. Leaves 2–5cm long,
rounded or cuneate at the base, usually
pinkish, marked with a black V. Flower heads
6–13mm across. Good ground-cover for a
moist shady site. *P. microcephalum* D. Don,
from Sikkim and Bhutan, with cordate,
acuminate leaves is now often used in hanging
baskets. Min. −5°C.

Polygonum runcinatum Buch.-Ham. ex D.
Don, syn. *Persicaria runcinata* (Buch.-Ham.)
Gross   A spreading perennial with leaves
amplexicaul at the base, with 1–4 pairs of basal
lobes and loose heads of pink or white flowers,
native of the Himalayas in Bhutan and Sikkim,
growing on roadsides and damp cliffs, at
1000–3800m, flowering in May–October.
Stems to 50cm high; leaves marked with a
black V. Good on a cool bank in leafy soil.
Min. −5°C, perhaps less if a hardier form
were to be introduced.

Ptilotus macrocephalus Poir.
(*Amaranthaceae*)   A tufted perennial with long
silky-hairy flower heads, native throughout
Australia, growing in many different habitats,
flowering in summer. Stems to 50cm. The
smaller and hairier *P. manglesii* (Lindl.) Muell.
with pink or white flowers is grown in alpine
houses in Britain. Min. −5°C, but needs
excellent drainage to survive frost.

Silene laciniata Cav. (*Caryophyllaceae*)
A perennial with narrow leaves and bright red
flowers, native of Mexico in the northern
Sierras and S California below 1700m (var.
major Hitchc. & Maguire), growing in dry
rocky places and open woods, flowering in
May–August. Plant with a deep taproot; stems
to 30cm; flowers 15–30mm across. For dry
well-drained soil. Min. −5°C, perhaps less.

Antigonon leptopus climbing on a fence near the coast in E Mexico

Dianthus 'Souvenir de Malmaison'

Dianthus 'Tayside Red' at Crathes

Polygonum runcinatum

Polygonum capitatum

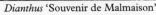

Aeonium tabuliforme in Tenerife

Aeonium holochrysum in Tenerife

Aeonium urbicum near Masca in Tenerife

Greenovia aurea in Tenerife

Aeonium glandulosum in Madeira

Aeonium arboreum 'Zwartkop' at Quinta de Palheiro Ferreiro in Madeira

Aeonium arboreum 'Atropurpureum'

Aeonium cuneatum on a mountain ridge in the laurel forest near La Laguna in NE Tenerife

The 35 or so species of *Aeonium* are found mainly in the Canary Islands with isolated species in Madeira, the Yemen and northern Africa. Many of the Canary species are confined to one or two islands. Most grow on cliffs and all need well-drained soil in sun or part shade. Min. −3°C for short periods if kept dry in winter.

Aeonium arboreum (L.) Webb & Berth. syn. *A. manriqueorum* Bolle (*Crassulaceae*)
A shrubby succulent with branched stems and terminal rosettes of leaves, blackish in 'Zwartkop', flushed red in 'Atropurpureum'. Native of Gran Canaria, growing on cliffs and rocks on the north coast and in the mountains at 300–1200m (and naturalized on the Californian coast), flowering in spring. Stems branched, to 1m. Rosettes 12–20cm across. Leaves spathulate, ciliate. Flowers yellow, in a conical pubescent inflorescence.

Aeonium cuneatum Webb & Berth.
A succulent perennial with groups of stemless rosettes and a tall leafy inflorescence, native of Tenerife, growing on cliffs in the forest and on mountain ridges at 600–800m, flowering in spring (March–April). Rosettes about 30cm across. Leaves usually glaucous, mucronate, ciliate. Flower stem about 1m; flowers golden yellow with 8–10 petals. This species is frequent in gardens in the Scilly Isles.

Aeonium glandulosum (Ait.) Webb & Berth. A succulent biennial or monocarpic perennial with flat rosettes and a widely branched inflorescence, native of Madeira, growing on shady cliffs, flowering in spring and early summer. Rosette 20–30cm across. Leaves flat in winter, upright in summer. Inflorescence to 25cm; flowers pale yellow.

Aeonium holochrysum Webb & Berth.
A succulent sub-shrub with branched stems and terminal rosettes with a dense conical inflorescence, native of Tenerife, Gomera, La Palma and Hierro, growing in dry rocky places at up to 1200m, flowering in spring (March–

April). Rosettes about 20cm across. Leaves green, mucronate, ciliate. Inflorescence about 20cm, glabrous; flowers golden yellow with 8–10 petals. Close to *A. arboreum*, but with narrower leaves and a denser, glabrous inflorescence.

Aeonium tabuliforme (Haw.) Webb & Berth.
A ground-hugging succulent with long-ciliate leaves, native of Tenerife, growing on shady cliffs along the north coast below 500m, flowering in spring–summer. Rosettes about 30cm across. Leaves spathulate. Flower stems about 30cm; flowers golden yellow with 8–10 petals. This needs cooler conditions than most and is striking for its very flat rosettes.

Aeonium urbicum (Chr. Sm.) Webb & Berth. A succulent monocarpic sub-shrub with single unbranched stems with a terminal rosette and a large inflorescence of pink or whitish flowers, native of Tenerife, growing on dry rocks, old roofs and on mountain ridges at up to 1100m, flowering in spring (March–April). Stems to 2m. Rosettes about 30cm across. Leaves often glaucous, red-edged, ciliate. Inflorescence about 80cm; flowers with 9–10 petals.

Greenovia aurea (Chr. Sm.) Webb & Berth. (*Crassulaceae*) A succulent perennial with groups of stemless rosettes and a leafy inflorescence, native of Tenerife, growing on dry cliff ledges and mountain ridges at 400–2000m, flowering in spring (March–April). Rosettes about 10cm across. Leaves usually glaucous, glabrous. Flower stem 15cm; flowers golden yellow with 30–35 petals, to 2.5cm across. *Greenovia* species have 18–35 petals and usually glabrous leaves; *Aeonium* have 6–12 petals and ciliate leaves.

Monanthes pallens (Webb & Christ) Christ (*Crassulaceae*) A dwarf succulent, native of the Canary islands, growing on shady, mossy slopes, flowering in spring. Rosettes 3–5cm across, white hairy; sepals 6–8, yellow; petals 6–8, white and red.

Aeonium cuneatum on Tresco

Monanthes pallens in Tenerife

The Little Karroo near Worcester, a wonderful habitat for succulents and bulbs, with *Cotyledon orbiculata*

Cotyledon orbiculata

Cotyledon macrantha at Les Cèdres

Dudleya saxosa near Palm Canyon

Kalanchoe pumila

Kalanchoe schimperana from Ethiopia, at Kew

Cotyledon macrantha L. (*Crassulaceae*)
A low succulent shrub with green leaves and nodding flowers, native of South Africa in the eastern Cape, flowering in winter. Stems to 1m. Leaves to 10cm long, edged red. Flowers about 18mm long, green with red tips. For dry soil with water in spring. Min. −3°C.

Cotyledon orbiculata L.   A very variable succulent shrub with whitish leaves and red, orange, yellow or rarely purple flowers, native of South West Cape Province to East Natal and the High Drakensberg, growing in dry, rocky and sandy places, flowering most of the year, but mainly in summer. Stems to 90cm; leaves variable, from cylindric to flat. Flowers nodding, about 12mm long. Var. *oblonga* (Haw.) DC., with oblanceolate or obovate leaves is found at up to 3000m in the Drakensberg and will survive frost if kept dry in winter (*shown in our book Perennials II, p. 57*). The forms with cylindrical leaves and

deeper red flowers are usually found in dry areas such as the Little Karroo (*shown here*). Other forms with broad leaves and deep red flowers are found along the coast and on low hills nearby.

Dudleya saxosa (Jones) Brit. & Rose subsp. **aloides** (Rose) (*Crassulaceae*)   A succulent with a rosette of glaucous leaves and flowers tubular at the base, native of SE California on the desert clopes of the San Jacinto and Laguna Mountains, growing in the shade of rocks and cliffs at 300–1600m, flowering in April–June. Rosettes about 15cm across. Flowering stems to 35cm, reddish. Flowers 10–12mm long. Min. 0°C. About 40 species of *Dudleya* are found in W North America, from the coast to the desert, some with few large rosettes, others with mats of small white rosettes as are found in *D. farinosa* (Lindl.) Brit. & Rose., a common rock garden plant.

Kalanchoe pumila Baker.   A small shrubby succulent with grey leaves and dense heads of upright pinkish flowers, native of Madagascar, flowering in spring. Stems sprawling, to 30cm. Leaves 2–3.5cm long. Flowers about 18mm long. For a sunny position in well-drained soil. Min. 0°C.
K. blossfeldiana Poelln., also from Madagascar, is the parent of several dwarf houseplants with upright vibrant-coloured flowers.

Kalanchoe schimperana A. Rich.   A leafy sub-shrubby succulent with thin fleshy leaves and large white flowers, native of Ethiopia in the Adowa district and in the Galla Highlands and of the Yemen, growing in rocky places, flowering in early spring. Shrub to 60cm. Leaves in two ranks, green, crenate. Flowers 7.5–9cm long with a long green tube and white lobes. This beautiful species, which is not commonly cultivated, was photographed at the Royal Botanic Gardens, Kew. Min. 0°C.

Kalanchoe pinnata naturalised in a forest in Bermuda

Kalanchoe manginii at Holly Gate Nursery, Ashington, Sussex

Kalanchoe porphyrocalyx in a hanging basket at Wisley

Kalanchoe pinnata flowers

Kalanchoe marnierana at Les Cèdres, Cap d'Antibes in January

Kalanchoe manginii Ham. & Perr.
(*Crassulaceae*)   A trailing perennial with fleshy
leaves and tubular reddish flowers, native of
Madagascar, probably epiphytic, flowering in
spring. Stems to 30cm. Leaves 12–20mm,
ovate-spathulate, to 8mm thick. Inflorescence
with adventitious buds and few flowers.
Flowers solitary or in pairs. Calyx pubescent.
Corolla 2.5–3.5cm long, pubescent outside.
Min. 0°C.

Kalanchoe marnierana (Mann. & Boit.)
Jacob   A shrubby succulent with rounded
leaves and umbels of hanging orange flowers,
native of SW Madagascar, flowering in winter.
Stems to 40cm, with stiff aerial roots. Leaves
about 3cm long, in two ranks on the stem,
greyish with a red edge and purple blotches
forming plantlets. Flowers about 2.5cm long,
very fleshy. Min. 0°C. Photographed in the
garden of M. Marnier-Lapostolle on Cap
d'Antibes, France.

Kalanchoe pinnata (Lam.) Pers. syn.
Bryophyllum pinnatum Lam.   A sprawling
perennial with thin fleshy leaves and loose
whorls of tubular hanging flowers with an
inflated calyx. Native area uncertain but now
widely distributed in the tropics and
subtropics, growing in dry shady places,
flowering much of the year. Stems to 2m;
leaves crenate, the lower simple, the upper
below the inflorescence often pinnate, forming
plantlets if detached and often while still on
the plant. Calyx about 3cm, streaked with red;
corolla to 4cm. Min. 0°C. Because of the ease
with which fallen leaves form plantlets, the
plant has become naturalized e.g. in New
Zealand, Natal and Madeira.

Kalanchoe porphyrocalyx (Bak.) Baill.
A sub-shrubby perennial with thin stems and
small fleshy leaves, native of Madagascar
where it grows as an epiphyte. Stems to 30cm.
Leaves 2–5.5cm long, obovate, unevenly
crenate. Flowers about 3cm long, in a
spreading few-flowered inflorescence. For
moist open, peaty soil in a hanging basket.
Min. 0°C.

'Tessa' and **'Wendy'**   Hybrids between
K. porphyrocalyx and *K. miniata*, are two
popular varieties for hanging baskets.

Kalanchoe 'Tessa' in a hanging basket at Wisley

Crassula multicava at Holly Gate Nursery

Crassula arborescens (Mill.) Willd.
(*Crassulaceae*)   A shrub or small tree with
thick succulent silver leaves, native of South
Africa in the Cape, from Worcester to Port
Elizabeth, growing on dry rocky slopes in
inland valleys, flowering in October–January
(summer). Stems to 3m, thick and trunk-like.
Leaves edged red, 2–5cm long. Flowers starry,
white becoming pink, in a branched
inflorescence. For very well-drained soil with
water mainly in winter. Min. −3°C.

Crassula coccinea L.   A succulent perennial
with overlapping opposite pairs of leaves and
flat-topped umbels of red flowers, native of
South Africa in the Cape, from Paarl to
Bredasdorp and on the Peninsula, growing in
rock crevices near the coast, flowering in
December–March (summer). Stems to 40cm.
Leaves edged red, to 2.5cm long, hiding the
stem. Flowers scarlet, pink or white, about
1cm across. For very well-drained soil, with
water all year. Min. −3°C.

Crassula fascicularis Lam.   A succulent
perennial with thin lanceolate leaves and
rounded heads of creamy flowers turning
pinkish, native of South Africa in the Cape,
from Clanwilliam to Paarl and Bredasdorp and
on the Peninsula, growing in fynbos, scrub and
sandy places near the coast, flowering in
August–December (spring). Stems reddish, to
40cm. Leaves to 3.5cm long, appressed to the
stem. Flowers cream with recurved reddish
tips, about 1cm across. For very well-drained
soil, with water all year. Min. −3°C.

Crassula multicava Lem.   A shrubby
spreading succulent with green leaves and
pinkish starry flowers, native of South Africa in
the E Cape and the Natal coast and midlands,
growing in rocky places and scrub, flowering
in September–October (spring). Stems to 1m,
sprawling and rooting. Leaves pitted with
small glands, 2–6.5cm long. Flowers starry,
white becoming pink, in a slender branched or
rounded inflorescence. For very well-drained
soil with water all year. Min. −3°C, overnight
only. *Crassula lactea* Sol. (*not shown*) from the
Cape, is more creeping with pairs of sessile
leaves. It is exceptionally shade-tolerant and
flowers in late autumn.

Crassula ovata (Mill.) Druce syn.
C. portulacea Lam.   A shrub or small tree with
thick succulent green leaves, native of South

Crassula ovata at Holly Gate Nursery, Ashington, Sussex, in January

Crassula vaginata on Ngeli Mountain

Crassula vaginata in Natal

Sedum praealtum in a garden in Bussaco, Portugal

Crassula coccinea in the Abbey Garden, Tresco

Crassula fascicularis on the Cape Peninsula

Crassula arborescens wild near Montagu

Sedum morganianum in Malawi

Africa in the Cape, from Uitenhage and Port Elizabeth to Natal, growing on dry rocky slopes, flowering in June–August (winter). Stems to 2.5m, thick and trunk-like. Leaves edged red, 2–4cm long. Flowers starry, white becoming pink, in a branched inflorescence. For very well-drained soil, with little water mainly all year. Min. −3°C. Does well outdoors in the mildest parts of California.

Crassula vaginata Eckl. & Zeyh.
A succulent perennial with thin lanceolate leaves and large flattish heads of yellow or creamy flowers, native of South Africa in Natal and the Drakensberg, growing in grassland in the mountains, and northwards to Arabia, flowering in December–January (summer).

Roots tuberous. Stems to 40cm. Leaves to 3.5cm long in a basal rosette, dying by flowering time. Flowers cream to yellow, about 8mm across. For very well-drained peaty soil, with water mainly in summer. Min. −5°C or lower if the tuberous root is protected.

Sedum morganianum Walth. *(Crassulaceae)*
A hanging succulent with closely crowded, greyish leaves and small pinkish to deep red flowers, native of Mexico but not yet found wild. Stems to 1m, hanging down, about 1.8cm in diameter with the appressed leaves. Leaves to 18mm long, incurved. Flowers from near the tips of the stems, 12mm across, on slender stalks. An unusual plant for a hanging basket in the shade; in warm areas often seen

hanging on a veranda. Needs rich well-drained but moist soil and protection from wind. Min. 0°C.

Sedum praealtum A. DC. A shrubby succulent with alternate shining green leaves and spreading inflorescences of bright yellow flowers, native of Mexico, formerly commonly grown as a windowsill plant and naturalized elsewhere in Mediterranean climates, flowering in spring and early summer. Stems to 1.5m; leaves 5–6.5cm, lanceolate, spathulate. Flowers 7–10mm across. For poor dry soil. Min. −5°C. *Sedum dendroideum* Sessé & Moç ex DC. is similar but with petals larger than the stamens and almost orbicular stalked leaves; said to be naturalized in Jersey.

233

Lotus berthelotii in a strawberry pot

Lotus maculatus in a Cretan jar

Chamaecytisus proliferus in Tenerife

Lotus glaucus on sea cliffs in Madeira

Adenocarpus foliolosus in Tenerife

Lotus sessilifolius

Adenocarpus foliolosus (Ait.) DC.
(*Leguminosae*)   An upright shrub with small crowded leaves and yellow flowers, native of Tenerife, Gran Canaria and Gomera, growing in heaths, woodland and pine forests at up to 1500m, flowering in March. Stems to 2m. Leaves with 3 lanceolate or obovate leaflets. Flowers in upright terminal racemes. Pods with black glandular swellings. For well-drained soil. Min. −5°C. *A. decorticans* Boiss., from S Spain is rather similar, with silvery leaves and peeling bark.

Chamaecytisus proliferus (L.) Link
(*Leguminosae*)   An upright shrub with green leaves and white flowers, native of Tenerife, Gran Canaria, Hierro and Gomera, growing in open forests and scrub at up to 1800m, flowering in March. Stems to 2m. Leaves with 3 lanceolate leaflets. Flowers in groups of 1–4, in the leaf axils. Pods black. For well-drained soil. Min. −5°C.

Lotus berthelotii Masf. (*Leguminosae*)
A silvery cascading sub-shrub with bright red and black flowers, native of the Cape Verde Islands and Tenerife, growing on cliffs in the cloud forest at 700–1200m, flowering mainly in spring. Stems hanging to 1m or more. Leaflets cylindric, linear, 10–18mm, folding up at night. Flowers about 2.5cm long, with a long curved keel. For a tall pot or hanging basket with well-drained but moisture-retentive soil. Min. 0°C. The flowers are adapted for bird pollination, like several other Canary endemics, in the apparent absence at present of sunbirds. This plant is now very rare in the wild and we searched for it on Tenerife without success. Fortunately it is widely cultivated.

Lotus berthelotii × maculatus   A hybrid between these two unusual species with silvery linear leaves closer to *L. berthelotii*, but with orange flowers.

Lotus jacobaeus L.   A lax evergreen perennial with blackish or brown flowers, native of the Cape Verde Islands, flowering mainly in summer. Stems to 30cm. Leaflets oblanceolate, acute. Flowers in heads of 1–6, the standard brown, yellowish outside. For a dry sunny position. Min. 0°C.

Lotus maculatus Breitf.   A greyish cascading sub-shrub with yellow and dark brown flowers, native of Tenerife, growing on cliffs on the north coast, flowering in spring. Stems hanging to 1m or more. Leaflets flat, linear, about 10mm. Flowers pointing outwards in groups of 2–4, about 2cm long with a long curved keel tipped red and a recurved standard with a brown stripe. For a tall pot or hanging basket with well-drained but moisture-retentive soil. Min. 0°C. Like *L. berthelotii* the flowers appear to be adapted for bird pollination in the absence of likely bird pollinators. This species is also extremely rare in the wild, but is easily propagated from cuttings.

Lotus sessilifolius DC syn. *L. mascaenis* hort. non Burchard   A dense silvery shrublet with yellow pea flowers, native of Tenerife, flowering in spring. Leaflets linear, 12–15mm long. Flowers in clusters of 3–7. For well-drained soil in a sunny position. Min. 0°C.

Lotus glaucus Ait.   A grey trailing shrublet with oblanceolate to obovate leaves and pale yellow to orange flowers, native of most of the Canary Islands and Madeira, growing on rocks and cliffs near the sea, flowering most of the year. Stems to 60cm. Leaflets 3–5mm. Peduncles about 4cm long with 1–3 flowers each, with a 9mm wide standard. For a dry sunny position. Min. 0°C.

Spartocytisus filipes Webb & Berth. (*Leguminosae*)   A spreading broom-like shrub with small white scented flowers, native of Tenerife, Gomera, La Palma and Hierro growing on dry, rocky mountains in the forest zone at up to 800m, flowering in March. Shrub to 1.5m high and more across, with green flexuous stems. Leaves soon falling in spring. Flowers in short racemes, with a red calyx. Pod black, hairy. Min. −5°C.
The Retama del Pico, *S. supranubius* (L.) Webb & Berth., has stout thick glaucous stems and dense clusters of flowers. It is common at high altitudes on Tenerife and La Palma and should be hardier in dry climates.

Lotus berthelotii (narrow leaf)

Lotus maculatus

Lotus berthelotii × *maculatus*

Lotus berthelotii

Specimens from Sellindge, Kent, April 24th, 2/5 life size

Lotus jacobaeus

Spartocytisus filipes on mountain cliffs above Masca in Tenerife in March

235

Kennedia nigricans

Chorisema ilicifolium in Kent

Kennedia macrophylla on Tresco

Brachysema celsianum at Kew

Oxylobium lanceolatum

Oxylobium ellipticum on Tresco

in loose heads, native of Western Australia, flowering in spring and summer. Stems to 3m or more. Leaflets 3–6cm long. Flowers with standard 13mm across. For good sandy but moist soil. Min. −3°C. In Australia all *Kennedia* species are used as ground-cover and as climbers, to cover fences etc.

Kennedia nigricans Lindl. A rampant climber with large dark green leaves and narrow black and yellow flowers in one-sided heads, native of Western Australia, flowering in spring and summer. Stems to 6m or more. Leaflets 3 or 1, to 12cm long. Flowers with standard 3cm long. For good sandy soil. Min. −3°C .

Kennedia rubicunda (Schneev.) Vent. A rampant evergreen climber with large dark green leaves and brownish-red flowers in loose heads, native of Victoria, New South Wales and Queensland, especially along the coast, flowering in late winter to spring. Stems to 3m or more. Leaflets 3, to 15cm long. Flowers with standard 4cm across. For good sandy soil. Min. −3°C. This species is said to be more drought-resistant than the others.

Kennedia stirlingii Lindl. A low climber or creeper with red flowers, native of Western Australia, flowering in spring. Stems forming patches to 2m across. Leaflets 3, to 6cm long, with leafy stipules. Flowers with standard 15mm across. For good sandy, but moist soil, preferring some shade. Min. −3°C.

Oxylobium ellipticum (Labill.) R. Br. (*Leguminosae*) An upright shrub with simple elliptic leaves and spikes of small yellow flowers, native from Queensland to Victoria and Tasmania, growing in scrub and open forest, flowering in spring–summer. Shrub to 2m; leaves to 3cm long. Flowers 1.2cm across. For well-drained but moist soil and will tolerate some shade. Min. −3°C. There are prostrate alpine forms. This species seeds itself on heathy sandy areas on Tresco, in the Isles of Scilly.

Oxylobium lanceolatum (Vent.) Druce An upright shrub with simple lanceolate leaves and spikes of small yellow flowers, native of Western Australia, growing in scrub, flowering in spring–summer. Shrub to 2m, in one form taller, forming a small tree; leaves to 12cm long. Flowers 1.25cm across. For well-drained but moist soil. Min. −3°C.

Brachysema celsianum Lem. syn. *B. lanceolatum* Meisn. (*Leguminosae*) A small dense shrub or scrambler with simple lanceolate, usually opposite leaves and small red flowers, native of Western Australia, growing in scrub, flowering in June–October (winter–spring). Shrub to 2m, in one form taller, forming a small tree; leaves to 10cm long, silvery beneath. Flowers to 2.5cm across with a short standard, solitary or in clusters. Best in well-drained soil but is tolerant of adverse conditions, even growing under mature *Eucalyptus*. Min. −5°C.

Chorisema ilicifolium Labill. (*Leguminosae*) A most attractive small dense shrub or scrambler with bristly holly-like leaves and masses of orange, yellow and purplish flowers,

native of Western Australia, growing in scrub, flowering in June–October (winter–spring). Shrub to 3m and as much across, sometimes scrambling with long thin shoots. Leaves to 8cm long, variable, sometimes lobed, with prickly teeth. Flowers to 1cm across, in loose leafy spikes. *C. cordatum* Lindl. is similar, with cordate, toothed or lobed but not prickly leaves and flowers usually deep orange, though a yellow form is known. Both do best in well-drained peaty sandy soil, not drying out. They should be pruned after flowering to keep them in shape. Min. −2°C for both. They are excellent plants for a cool greenhouse.

Kennedia macrophylla (Meissn.) Benth. (*Leguminosae*) A rampant climber with large light green leaves and brownish-red flowers

Kennedia rubicunda

Brachysema celsianum

Chorisema ilicifolium

Kennedia nigricans

Kennedia stirlingii

Specimens from the old Australia House at Kew, February 7th, 3/5 life size

Psoralea pinnata on the Robinson pass, near Oudtshoorn in October

Hypocalyptus sophoroides (Berg.) Baill. (*Leguminosae*)   An upright shrub with long heads of bright pink flowers, native of South Africa from the Cedarberg to Caledon, the Langkloof and Swarteberg, growing by streams in the mountains, flowering in September–November (spring). Shrub to 4m, with maroon stems. Leaves glaucous, trifoliolate. Flower heads about 10cm long. Standard with a yellow centre. For well-drained but moist peaty soil. Min. −5°C, perhaps less for short periods.

Lotononis trisegmentata E. P. Phillips (*Leguminosae*)   An upright sparse shrub with small silvery leaves and blue and yellow flowers, native of South Africa in the Drakensberg, in the E Cape and Natal at 1800–2400m, growing by streams and in gullies, flowering in summer. Shrub to 2m. Leaflets linear, pointed. Flowers with a blue, yellow-based standard and greenish-yellow wings. For well-drained but moist peaty soil. Min. −10°C, perhaps less for short periods.

Podalyria calyptrata (Retz.) Willd. (*Leguminosae*)   A low spreading shrub or small tree in a sheltered site, with dark green leaves and large pink and white flowers, native of South Africa on the Cape Peninsula, east to Bredasdorp, growing on rocky slopes, by streams and on forest margins, flowering in spring. Shrub to 4m high and 1m across, or taller in old specimens. Leaflets obovate, orbicular or lanceolate, dark green above, silky below with brownish hairs. Bracts enclosing the flower buds, forming a cap as they fall. Flowers white with a mauve-pink edge to the broad 2-lobed standard, to 4cm across. A particularly lovely shrub for well-drained sandy soil. Min. −5°C.

Podalyria cordata R. Br.   An upright shrub with dark green leaves with sparse silky hairs and bright magenta-pink flowers, native of South Africa in the Cape, growing in wet peaty places in the mountains between Paarl and Caledon, flowering in October (late spring). Stems to 1m, usually less. Leaves about 2cm long, folded upwards. Bracts not enclosing the buds. Flowers 4cm across, the calyx densely covered with rusty-brown hairs. For peaty sandy soil. Min. −5°C. Photographed on the Franshoek Pass near Stellenbosch in October.

Psoralea aphylla L. (*Leguminosae*)   An upright or arching broom-like shrub with few small leaves and blue flowers, native of South Africa from Clanwilliam to Worcester, the

Psoralea pinnata in the Abbey Gardens, Tresco in June

Eriosma cordatum near Nottingham Road, Natal

Hypocalyptus sophoroides

Hypocalyptus sophoroides on the Swartberge pass near Oudtshoorn in October

Podalyria cordata on Franshoek pass

Psoralea aphylla near Dido Road on the Cape Peninsula in October

Peninsula and Riversdale, growing by streams, on wet rocks and in marshy places, flowering in October–February (summer). Shrub to 3m. Leaflets linear, pointed. Flowers with pale wings and a dark standard. For well-drained but moist, peaty soil. Min. −5°C, perhaps less for short periods.

Psoralea pinnata L. An upright, bushy shrub with narrow, pinnate leaves and bluish flowers, native of South Africa from Clanwilliam to the E Cape, Natal and the Transvaal, growing by streams and on wet rocks, flowering most of the year. Shrub to 4m. Leaflets linear, pointed. Flowers pale with dark veins. For well-drained but moist peaty soil. Min. −5°C, perhaps less for short periods.

Eriosema cordatum F. Mey. (*Leguminosae*) A low perennial with large trifoliate leaves and spikes of brownish-orange flowers, native of South Africa in Natal, growing in grassland, flowering in October (late spring). Stems to 20cm, from a deep wiry perennial rhizome. Leaflets about 10cm long. Flowers 1cm across with dark-veined standards. For deep rich soil, with water in summer. Min. −10°C, perhaps.

Podalyria calyptrata on the Cape Peninsula

Lotononis trisegmentata in the NE Cape

239

Sutherlandia frutescens

Sutherlandia frutescens wild on the coast with Cape Hangklip behind

Crotalaria laburnifolia subsp. *laburnifolia*

Crotalaria capensis

Crotalaria agatiflora subsp. *imperialis*

Crotalaria agatiflora subsp. *imperialis*

Sutherlandia microphylla in NE Cape

Crotalaria agatiflora Schweinf. subsp.
imperialis (*Leguminosae*)   A large shrub with
horizontal racemes of huge hanging greenish
flowers, native of tropical E Africa, flowering
in winter–spring. Shrub to 4m. Leaflets 3,
ovate, 2.5–7cm long. Racemes to 60cm.
Flowers 5–10cm across. A very striking
species, growing well outdoors in sheltered
positions in S California, S Australia and on
the Riviera or in a frost-free greenhouse, kept
rather dry. Min. −3°C. Most *Crotalaria*
species have yellow flowers but several such as
the African *C. purpurea* and the Australian
C. cunninghamii R. Br. are beautifully marked
with red or purple.

Crotalaria capensis Jacq.   A spreading
shrub with hanging branches and spikes of
large yellow flowers, native of South Africa
from Knysna to the E Cape and N Natal,
flowering in August–December (spring–
summer). Stems to 3m; leaflets 3, elliptic to
obovate, 1.5–7cm long. Racemes 10–15cm
long; flowers about 5cm, yellow with a red
blotch on the standard. For any good well-
drained soil. Min. −5°C.

Crotalaria laburnifolia L. subsp.
laburnifolia   An upright shrub with erect
racemes of large hanging yellow flowers, native
of E Africa in Malawi, growing on mountain
slopes (with subsp. *australis* (Bak. fil.) Polhill,
in Natal) flowering in November–July, and in
N Australia growing in sandy places along
large rivers, flowering in March–July (winter).
Shrub to 3m. Leaflets obovate. Flowers about
4cm across with a very strongly curved and
pointed keel. Back of standard and tip of keel
often marked with brownish-red. For well-
drained soil. Min. 0°C.

Sutherlandia frutescens (L.) R. BR.
(*Leguminosae*)   A soft upright or spreading
shrub with greyish leaves, red flowers and
papery inflated seed pods, native of southern
Africa from the Cape northwards, mainly near
the coast, growing in scrub on rocky hills,
flowering in July–December (spring–early
summer); it is also widely grown elsewhere and
sometimes naturalized. Shrub to 1.2m. Leaves
with leaflets 3 or more times as long as wide.
Flowers 14–24mm long; pods 1.3–2 times as
long as wide, the stipe strongly down-curved
from the calyx. For well-drained sandy soil.
Min. 0°C. The six or so species of *Sutherlandia*
are all very similar and being revised at present
(*see bibliography in volume 2*).

Virgilia oroboides in the Kirstenbosch Botanic Garden

Sutherlandia microphylla Burch. ex DC.
An upright sparse shrub with narrow leaflets,
red flowers and swollen papery seed pods,
native of South Africa in the NE Cape
Province, growing on dry rocky hills and sandy
roadsides, flowering in November–December
(spring–early summer). Shrub to 1.4m. Leaves
with leaflets 3 or more times as long as wide.
Flowers 19–27mm long; pods 2.3–4 times as
long as wide, the stipe strongly down-curved
from the calyx. For well-drained sandy soil.
Min. −5°C.

Sutherlandia montana Phillips & Dyer
A dense spreading or prostrate shrub with
large red flowers and swollen papery seed
pods, native of the Drakensberg in the NE
Cape and Natal, growing on rocks, by streams,
on cliffs and in scrub at 1500–3000m,
flowering in November–December (spring).
Shrub to 1m; leaflets 2–3 times as long as
wide. Flowers 30–45mm long. Pods 2–4 times
as long as wide, the stipe exserted nearly
straight from the calyx. For very well-drained
soil in a sheltered position; propagate from
seed or soft cuttings. Min. −5°C, perhaps less
if dry. Plants from Naude's Nek, NE Cape
(C. D. & R. 151).

Virgilia oroboides (Bergius) Salter
(*Leguminosae*)   A tree with pinnate leaves and
masses of pale pink flowers, native of South
Africa in the Cape, from the Peninsula east to
Mossel Bay, growing on the edges of forest and
along streams and commonly planted,
flowering in November–April. Tree to 10m.
Leaves with rounded leaflets. Flowers in short
racemes with wide wings. A good flowering
tree for Mediterranean areas. Min. −5°C.

Virgilia oroboides

Sutherlandia montana

241

Indigofera decora in the garden at Isola Bella, Lago Maggiore

Dalea bicolor at the Living Desert Reserve, Palm Desert, California

Dalea schottii wild in the desert near Palm Springs

Lathyrus splendens in California

Lupinus albifrons wild on grassy hills in Marin Co.

Anagyris foetida L. (*Leguminosae*) An upright shrub with large dull yellow flowers, native of the Mediterranean region from N Africa and Spain to N Iraq and Arabia, growing on rocky slopes, in scrub near the sea and in woods at up to 1000m in Turkey, flowering in March–May. Plant strong-smelling. Leaves with 3 leaflets. Flowers 20–25mm long, the standard blotched with black. Drought-tolerant, for well-drained soil. Min. −5°C.

Dalea bicolor Humb. & Bonpl. (*Leguminosae*) A silvery-hairy sub-shrub with upright spikes of pinkish-purple flowers, native of Baja California, growing in sandy deserts, washes and dry slopes, flowering in March–April. Stems upright, to 50cm. Leaves about 7cm long. For dry well-drained soil. Min. −5°C, if dry. Close to *D. mollis* Benth., which is more creeping with whitish flowers.

Dalea schottii Torr. A twiggy bush with greenish stems and deep blue flowers, native of California, Arizona and North West Mexico, growing in sandy washes in deserts, below 300m, flowering in March–May. Stems to 3m high and wide; leaves usually simple, linear, 1–3cm long, lasting into the flowering season. Racemes lax, 5–10cm long, with flowers 8–10mm long. *D. spinosa* Gray, is similar, with silvery-silky shoots. Both are good drought-resistant shrubs for desert soils. Min. −5°C.

Ebenus cretica L. (*Leguminosae*) A small silvery shrub with dense spikes of bright pink flowers, native of Crete, growing on cliffs, gorges and rocky hills, flowering in spring. Shrub to 50cm. Leaves with 3–5 leaflets. Bracts papery. Flowers 1–1.5cm long, occasionally white. For well-drained stony soil in full sun. Min. −5°C.

Indigofera decora Lindl. (*Leguminosae*) A sub-shrub with loose spikes of pale mauve-pink flowers, native of S Japan in Honshu and Kyushu and to C China, growing on river banks and on old walls, flowering in May–July. Stems to 1.5m, dying down in cold winters. Leaves 7–20cm long with 9–13 leaflets 2.5–4cm long. Racemes 10–20cm, with 20–40 flowers about 18mm long, the standard white with reddish purple veins at the base, the wings pink. Easily grown in a warm sheltered position and best in warm summer climates. Min. −10°C.

Lathyrus splendens Kell. (*Leguminosae*) A most beautiful climber with bright crimson or deep red flowers, native of California and N Mexico, from E San Diego Co. southwards, growing on dry slopes in chaparral, below 1000m, flowering in March–June. Stems to 3m, climbing by tendrils. Leaflets 6–10, linear to oval, 2–7cm long. Flowers 4–12, 3–4cm long. A very rare plant, photographed here at the Theodore Payne Foundation near Pasadena, which preserves and distributes Californian native plants.

Lupinus albifrons Benth. (*Leguminosae*) A rounded shrub with spikes of blue or purplish flowers, native of California in the Coast Ranges, from Humboldt Co. to Ventura Co. and in the foothills of the Sierras from Shasta Co. to Tulare Co. (with var. *eminens* [Greene] C. P. Sm., from Siskiyou Co. to San Diego Co.) growing in sandy and rocky places and on heathy hills, below 1700m, flowering in March–June. Shrub to 1.5m high and 2m wide. Leaves appressed silky, the leaflets 7–10, 1–3cm long. Inflorescence 8–30cm long with whorls of flowers 10–14mm long, the upper petal pubescent on the back, the keel with a long slender point, ciliate along the upper edge. For well-drained soil. Min. −5°C for coastal forms, perhaps less for those from inland. In *L. arboreus* L., which is usually yellow but can be blue, the banner is glabrous on the back and the keel does not have a slender point.

Anagyris foetida in S Turkey

Ebenus cretica

Clianthus formosus in King's Park Botanic Gardens, Perth

Clianthus puniceus white form

Clianthus puniceus pink form, in Devon, now dead

Castanospermum australe in Sydney Harbour Botanic Gardens

Castanospermum australe A. Cunn. & C. Fraser ex Hook. (*Leguminosae*) A handsome tree with long shining pinnate leaves and clusters of red or yellow flowers on the old wood, native of Vanuatu, New Caledonia and N Australia from the Cape York Peninsula to the Bellinger River in NSW, growing in rainforest and coastal scrub by rivers, flowering in September–November. Tree to 30m, but shorter to 8m in cooler areas. Leaves 30–45cm long with 8–17 leaflets, 7–12cm long. Flowers 3–4cm long with the standard reflexed, much visited by nectar-feeding parrots. Seed pods 10–25cm, with 3–5 seeds. Needs well-drained soil. Min. −5°C. The chestnut-like seeds contain castanospermine which has been used as an experimental drug in the treatment of AIDS.

Clianthus formosus (G. Don.) Ford & Vick. syn. *C. dampieri* Cunn. ex Lindl., *Swainsona formosa* (G. Don) J. Thompson (*Leguminosae*) Sturt's Desert Pea A prostrate annual or perennial with silky-hairy leaves and huge red flowers with a black blotch, native of much of the drier parts of Australia, growing in sandy or stony places in full sun, often over limestone, flowering in May–March (winter), though in spring–summer in cultivation in cool climates. Plants to 4m across. Leaflets 9–21, to 3cm long. Flowers to 7.5cm long, sometimes all red or rarely red and white. Min. −2°C. This spectacular plant has the reputation of being very difficult to grow. It is usually grown as an annual and needs excellent drainage, full sun and a good circulation of dry air if it is under glass. In hot climates the seed should be sown in autumn, in cool climates in early spring. Sow the seed either in its final position or in small pots so it can be put out without root disturbance. Plants need either a raised sandy bed about 30cm above the surrounding soil or a very deep pot, clay drainpipe or chimneypot. Fill with very sandy sterilized soil

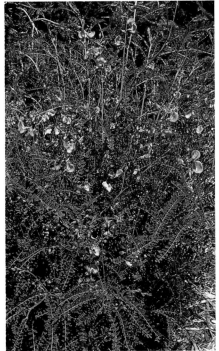

Swainsona galegifolia

Swainsona galegifolia 'Albiflora' in the Huntington Gardens, California

Templetonia retusa

with limestone chippings and top dress with 3cm of sand. Water sparingly and only from below once the seedlings are established and keep the foliage dry. Liquid fertilizer can be used to improve growth. In a hot dry summer, plants will do well outside on a sunny patio. Seedlings have been grafted successfully onto both *Colutea arborescens* and *Clianthus puniceus* to make the plants more perennial.

Clianthus puniceus (G. Don.) Sol. ex Lindl. A spreading shrub with dark green pinnate leaves and hanging bunches of large red, pink, or greenish-white flowers, native of New Zealand on North Island, in the inlets of the Bay of Islands, on the coast near Thames and inland at Lake Waikaremoana, growing in scrub and forest, flowering from winter to spring in gardens. Spreading shrub to 3m; leaves with up to 31 leaflets to 4.5cm long. Flowers to 8cm long. For any good soil in a warm position in frosty climates. Min. −5°C, perhaps lower for short periods if well sheltered, but soon killed by freezing winds. The colour forms are variously called by fancy names and come largely true from seed.

Hardenbergia violacea (Schneev.) Stearn (*Leguminosae*) An evergreen climber with single leaflets and masses of small purple flowers, native of most of Australia, in various habitats, flowering in spring. Stems to 2m; leaflets ovate to narrowly lanceolate, 3–13cm long. Flowers 8mm long, in dense racemes, the standard with a greenish-yellow centre. For any well-drained soil. Min. −5°C.

Swainsona galegifolia (Andr.) R. Br. (*Leguminosae*) A delicate soft-growing shrub with pinkish mauve, or white in **'Albiflora'** or rarely deep red or orange flowers in upright spikes, native of Victoria, New South Wales and Queensland, in various habitats, flowering most of the summer. Stems to 1m; leaves pale green, pinnate, leaflets 8–15mm. Flowers 15–20mm across. For moist sandy soil in a sunny position. Min. −3°C.

Templetonia retusa (Vent.) R .Br. (*Leguminosae*) A rounded or spreading shrub with simple leaves and red or rarely yellow flowers with a reflexed standard, native of South and Western Australia, growing on limestone, flowering in winter–early spring. Shrub to 2m tall, 3m wide. Leaves to 4cm, oblanceolate, retuse at apex. Flowers with standard about 2cm long. For well-drained limestone soil. Plants resistant to salt-spray. Min. 0°C.

Hardenbergia violacea

245

Tipuana tipu in Sydney Harbour Botanic Gardens

Erythrina livingstoniana wild near Monkey Bay, Malawi

Erythrina livingstoniana

Erythrina acanthocarpa E. Mey.
(*Leguminosae*) A low sparse thick-stemmed
shrub with scarlet, yellow- and green-tipped
flowers, native of South Africa in E Cape
Province, flowering in spring. Stems to 2m;
leaflets to 2.5cm long, 4cm wide, leathery,
glaucous, especially beneath. Flowers with
standard to 5cm long, 4cm wide. Fruit prickly.
Min. −5°C.

Erythrina caffra Thunb. A spreading shrub
or tree with angular spiny branches and short
spikes of red flowers, native of South Africa in
the Cape from Humansdorp eastwards to NE
Natal, growing in forest along the coast and by
rivers, flowering in August–September (spring)
before the leaves. Tree to 20m; leaflets to 9cm
long. Flowers with standard to 5.5cm long,
3.5cm wide. Drought-resistant in summer;
prune after flowering. Min. −5°C. Commonly
planted as a street tree in warm dry areas of
California where it is leafless from January
before flowering in March. *E. coralloides*
A. DC., from Mexico, has narrower flowers in
short dense heads.

Erythrina crista-galli L. A deciduous shrub or small tree with spiny branches and long spikes of large red flowers, native of South America east of the Andes, from Brazil to Argentina, flowering summer–autumn. Tree to 9m; leaflets to15cm long. Flowers held upside down, with recurved standard to 5.5cm long, 3.5cm wide. In frosty climates this can be grown as an herbaceous plant, sending up stems in spring from a woody rootstock. It flowered well at Wisley, Surrey, in a warm corner with the rootstock protected in winter. Min. −5°C. Commonly grown as a tree in warm areas. Give water in summer and prune after flowering.

Erythrina livingstoniana Bak. A large deciduous tree, like a brilliant red-flowered horse chestnut, native of Malawi, Mozambique and Zimbabwe, growing in rocky and sandy places, flowering in December (summer). Tree to 25m; leaflets to 17cm long, 3-lobed. Flowers with standard to 4cm long and wide. Pod deeply narrowed between the seeds. Min. −5°C. Photographed in Malawi near Monkey Bay.

Erythrina lysistemon Hutch. A large semi-evergreen tree with narrow scarlet flowers, native of South Africa in Natal and the Transvaal, growing in rocky and sandy places, flowering in spring. Tree to 10m, usually less; leaflets to 17cm long, ovate, tapering at apex. Flowers with standard to 6cm long, 2cm wide. Pod narrowed between the seeds. Min. −5°C. Photographed in the Huntington Gardens, Pasadena, California.

Sesbania punicea Benth. (*Leguminosae*) A graceful shrub with hanging branches and orange flowers, native of Brazil, Uruguay and NE Argentina, but naturalized in the SE United States and in South Africa, flowering in summer. Shrub to 1.8m. Leaves pinnate, the leaflets 2.5cm. Flowers about 2cm. Pods 4-winged, leathery. For good but well-drained soil. Prune after flowering. Min. −10°C for short periods. *S. grandiflora* (L.) Poir., from N Australia has larger curved red, pink or white flowers and long pods to 50cm.

Tipuana tipu (Benth.) Kuntze (*Leguminosae*) A large spreading tree with pinnate leaves and pendulous panicles of yellow flowers, native of Brazil, Argentina and Bolivia, flowering in summer. Deciduous or semi-evergreen tree to 35m; leaflets 11–20, 2.5–6cm long, downy beneath. Standard 2cm long and wide. A commonly planted tree in warm countries, fast-growing when young. Min. −6°C.

Erythrina acanthocarpa in the Huntington Gardens, California in April

Sesbania punicea in Natal

Erythrina lysistemon

Erythrina caffra

Erythrina crista-galli

Acacia dealbata in Lawrence Johnston's garden at La Serre de La Madonne in January

Acacia 'Exeter Hybrid' in the Temperate House at Kew

Acacia podalyriifolia in the Jardin Exotique du Val Rameh, Menton

Acacia dealbata A. Cunn. (*Leguminosae-Mimosoideae*) Silver Wattle, Mimosa   An upright large shrub or tree with grey bipinnate leaves and spikes of yellow globular scented flower heads, native of New South Wales, Victoria and Tasmania, growing in dry forest, flowering in July–October (winter). Tree fast-growing to 10m; branches white, hairy when young; leaves about 10cm long, with 10–25 pairs of pinnae about 3cm long. Pods 7–10cm, blue-green, not constricted between the seeds. For well-drained preferably moist soil, but stands drought and wet. Min. −10°C. This species is grown in many other parts of the world and is especially common in S France where it is used as a cut flower. The variety 'Mirandole' is said to be the hardiest. 'Pendula' is a lovely weeping form.
'Kambah Karpet' is a prostrate ground-covering form, grown in Australia.

Acacia paradoxa DC. syn. *A. armata* R. Br. A spreading shrub with slender branches and small flat leaves (phyllodes) with a pair of spiny stipules at the base, the globular flower heads borne singly in the leaf axils, native of Queensland, Western Australia, New South Wales, South Australia, Victoria and Tasmania, flowering in August–October. Shrub to 4m; leaves 1–3cm long, 0.5cm wide, flat with a prominent midrib off-centre. Flower heads 6mm across. Pods 4–8cm, usually hairy. A very tough plant which stands drought and wet well. Lime-tolerant and stands salt winds. Min. −5°C.

Acacia podalyriifolia A. Cunn. ex G. Don Queensland Silver Wattle   A silvery-white shrub with long slender branches, flat soft ovate or oblong leaves (phyllodes) and globular flower heads in long branched racemes, native of New South Wales and Queensland, flowering in July–October (winter–early spring). A tall open shrub to 5m; leaves 2–4cm long, 1.5–3cm wide with 1 clear nerve. Pods 6–8cm, flat, glaucous. Needs well-drained soil, but is otherwise tolerant. This lovely silver shrub is one of the most commonly cultivated species in Australia and grows well in S

France. It can be pruned hard after flowering. Min. −3°C.

Acacia 'Exeter Hybrid' syn. *A. × veitchiana* hort.   A tall shrub or small tree with long slender weeping branches, flat narrowly lanceolate leaves (phyllodes) and flowers in long slender spikes, flowering in winter–early spring. A tree to 5m; leaves scattered or in groups, dark green, 1.5–5cm long, 2–4mm wide with 1 or 3 nerves and a fine sharp point. Pale yellow flowers in spikes around 7cm long. Pods not seen. Needs moisture-retentive well-drained soil, but dislikes drought. Prune after flowering. This is one of the best winter-flowering trees for a tall conservatory and will make a lovely weeping tree outside in mild climates. It is variously considered a hybrid between *A. longifolia* and *A. riceana* or a form of *A. riceana* Henslow, a Tasmanian species, which usually has narrower leaves. Min. −3°C.

Acacia vestita Ker-Gawl.   A silvery shrub with long pendulous branches, flat ovate or elliptic softly-hairy leaves (phyllodes) and globular flower heads in long racemes, native of New South Wales, growing in dry forest, often in sheltered gullies, flowering in August–October (winter–early spring). A tall open shrub to 6m; leaves 1–2 cm with wavy edges, soft, hairy and grey-green. Pods 4–8cm, flat, glaucous. One of the more tolerant species for damp conditions, but will not stand drought. Min. −3°C. Grows from cuttings. Photographed in Malawi.

Acacia dealbata 'Kambah Karpet' in Canberra

Acacia vestita in Malawi

Acacia paradoxa in the cold house at Wisley

Acacia saligna in California

Acacia melanoxylon naturalised in Madeira

Acacia glaucoptera in the Huntington Gardens, California in April

Acacia calamifolia Sweet ex Lindl.
(*Leguminosae*) An upright or spreading shrub
with long slender flat leaves (phyllodes) and
1–4 globular flower heads in the leaf axil,
native of New South Wales, Victoria and
South Australia, growing in dry woodland,
flowering in July–November. Shrub to 5m;
leaves 5–20cm long and 1–5mm wide, flat,
ending in a curved point. Pods 12–20cm,
narrow, straight or curved, slightly constricted
between the seeds. For well-drained soil, but
stands drought and wet. Lime-tolerant. Min.
−3°C.

Acacia glaucoptera Benth. A spreading
shrub with long flat greyish stems formed by
the wing-like phyllodes and 1 globular flower
head in the leaf notch, native of Western
Australia, flowering in August–November.
Shrub to 1.5m tall and more across; stems
2.5cm wide, the young growth sometimes
purplish. Pods 4–5cm, circular, slightly
constricted between the seeds. For well-
drained soil, but stands drought. Somewhat
lime-tolerant. Min. 0°C.

Acacia mearnsii De Wild. Black Wattle
An upright large shrub or tree with greyish
bipinnate leaves and spikes of pale yellow
globular scented flower heads, native of New
South Wales, Victoria, South Australia and
Tasmania, growing in dry forests, flowering in
September–December (spring). Tree fast-
growing to 25m; leaves 6–15cm long with
10–25 pairs of pinnae. Pods 5–15cm, dark
brown or black, very constricted between the
seeds. For well-drained soil, but stands
drought and wet. Min. −5°C. This species is
commonly naturalized in warm semi-arid
climates and is a pest in parts of South Africa,
destroying the natural vegetation and
regenerating quickly after fire.

Acacia melanoxylon R. Br. Blackwood
An upright or spreading large shrub or tree
with flat leaves (phyllodes) and large globular

Acacia mearnsii naturalised in Madeira

Acacia calamifolia at Kew

Acacia mearnsii in Madeira

flower heads in short racemes in the leaf axil, native of Queensland, New South Wales, Victoria, South Australia and Tasmania, growing in wet, cool forest, flowering in July–October (early spring). Tree to 30m; leaves 7–15cm long and 1–3cm wide, flat, elliptic. Flowers cream to pale yellow. Pods 5–15cm long and about 1cm wide, slightly twisted. For moist well-drained soil and prefers cool climates, growing well in western Britain. It can become a nuisance by suckering. Min. −10°C.

Acacia saligna (Labill.) H. Wendl. syn. *A. cyanophylla* Lindl. An upright shrub or small tree with long, slender, often hanging, branches and long, narrow flat leaves (phyllodes), and globular flower heads in short racemes in the leaf axil, native of Western Australia, flowering in August–November. Tree to 10m; leaves 8–30cm long, 1–8cm wide, flat with a prominent midrib. Pods 5–15cm, narrow, slightly constricted between the seeds. For well-drained soil, but stands

drought and wet well. Lime-tolerant and stands salt winds. Min. −5°C.

Acacia trigonophylla Meisn. A small spreading shrub with winged stems, decurrent phyllodes ending in a curved point and globular flower heads, 1 in each leaf axil, native of Western Australia, flowering in October–November. Shrub to 2.5m; leaves triangular, ending in a curved point. Flower heads about 1.5cm across; pods 5–7.5cm, flat with thickened margins. For well-drained soil, but stands drought and wet and prefers light shade. Prune after flowering. Min. −3°C.

Acacia trigonophylla in Perth

Acacia pravissima

Acacia verticillata

Acacia baileyana

Acacia lineata

Acacia longifolia

Acacia adunca

Acacia decora

Acacia cultriformis

Acacia decurrens

Acacia cardiophylla

Acacia mucronata

Acacia retinodes

Specimens from Hollington Nurseries, Newbury, February 10th, 2/5 life size

Acacia adunca A. Cunn. ex G. Don.
An upright shrub or small tree with slender branches and narrow flat leaves (phyllodes) and globular flower heads in a long raceme in the leaf axil, native of Queensland and New South Wales, flowering in April–November. A bushy and very floriferous tree to 8m; leaves 7–15cm long and 2–4mm wide, flat, linear. For well-drained soil, but stands drought and wet well. Good for subtropical areas. Min. −5°C.

Acacia baileyana F. Muell. Cootamundra Wattle A spreading dense large shrub or small tree with greyish bipinnate leaves and long spikes of bright yellow globular scented flower heads, native of S New South Wales, only in the West Wyalong district, growing in mallee on acid soils, flowering in July–September (winter–spring). Tree fast-growing to 8m; leaves about 10cm long with 10–25 pairs of pinnae, each 2–5cm long. One of the most beautiful and popular species; 'Purpurea' has purplish young growth and there is a golden-leaved form 'Aurea'. For well-drained soil, but stands drought and wet. Prune after flowering to keep in shape. Min. −5°C.

Acacia cardiophylla A. Cunn. ex Benth. Wyalong Wattle A spreading dense large shrub or small tree with greyish bipinnate leaves and long spikes of 9–20 bright yellow globular, scented flower heads, native of New South Wales, growing on stony ridges and stream banks, in mallee, flowering in August (spring). Shrub to 4m; leaves 2.5–6cm long with 12–15 pairs of pinnae, each about 1cm long. Pinnules 1–2mm, ovate, hairy. A beautiful species with small delicate leaves and scented flowers. For well-drained soil and full sun, but stands drought well. Prune after flowering to keep in shape. Min. −5°C.

Acacia cultriformis A. Cunn. ex G. Don. A grey shrub with drooping slender branches, flat knife-shaped or almost triangular leaves (phyllodes) and flower heads globular or elongated in long branched racemes in the upper leaf axils, native of Queensland and New South Wales, growing on rocky ridges, flowering in August–November. A bushy shrub to 4m; leaves 1–2.5cm long and 8–12mm wide with thickened edges. Needs very well-drained soil, but stands drought well. Min. −5°C.

Acacia decora Rchb. An upright shrub with slender branches, crowded, narrow flat leaves (phyllodes) and globular flower heads in racemes that are usually longer than the leaves, native of Queensland, New South Wales and Victoria, flowering in August–October. A shrub to 5m; leaves 2–5cm long, 5–10mm wide, flat, linear, slightly curved. Flowers golden-yellow. For well-drained soil, but stands drought and wet well. Often planted as a windbreak and can be pruned to keep in shape. Min. −5°C.

Acacia decurrens (Wendl.) Willd.
A spreading dense large shrub or small tree with green bipinnate leaves and long spikes of bright yellow globular scented flower heads, native of New South Wales and naturalized elsewhere, often growing on river banks, flowering in July–November (winter–spring). Tree fast-growing to 15m; leaves about 15cm long with 6–12 pairs of pinnae. Flowers deep golden-yellow. A popular species, planted in parks and large gardens in Australia; similar to *A. dealbata*, but with green not grey leaves. Min. −5°C.

Acacia lineata A. Cunn. ex G. Don
A small spreading shrub with hairy branches, flat linear-lanceolate curve-pointed leaves (phyllodes) and single or paired globular flower heads in the leaf axils, native of Queensland, Victoria, South Australia and New South Wales, flowering in August–November. Shrub to 3m; leaves 1–2cm long, 1–4mm wide, flat with a prominent vein near the upper edge. For well-drained soil; stands drought well. Min. −5°C.

Acacia longifolia (Andr.) Willd.
A spreading shrub or small tree with narrow flat leaves (phyllodes) and narrow elongated flower heads, native of New South Wales, Victoria, South Australia and Tasmania, flowering in July–October. A fast-growing, very variable tree to 10m; leaves 7–15cm long, 1–2.5cm wide, flat, narrowly elliptical, straight or slightly curved. Flowers bright-yellow in rods 2–6cm long. Easily grown in well-drained soil. Min. −5°C.

Acacia mucronata Willd. ex H. Wendl.
An upright or spreading shrub with narrow flat leaves (phyllodes) and elongated flower spikes in racemes that are usually much shorter than the leaves, native of Tasmania, with var. *longifolia* Benth., in New South Wales and Victoria, flowering in August–November. A shrub to 6m and as much across. Leaves very variable, 3–20cm long, 3–10mm wide, flat, linear, slightly curved. Flowers cream to yellow. Pods 6–15cm, narrow, straight. For well-drained soil and very tolerant of drought. Min. −5°C.

Acacia pravissima F. Muell. A blue-grey shrub or small tree with drooping slender branches, flat triangular leaves (phyllodes) and globular flower heads in long branched racemes in the upper leaf axils, native of New South Wales and Victoria, growing mainly in mountains south of Canberra, flowering in September–October (spring). A tall open shrub or tree to 8m; leaves 0.5–2cm long and about 1cm wide with 2–3 clear nerves. This is one of the hardiest and most tolerant species to grow in cool moist climates and does well outside in W Britain. Unfortunately it is difficult to root from cuttings. Min. −10°C. **'Golden Carpet'** is a low-spreading form with weeping branches, cultivated in Australia.

Acacia retinodes Schltdl. Swamp Wattle
An upright shrub or small tree with long, slender, often hanging, branches and long narrow flat leaves (phyllodes). Flower heads small, globular in short racemes in the leaf axils, native of South Australia, Victoria and Tasmania, flowering most of the year. Tree to 8m; leaves 5–20cm long and 0.5–2cm wide, flat, pointed with a prominent midrib. Best in well-drained soil, but stands drought and wet well. Lime- and salt-tolerant and stands salt winds. Commonly planted in southern Europe and California. Min. −5°C.

Acacia verticillata (L'Herit.) Willd. Prickly Moses An upright or spreading bristly shrub with whorls of 6 short stiff leaves (phyllodes) and ovoid or rod-like flower heads, native of New South Wales, South Australia, Victoria and Tasmania, flowering in June–October (winter–spring). A tall open shrub to 6m; leaves 1–2cm with a sharp point. Needs well-drained moist soil and some shade, but is otherwise tolerant. Will grow from cuttings. The roots smell of garlic. Min. −5°C.

Acacia retinodes in California

Acacia pravissima 'Golden Carpet' in Canberra

Acacia karroo in the Hanbury Botanic Garden, La Mortola, Ventimiglia in September

Calliandra californica in a dry garden in Palm Springs

Calliandra haematocephala in the Huntington Gardens, California in April

Acacia berlandieri Benth. Huajillo
A spreading shrub or small tree with long narrow pinnae and widely branched clusters of pale yellow globular heads, native of S Texas and N Mexico, growing in semi-desert, flowering in spring. Flowers sweetly scented and a good source of honey. For dry areas, tolerant of heat and drought. Min. −5°C, perhaps less. *Acacia farnesiana* (L.) Willd. (*not shown*), is native of Arizona south to Argentina, often grown for its very sweet scent. It has spines 1–3cm long and leaves with 2–8 pairs of pinnae. It can be grown in a pot under glass to flower in winter and makes a small tree in the open garden. Min. −3°C.

Acacia karroo Hayne   A spreading thorny tree with bipinnate leaves and globose heads of flowers, native of Africa in the Cape, from Worcester eastwards and north to the tropics, growing on dry hills, flowering in summer. Tree to 22m; leaves with 2–6 pairs of pinnae. Flower heads 5mm across in open clusters of 5–8. Pods curved, constricted between the seeds. For dry poor soils. Min. −5°C.

Calliandra californica Benth (*Mimosoideae*) Fairy Duster A low spreading shrub with pinnate leaves and bright crimson flowers in solitary heads with long stamens, native of N Mexico, in Baja California growing in desert scrub, usually below 1500m, flowering much of the year. Shrub to 1m high; leaves with 6–9 pairs of pinnae. Stamens 1.5–2cm long. Similar to *C. eriophylla*, but with larger leaves. In gardens in Palm Springs the flowers of this species are

Calliandra eriophylla at the Living Desert Reserve, Palm Desert, California

Calliandra portoricensis at Kew

much visited by hummingbirds. For desert conditions or dry well-drained soil with a little water to keep it flowering through the summer. Min. −3°C.

Calliandra emarginata (Humb. & Bonpl. ex Willd.) Benth.   A shrub with pinnate leaves and crimson flowers in dense heads with long stamens, native from S Mexico to Honduras, flowering most of the year. Shrub to 3m high; leaves with only 1 pair of pinnae; leaflets in 1–5 pairs, 3–6cm long, oblique, elliptic or obovate. Flower heads about 7cm across. Flowers with stamens about 3cm long, deep crimson to nearly white. For warm sheltered positions. Min. 0°C.

Calliandra eriophylla Benth. Fairy Duster A low-spreading shrub with small pinnate leaves and rose-pink to purplish-pink flowers in solitary heads with long stamens, native of S California to W Texas and to N Mexico in Baja California, growing in desert scrub, in sandy washes and gullies, usually below 1500m, flowering in February–March. Shrub to 1.2m high; leaves with 2–4 pairs of pinnae. Stamens 1.5–2cm long. Pods 5–7cm, silvery with a red edge. For desert conditions or dry well-drained soil. Min. −3°C.

Calliandra haematocephala Hassk.
A shrub or small tree with pinnate leaves and white and rose-pink flowers in dense heads with long stamens, native of Bolivia, flowering in October–March (winter). Shrub to 6m high, fast-growing to 3m; leaves to 20cm with 1 pair of pinnae and 5–10 pairs of leaflets to 8cm. Stamens about 3cm long. Pods 6–10cm, smooth. Flowers with stamens white at base, reddening above. For light well-drained soil and ample water in dry periods. Min. −3°C or less in colder areas with wall protection.

Calliandra portoricensis (Jacq.) Benth. Small tree or shrub with bipinnate leaves and white flowers in solitary heads with long stamens, native of Central America, flowering in June–July. Shrub to 3m or tree to 6m; leaves with 2–7 pairs of pinnae; leaflets overlapping. Stamens about 2cm long. Pods to 13cm. For moist conditions in partial shade. Min. 0°C.

Calliandra emarginata in the Huntington Gardens, California in April

Calliandra californica detail

Acacia berlandieri in California

The spectacular flowers of *Delonix regia*, the Gul Mohur tree, in Malawi

Bauhinia variegata in Hong Kong

Bauhinia forficata at Clos du Peyronnet

Bauhinia tomentosa in the garden near Blantyre, Malawi

Bauhinia × blakeana Dunn. (*Leguminosae-Caesalpinoideae*) An evergreen or briefly deciduous shrub or small spreading tree to 12m, with characteristically bilobed leaves and purple flowers mainly in autumn–early winter. A hybrid between two E Asian species, probably *B. purpurea* and *B. variegata*, commonly cultivated especially in Hong Kong and N Australia. Leaves bluish-green, to 20cm long, bilobed to about a third with rounded lobes. Flowers about 15cm across, maroon-red to pink, with petals not overlapping. Needs a warm climate and can be grown in a large pot, watered well in summer. Min. −3°C for short periods. The unusual two-lobed leaves of this genus reminded Linnaeus of the Bauhin brothers, Jean and Caspar, who together wrote the *Pinax*, a list with synonyms of all the plants then known, published in 1623.

Bauhinia faberi Oliv. A small shrub or scrambler with the characteristic bilobed leaves and heads of small white flowers, native of China where it is common in W Yunnan and W Sichuan, growing by roadsides and on dry open hillsides at up to 2000m, flowering in May. Shrub to 2m. Leaves lobed to a third, to 5.5cm long or 6–12mm in var. *microphylla* Oliv., from the Min Valley. Petals to 1cm long. This is one of the hardiest species and would be a useful parent of dwarfer, hardier *Bauhinias*. Min. −10°C.

Bauhinia forficata Link. syn. *B. candicans* Benth. An evergreen or deciduous shrub or tree with large narrow-petalled white flowers, native of Brazil, flowering in summer. Tree to 15m, often leaning or twisted with spiny branches; leaves to 12cm long, bilobed to halfway, with pointed lobes. Flowers opening at night and shrivelling on hot days. Petals linear to lanceolate, 5–10cm long and to 2.5cm wide. One of the hardier species. Min. −7°C.

Bauhinia tomentosa L. A small shrub bearing lovely open bell-shaped pale yellow flowers with a reddish spot inside, native of India, Sri Lanka, SE Asia and E Africa, flowering most of the year. Shrub to 5m, but usually about 2m; leaves to 8cm, bilobed to one third. Petals to 6cm long. Easily grown in subtropical climates, even in semi-arid areas. Min. 0°C.

Bauhinia variegata L. Orchid tree
A spreading usually deciduous shrub or tree with characteristic bilobed leaves and large pink to purple flowers, native of E Asia from Pakistan to S China, flowering mainly in winter–early spring. Tree to 12m; leaves bluish-green, to 20cm, bilobed to a third. Petals usually obovate, overlapping, 4–6cm long, the uppermost heavily feathered with dark purple. For a warm sunny position. Min. −5°C. *B. purpurea* L. from the same area, differs in its more deeply lobed leaves (to half), its mainly autumn flowering and its non-overlapping petals.

Bauhinia variegata 'Candida' syn. *B. candida* Roxb. A white-flowered form of *B. variegata*, with flowers marked with green.

Delonix regia (Bojer) Raf. (*Leguminosae-Caesalpinoideae*) Poinciana, Flamboyant, Gul Mohur tree A large wide-spreading

Schotia brachypetala flowering on the branches in the Botanical gardens in Pietermaritzburg, Natal

Bauhinia variegata 'Candida'

Bauhinia faberi wild on dry hills near Dali, Yunnan in May

deciduous tree with pale green feathery leaves and bright red flowers, native of Madagascar near the west coast S of Maintirano in the Antsengy Forest Reserve, growing on steep rocks, but now common in India, SE Asia and even naturalized in S Florida. Tree to 15m and as much across. Leaves with up to 40 pairs of pinnae, folding at dusk. Flowers about 10cm across. Seed pods woody, reddish-brown to 60cm long, taking 2 years to ripen. For any well-drained site; a beautiful shade tree, but has greedy and invasive roots spreading at least 10m from the trunk. There is a variety with golden-yellow flowers. Min. 0°C.

Schotia brachypetala Sond. (*Leguminosae-Caesalpinoideae*)   A large shrub or wide-spreading tree with pinnate leaves and small crimson flowers often emerging from old branches, native of SE Africa from Zimbabwe and Mozambique to Natal, flowering in summer. Tree to 10m; leaves to 17cm with 4–7 pairs of leaflets. Flowers with a red 4-lobed calyx to 2cm long and minute petals. Min. −5°C, perhaps.

Bauhinia × *blakeana* in the Huntington Gardens, California in April

Cassia alata wild in the hills near Copala above Mazatlán, Mexico in October

Caesalpinia gilliesii (Wall. ex Hook.) Benth. (*Leguminosae-Caesalpinoideae*) A deciduous or evergreen shrub or small tree with ferny leaves and racemes of yellow flowers with long red stamens, native of Uruguay and Argentina, flowering in spring–summer. Shrub fast-growing to 3m. Young shoots glandular-hairy. Leaves about 20cm. Petals about 2cm; stamens to 7cm long. An exotic plant to attract hummingbirds; for any soil with heat and water in summer, drier in winter. Will usually resprout if cut down by frost in winter. Min. −10°C.
Caesalpinia pulcherrima (L.) Sw. syn. *Poinciana pulcherrima*, the Flamboyant tree, differs in its larger, usually red petals and eglandular young shoots. It needs more heat to grow and flower well and is good in S California.

Caesalpinia mexicana Gray An evergreen shrub or small tree with pinnate leaves and racemes of yellow flowers, native of Mexico, flowering most of the year. Tree to 10m; leaflets to 2.5cm long, 2cm wide; racemes about 30cm; flowers about 3cm across. Min. −5°C.
Caesalpinia decapetala (Roth.) Alston, has rather similar flowers, but is a thorny and often rampant climber, native from India east to Japan. It will succeed on a wall in N Europe. Min. −10°C.

Calliandra grandiflora (L'Hérit.) Benth. (*Leguminosae-Mimosoideae*) Large-flowering Sensitive Plant A tall shrub with ferny leaves and small greenish flowers with long red stamens, native of Mexico and the West Indies, growing in openings in evergreen oak forest in the mountains, flowering in autumn–winter. Shrub to 2m; leaves pinnate with linear leaflets. Stamens about 10cm long. In spite of its superficial resemblance to *Ceasalpinia gilliesii*, this plant is close to the other *Calliandra* species (*shown on p. 255*). It was grown in Europe in the 18th century and was illustrated, with two attendant hummingbirds, by Dr Robert Thornton in the famous *Temple of Flora* in 1812. *C. houstoniana* (Mill.) Standl. from S Mexico and Honduras is rather similar.

Cassia alata L. syn. *Senna alata* (L.) Roxb. (*Leguminosae-Caesalpinoideae*) A shrub or tree with large pinnate leaves and erect spike-like racemes of yellow flowers, native of C America, tropical Africa and SE Asia, growing on rocky hillsides, flowering in autumn–winter. A tree to 10m, but usually a wide shrub to 4m. Leaves with 7–14 pairs of leaflets, each 7–14 cm long and 3–13.5cm wide. Racemes to 60cm; flowers about 3cm across. A bold and striking shrub for a warm position. Min. 0°C.
C. magnifolia F. Muell., from N Australia is rather similar, but has shorter racemes.

Cassia corymbosa Lam. syn. *Senna corymbosa* (Lam.) Irwin & Barnaby A spreading shrub with short racemes of yellow flowers, native of Uruguay and Argentina and naturalized in parts of California, Texas and S Carolina, flowering in spring–autumn. Shrub to 4m; leaflets 25–80mm long, 5–15mm wide; flowers about 30mm across. Easily grown in any well-drained soil. Min. −5°C.

Cassia didymobotrya Fres. syn. *Senna didymobotrya* (Fres.) Irwin & Barnaby An upright evergreen shrub with spike-like racemes of yellow flowers from blackish buds, native of tropical Africa, S India to Malaysia

Cassia corymbosa in Cornwall

Cassia phyllodinea in Canberra

Petalostylis labicheoides in Perth

Caesalpinia mexicana in California

Calliandra grandiflora above Tequila

Caesalpinia gilliesii in a garden at Palm Springs in April

Cassia didymobotrya in Natal

Cassia spectabilis in Malawi

and naturalized elsewhere in the tropics, growing in waste places, flowering in winter–early summer. Stems to 3m; leaves with 8–18 pairs of leaflets about 5cm long. Racemes to 30cm; flowers about 4cm across. A heat-loving shrub requiring water in summer until well-established. Min. −3°C.

Cassia phyllodinea R. Br. syn. *Senna artemisiodes* (DC.) Randell subsp. *petiolaris* Randell   A rounded or prostrate shrub with silky silvery leaves reduced to curved phyllodes and short racemes of flowers, native of Australia from Queensland to New South Wales and South Australia, growing on dry plains inland, flowering most of the year when watered, otherwise mainly in winter. Shrub to 2.5m. Phyllodes 1–5cm long and 0.5cm wide, greyish, sometimes with 1–2 pairs of leaflets. Flowers about 12mm across. Good for semi-desert conditions. Min. −5°C or lower for short periods.
C. artemisioides Gaud. ex DC., from the

Northern Territories, New South Wales and South Australia, is an attractive shrub with 4–8 pairs of silvery terete leaflets. A better garden plant in less dry climates. Min. −5°C.

Cassia spectabilis DC. syn. *Senna spectabilis* (DC.) Irwin & Barnaby   A large spreading shrub or small tree with lush green leaves and large broad loose racemes of flowers, native of Central and South America. Tree to 20m. Leaves with 8–20 pairs of leaflets, 17–45mm long, variable in width. Flowers 5–8cm across, long-stalked. For a moist climate. Min. 0°C.

Petalostylis labicheoides R. Br. (*Leguminosae-Caesalpinoideae*)   A rounded evergreen shrub with pinnate leaves and yellow *Cassia*-like flowers, native of the drier regions of Australia, growing in sandy places and rocky ridges, flowering mainly in spring. Shrub to 3m high and as much across. Leaflets to 2cm; flowers to 4cm across. For a well-drained soil in full sun. Min. −3°C.

259

Rosa banksiae × *gigantea* with *Wisteria* in Joanna Millar's garden near Vence in Alpes Maritimes

Rosa banksiae var. *normalis* wild near Dali, Yunnan

Cascades of *Rosa banksiae* var. *normalis* wild in NW Sichuan

Rosa banksiae 'Lutea' in Spain

Rosa banksiae 'Lutescens' at La Mortola

Of the thousands of roses in cultivation, there are some which are definitely happier in warm climates or grown under glass. It is sad that nearly all modern rose breeders concentrate on roses which are hardy; few bother to breed any for subtropical climates and thereby fail to make use of some of the exciting tender species. Most modern roses do however thrive in places as warm as S California and David Austin's English Roses do very well there too. Many of the roses shown here originated in warm parts of China or were bred in France in the 19th century from Chinese roses. They are definitely tender and do best in subtropical areas. They are still among the most beautiful and distinct roses grown today.

Rosa banksiae R. Br. in Ait. var. **banksiae** syn. 'Alba Plena' The double white was the first form of *R. banksiae* to be named. It was brought from China to Kew by William Kerr in 1807. The white form now cultivated in Europe is less thorny and has larger, softer leaves than the form commonly seen in the Lijiang Valley in SW China (*illustrated here*). The Lijiang Valley form makes an arching shrub and is planted to make hedges animal-proof. It appears to be a double form of the wild type, whereas the European double white looks like a white form of the double yellow 'Lutea'. Easily grown and once-flowering in early spring. Min. −10°C.

Rosa banksiae R. Br, in Ait. **'Lutea'** is the double yellow and **'Lutescens'** the single yellow form of *R. banksiae*. Both are ancient Chinese garden plants of unknown origin and may be hybrids with a yellow tea rose as their leaves have something of the tea rose texture – larger and softer than those of the wild *R. banksiae*. 'Lutea' was introduced to Europe by John Parks in 1824. It is a lovely plant for a conservatory, early-flowering and almost thornless. In warm climates it is magnificent, a large free-flowering climber. Min. −10°C.

Rosa banksiae Aiton var. **normalis** Regel This is the wild type of *R. banksiae*, common

Rosa banksiae var. *banksiae* planted in hedges in the Lijiang Valley

in hedges, growing into trees or hanging down steep rocky hillsides at low altitudes below 2000m, from Hubei and Gansu to Yunnan. It flowers well before any of the white roses of the synstylae section, usually in March–June according to altitude. The small flowers, about 2cm across, are in umbels. Min. −10°C. There is also a single white cultivar which has the leaf characters of the yellow and may be a sport of the cultivated double white.

Rosa banksiae × R. gigantea A beautiful rose which is probably of this parentage is grown by Joanna Millar at her garden in S France near Grasse. The long branches arch down, with umbels of about 5 large flowers from every leaf bud of the previous year.

Rosa banksiae var. *banksiae* in Spain

Rosa rubus forming huge, arching shrubs in NW Sichuan in May

Rosa rubus

Rosa laevigata in Menton in April

Rosa phoenicea climbing into a pomegranate tree near Antalya in May

Rosa bracteata Wendl.   A dense thorny climber with small shiny rounded evergreen leaflets and large white flowers over a long season, native of SE China and Taiwan, flowering from late spring onwards. Stems to 6m; leaflets 5–11, to 5cm long; flowers to 10cm across, solitary, the stalk hidden by soft hairy bracts. Introduced in 1793 by Lord Macartney's embassy to the emperor of China. This is a good rose for a warm climate but does not flower very freely outside in England, though it survives on warm walls in S England. Min. −10°C.

Rosa cymosa Tratt. syn. *R. microcarpa* Lindl. A climbing or cascading rose with large flat corymbs of very small flowers, native of most of China from W Sichuan and Hubei eastwards, growing in warm humid areas, in hedges and river gorges at up to 1300m, flowering in April–June (late spring) well after *R. banksiae*. Stems to 5m; leaflets 5–7, narrowly ovate, often acuminate; flowers about 1.5cm across. Styles exserted but not united. Hips about 5mm across, greenish to dull red. Probably needs similar treatment to *R. banksiae*. Min. −10°C, perhaps.

Rosa laevigata Michx. Cherokee Rose A rampant climber, or if pruned or grazed, a dense shrub, with shiny evergreen leaves and large white flowers, native of China from Sichuan and Hubei to Taiwan and found wild as an introduction in Japan and in SE North America, growing in scrub and rocky places at up to 1000m, flowering in January (in Hong Kong)–June. Stems to 10m or more; leaflets 3; flowers to 10cm across; ovary bristly.

Introduced to America in the early 17th century. Easily grown and beautiful in areas which are warm enough for it to flower well. Min. −10°C, and cut to the ground in hard winters even in S England.

Rosa phoenicea Boiss.   A climber or large shrub with arching branches, hairy coarsely-toothed leaflets and corymbs of rather small very fragrant white flowers, native of NE Greece to S Turkey eastwards to Siirt, Syria and Lebanon, growing in hedges and in scrub mainly near the coast at up to 1100m, flowering in May–June. Stems to 5m; leaflets usually 5, 2–4.5cm long, densely short-hairy beneath, with distinct very broad, coarse teeth. Flowers 3–5cm across. This is significant as one of the likely parents of the original Damask rose, the other being *R. gallica*. We found it common along the south coast of Turkey around Antalya but the seeds we collected have not germinated and it awaits reintroduction. Probably not very hardy.

Rosa rubus Lév. & Vaniot   A climber or large shrub with arching branches, hairy bramble-like leaves and corymbs of large, very fragrant creamy-white flowers, native of W China in W Hubei and Guizhou to SW Sichuan, growing in hedges and rocky hillsides, usually below 1800m, flowering in May–June. Stems to 6m; leaflets densely short-hairy beneath, usually 5, ovate, acuminate, the terminal about 8.5cm long. Flowers about 5cm across. This is one of the finest of the synstylae for its large well-scented flowers. Min. −15°C.

Rosa cymosa on Omei Shan

Rosa bracteata at Kew

Rosa chinensis var. spontanea near Pingwu, NW Sichuan

Rosa chinensis var. spontanea in NW Sichuan, showing colour change

Shrub-covered hills near Pingwu, NW Sichuan, habitat of Rosa chinensis var. spontanea

Rosa chinensis Jacq. var. **chinensis**
(*Rosaceae*)   This species and the tea rose are
the ancestors of all the modern large repeat-
flowering roses grown in the world today. The
first description of *Rosa chinensis* was given in
1768 by Nicolaus von Jacquin, a botanist and
gardener born in Holland of French parents,
working in Vienna. His illustration in
Observationum Botanicarum 3:7, t.55 and
description of the flowers was of 'Slater's
Crimson China' although it was introduced to
Europe later than 'Parson's Pink'. Four early
cultivars of *Rosa chinensis* are shown here:
'Parsons' Pink China' syn. 'Old Blush',
'Monthly Rose', *R.* × *odorata* 'Pallida'   This
was the first China rose to come to Europe and
its date of introduction to Sweden is variously
given as 1763 by a Capt. Ekeberg, or 1752 by
Peter Osbeck, a pupil of Linnaeus. In any case,
it was grown in London by 1789 and in Paris
by 1798. It was introduced into commerce
from the garden of Mr Parsons of
Rickmansworth near London in 1793 and
from him derived its common English name. It
is an ancient Chinese garden rose, known from
10th-century paintings and still grows in China
today where it (and 'Slater's Crimson') are
both known as *ue ji* (monthly). These Chinese
repeat-flowering roses are usually dwarf plants,
in contrast to the once-flowering wild China
rose *Rosa chinensis* f. *spontanea*, which is
usually a large arching shrub, but can become
a tall climber if growing up through trees. The
dwarfs were doubtless selected by Chinese
gardeners for their perpetual flowering and
small size. The several-flowered stems of many
of these pink China roses suggest that they
may be hybrids with *Rosa multiflora* or some
other many-flowered rose, since wild *R.
chinensis* always has a single flower on each
stem. They may also have *R. gigantea* in their
ancestry and are sometimes listed under *R.* ×
odorata (Andr.) Sweet. 'Parsons' Pink China'
is still a good garden rose in a mild climate,
long-lived, flowering throughout the summer

'Single Red China' in Devon

Rosa chinensis var. chinensis
'Slater's Crimson China'

'Single Pink China' in Chengdu

'Parson's Pink China' in a village garden in NW Sichuan

and autumn and growing well in humid summers. Min. −15°C.

'Single Pink China' This may be a single sport of 'Parsons' Pink', but is also an old Chinese variety, still to be found growing in gardens in China in Chengdu, for example, where it forms a bush around 2m tall. In cool gardens in England it is usually much smaller, to 60cm. For a warm position. Min. −10°C.

'Single Red China' syn. 'Rose de Bengale', 'Miss Lowe', 'Sanguinea' First recorded in 1887. A beautiful single red rose, forming a dwarf bush in the open, but climbing to 3m or more if supported. Flowers about 7cm across, deep crimson in hot weather, paler in autumn. There may be two very similar clones in this group, the larger 'Sanguinea', the smaller 'Miss Lowe'. Like 'Mutabilis', this rose probably also belongs to *R.* × *odorata.* For a sheltered position and tolerant of partial shade. Min. −10°C.

'Slater's Crimson China' syn. 'Semperflorens', 'Old Crimson' A dwarf double, perpetual-flowering rose introduced from China by Gilbert Slater of Knot's Green, Hertfordshire in about 1791. This appears to be the same clone as the specimen on which Jacquin based his name *R. chinensis.* It is still grown in China and when filming the *Quest for the Rose,* we found it growing in the sluice operator's garden outside Ping-Wu, near where the wild *R. chinensis* grows. It is also illustrated in the Reeves drawings of Chinese garden plants painted in Canton in about 1815. It is a dwarf, rather feeble plant, free-flowering but seldom showy. Min. −10°C.

'Mateo's Silk Butterflies' This beautiful continual-flowering hybrid was the best of several seedlings raised by Kleine Lettunich in 1990 in California by crossing 'Mutabilis' with 'Francis E Lester', a climbing single hybrid musk. It makes a round bush to 2m across, covered with heads of delicate flowers which open yellowish and fade to deep pink. Does best in a hot climate, given ample water. Min. −10°C.

'Mutabilis' syn. 'Tipo Idéale', *R.* × *odorata* 'Mutabilis' An ancient Chinese garden rose seen in China recently by Mikinori Ogisu but now rare there, though commonly grown in England. Its date of introduction to Europe is not known but it was first recorded in Italy in 1896. The large loose flowers suggest that this

is probably a hybrid with *R. gigantea* but the changing colour of the flowers, from pale orange to deep pink is typical of wild *R. chinensis.* 'Mutabilis' usually makes a bush up to 1.5m, but if trained on a wall, as at Kiftsgate Court, can reach 6m. Min. −15°C.

Rosa chinensis Jacq. var. *spontanea* (Rehder & Wilson) Yu & Ku syn. 'Henry's Crimson China' The wild China rose is usually a large arching evergreen shrub but can become a tall climber if growing up through trees, native of W China from SW Sichuan, near Leibo and at the foot of Omei Shan, to S Gansu and W Hubei, growing by rivers, in mountain scrub and in open grassy places at 800–1950m, flowering in April–May, at the same time as *R. banksiae.* Stems to 5m when climbing, but usually an arching shrub to 3m. Shoots with sharp recurved thorns. Leaves with 5–7 leaflets, shiny dark green above, glabrous beneath with stalked glands on the narrow stipule. Flowers 5–6cm across, solitary, formed on short shoots on the previous year's wood; petals usually red but in some populations varying in colour from nearly creamy-white with a pink edge to blackish-crimson, sometimes pink with a darker eye, always solitary. Hips smooth, not very large, ripening orange. Easily grown but needs a warm position to flower; in England a greenhouse or very warm wall, but it should do well outside in Australia, in California and from Virginia southwards. Min. −15°C.

'Mutabilis' at Mottisfont

'Mateo's Silk Butterflies' in Devon

Rosa gigantea by a dry stream in Yunnan

'Lijiang Road Climber' over a village house near Lijiang

Rosa gigantea in Yunnan

'Bella Blanca' in Descanso gardens

'Bella Portugaisa' in Descanso gardens

'Park's Yellow Tea-scented China'

'Maréchal Neil' in the greenhouse

'Fortune's Double Yellow'

'La Folette' at Clos du Peyronnet, Menton

'Chromatella' in Berkeley Botanic Garden

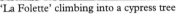

'La Folette' climbing into a cypress tree

Rosa gigantea Coll. ex Crépin   A large arching shrub or climber into trees with 5–7 usually acuminate leaflets and large white or yellowish flowers, native of SW China from Mengzi and Kunming west to Burma and Manipur near Ukhrul, growing in forest, in ravines in mountain scrub and hedges, at 1500–2500m, flowering in March–May. Stems to 30m; leaflets with a curved acuminate apex, glaucous beneath; flowers to 15cm across. In Yunnan plants of this rose are not common, and vary in size, often being rather small and pure white (*as shown here*), in the hills west of Kunming. The plants described by Kingdon Ward in Manipur were exceptionally large, yellow in bud. Another variety with a large pale pink single flower 12cm across was growing in a village by the road between Dali and Lijiang. Forrest recorded this form in the Lijiang Valley in 1906 but we did not see it, though the 'Lijiang Road Climber' (*described below*) was common. This species is best in warm climates such as S France and California but may be grown outside in S England on a warm wall. Min. −10°C, perhaps but variable according to provenance.

'La Folette'   A *Rosa gigantea* hybrid raised by Busby, the 3rd Lord Brougham's gardener at Cannes in about 1910. It is now popular all over the Mediterranean and will grow and flower well in a large conservatory or on a very warm wall in cooler areas. It is a rampant climber, pushing up into trees and hanging down with cascades of huge salmon-pink

flowers. Charles Quest-Ritson describes Lord Brougham's garden at Château Eléonore and its fantastic collection of roses. The original *Rosa gigantea* collected in Burma by Sir Henry Collett flowered here for the first time in Europe in 1898. Min. −15°C.

'Bella Portugaisa'   Raised by Cayeux in about 1905. *R. gigantea* × perhaps 'Reine Marie Henriette' (a climbing HT). Plant very rampant to 10m or more. Flowers pale flesh-pink, loosely double with long buds, in spring only. Min. −10°C.

'Bella Blanca'   syn. 'White Belle Portugaise' A pure white sport of 'Bella Portugaisa' of unrecorded origin.

'Fortune's Double Yellow'   syn. 'Beauty of Glazenwood', *R.* × *odorata* 'Pseudindica' An old Chinese rose discovered in the garden of a rich mandarin at Ningpo by Robert Fortune in 1845. Flowers bronzy or fawn yellow, sometimes shot with pink and purple mainly in spring. Stems to 20m or so when old, very thorny when young. Min. −10°C.

'Chromatella'   syn. 'Cloth of Gold' A Noisette raised at Angers by M. Coquereau in 1843 and introduced by Vibert. A climber with globular nodding rich golden-yellow flowers in spring–summer, again in autumn. A good grower but shy-flowering until established. Best in a warm climate such as California or Australia. Min. −10°C.

'Lijiang Road Climber'   A semi-double once-flowering climber common in the villages and hedges between Dali and Lijiang and in the Lijiang Valley. This is probably a hybrid between *R. gigantea* and cultivated *R.* × *odorata*, so would be classed as a climbing Tea. E. H. Wilson reports white, yellow, buff or pale rose-pink forms cultivated in W Yunnan; we saw a yellow one in the park in Lijiang very close to 'Parks' Yellow', but none were as common as this pink, of which two slightly different clones were grown. Min. −15°C.

'Maréchal Neil'   A Tea-Noisette raised by Pradel in 1864, a seedling of 'Isabella Gray'. Flowers large with a good scent. This was the most famous greenhouse rose of the 19th century and is still lovely; not too rampant with pale yellow nodding flowers from almost every leaf bud. It flowers in early spring under glass, later in the open where the colour is a more golden yellow. Very healthy indoors and easily grown; mainly once-flowering with some late-summer flowers. Min. −10°C.

'Parks' Yellow Tea-scented China'   syn. *R. odorata* 'Ochroleuca'   An old Chinese garden rose introduced to Europe from Canton in 1824 by John Parks who had been sent by the Horticultural Society to bring back plants from China. A strong grower to 3m or more, with graceful pale yellow flowers with a pinkish flush in the centre, produced only in summer. This was important as a parent of the climbing Tea roses. Min. −10°C.

'Albéric Barbier' by a chaikana in Turkey

'Rêve d'Or' in Eccleston Square

'Albéric Barbier'

'Souvenir de la Malmaison'

'Ramona' at Mottisfont

'Céline Forestier' at Knightshayes, Devon

'Mme Grégoire Staechelin' in the greenhouse in May

'Cooper's Burma Rose' at Sellindge, Kent

'Happenstance' in California

'Noëlla Nabonnand' at La Mortola

'Albéric Barbier' A small-flowered climber raised by Barbier in 1900. Parentage: *Rosa luciae* × 'Shirley Hibberd', a yellow Tea. This is a wonderful rose in hot dry climates and flowers with great profusion, forming a very large dense shrub or a climber on an arbour. To 6m or more; once-flowering with a scattering of later flowers. A group of six or more similar climbers were raised by Barbier and all are beautiful with medium-sized elegant flowers in loose sprays, with some of the colouring of Tea roses. Min. −15°C .

'Céline Forestier' A Tea-Noisette raised by Trouillard in 1842. Flowers pale yellow with a deeper-coloured and very tight centre produced throughout the season. Usually a rather short climber, but up to 5m in a warm position. Min. −10°C.

'Colombia' climbing A Hybrid Tea raised by Hill in 1916, the climber introduced by Vestal in 1923. Flowers rich pink with a good rich scent; a good rose for a conservatory as it is healthy and flowers almost continuously without being too rampageous. Stems reach about 3m or less if kept in a pot. Not often seen in Europe but commoner in California. Min. −15°C.

'Cooper's Burma Rose' syn. 'Cooperi' A hybrid of *R. laevigata* probably with *R. gigantea*. It was raised at Glasnevin from seeds sent to Ireland by Roland Cooper, collected in Burma in around 1926. It differs from *R. laevigata* in its red stems, looser leaves with 5 leaflets and floppier petals; from *R. gigantea* in its very shiny, not acuminate leaflets and slightly bristly ovary. Flowers scented, 5cm across. A rampant grower to 10m or more, flowering more freely than *R. laevigata* and slightly hardier; damaged by −10°C, even on a warm wall.

'Happenstance' A mystery rose, probably a sport or seedling of 'Mermaid', which appeared in California in the mid-20th century. It forms a mat of shiny small leaves and has 'Mermaid'-like pale yellow flowers

An unusual rose for ground-cover. Min. −15°C, perhaps.

'Mme Grégoire Staechelin' syn. 'Spanish Beauty' A climbing Hybrid Tea raised by Pedro Dot in Spain in 1927. Parentage: 'Frau Karl Druschki' × 'Chateau de Clos Vougeot'; the result of this cross is a very fine once-flowering climber similar to *R. gigantea* with large slightly nodding flowers but broader leaflets. A free-flowering rose which responds to feeding well, reaching 6m. Min. −15°C.

'Noëlla Nabonnand' A climbing Tea-style rose raised by Nabonnand in 1900. Parentage: 'Reine Marie Henriette' (climbing HT) × 'Bardou Job' (Bourbon × HP). A strong-growing rose with lovely buds and wonderful, huge semi-double flowers of the deepest crimson velvet. This is valuable in warm climates for flowering in winter. Min. −15°C, perhaps.

'Ramona' A sport of 'Anemone', a cross between *R. laevigata* and a Tea rose, found in California in 1913. A not very robust climber with lovely scented flowers mainly in spring, but with a few later. 'Anemone' itself is similar but paler. Both need a warm position and good cultivation to do well. Min. −10°C.

'Rêve d'Or' syn. 'Condesa da Foz' A Noisette raised by Ducher in 1869, a seedling of 'Mme Schulz'. A climber with buff-yellow fully-double well-scented flowers, throughout the season. A vigorous rose with coppery foliage said to do especially well in Florida and good in California too. Height 3–5m. Min. −15°C, perhaps.

'Souvenir de la Malmaison' A climbing sport of the Bourbon raised by Béluze in 1843, the climber introduced by Henry Bennett in England in 1893. An excellent and most beautiful rose with very double, large, flat, palest pink flowers, produced mainly in spring. Growth to 6m, though usually less. Min. −15°C, perhaps.

'Colombia' climbing

Rosa × micrugosa

'Lady Ann Kidwell' in California

'Rival de Paestum'

'Niphetos'

'Hume's Blush' in NW Sichuan

'Louis XIV'

Rose in Yufeng lamasery, Lijiang

'Hume's Blush Tea-scented China'

'Sophie's Perpetual'

'Hermosa'

'Safrano' in Berkeley Botanic Gardens, California

A fine bush of 'Le Vésuve' at Mottisfont

'Le Vésuve'

Rosa × *odorata* (Andr.) Sweet **'Hume's Blush Tea-scented China'** This is the rose which was originally named *Rosa* × *odorata*, the name for hybrids between *R. gigantea* and *R. chinensis*. It was introduced to England from China in 1810 and grown in the garden of Sir Abraham Hume at Wortlebury; Hume was a keen chrysanthemum grower and the rose would have come with a cargo of chrysanthemums from the Fan Tee Nursery in Canton. 'Hume's Blush' was illustrated by Redouté in around 1820 but had become lost in Europe by the mid-20th century until it was rediscovered growing in Bermuda. We saw this rose growing in the sluice-keeper's garden at Pingwu, NW China, along with other ancient Chinese garden roses; it formed either a bush, or (*as shown here*), a cascade hanging over a wall. Repeat-flowering but probably not very hardy. 'Hume's Blush' soon became one of the chief parents, with 'Parks' Yellow', of the dwarf Tea roses, an important group throughout the 19th century and still very good in warm climates such as California and Australia.

'Hermosa' This China-like rose is usually classed as a Bourbon, that is a cross between a China and an Autumn Damask, but it is a back-cross to a China again, as it is supposed to have arisen from 'Parsons' Pink' × 'Mme Desprez', raised by Marchesseau in 1834. It is still a fine rose, well-scented with rich pink very double flowers, good in autumn. Very free-flowering in warm wet climates, but hardy too. Height usually about 1m, but a climbing sport called 'Setina' appeared in America in 1879.

'Lady Ann Kidwell' A distinct and lovely rose introduced by Krebs in 1948 and then rediscovered by Fred Boutine in a nursery in Pasadena. This is one of the poly-pom roses which originated from Tea roses crossed with *R. multiflora*, or a double form or hybrid of it, and are thus close in parentage to 'Parsons' Pink'. Poly-poms are free-flowering roses with branching stems of small but lovely flowers and grow well in California and Mexico. The group includes 'Mlle Cécile Brunner' which is shell-pink and 'Perle d'Or' which is pale pinkish-yellow, both of which have climbing sports. They can make rounded bushes to 2m across or climbers to 6m. Min. −15°C.

'Le Vésuve' syn. 'Lemesle' Raised by Laffay in 1825 and generally classed as a China, though this is definitely a small-flowered Tea rose. The flowers vary in colour from pink and buff to scarlet and crimson, depending on temperature, showing the influence of the wild *chinensis*. It is an easily grown and beautiful rose, flowering in cold areas in early summer and even better in autumn, given sufficient water. If pruned lightly it will form a dense thorny shrub about 1.2m tall and more across. A climbing sport appeared in France in 1904 but I have never seen it. Min. −15°C.

'Louis XIV' A small much-branched rose with the deepest, richest red flowers fading maroon with a heavy scent. Raised by Guillot fils in 1859, a seedling of 'Général Jacquéminot'. Its parentage makes it a Hybrid Perpetual but it has some of the delicacy of the Tea roses; the flowers are rather flat, an HP character. A good rose for a pot or a warm climate outdoors, but dislikes cold wet conditions. Height less than 1m. Min. −15°C.

R. × *micrugosa* A cross between *R. roxburgii* var. *normalis* (formerly called *R. microphylla*) and *R. rugosa*, found in the garden of the Strasbourg Botanical Institute before 1905. This makes a large dense shrub with brown peeling bark and bristly yellowish hips. The flowers are produced over a long season, from late spring–autumn. This rose should do well in warm, wet subtropical climates, as *R. roxburghii* is a common plant around the edges of paddy fields in W China, and *R. rugosa* is good on mild wet coasts such as Scotland and NE Japan.

'Niphetos' A Tea rose raised by Bougère before 1841, with a flower of classic shape; a long tapering pure white bud, the centre of the flower pale lemon yellow on opening, becoming white. Height around 1m; the climbing form, said to be finer than the dwarf, which appeared in America in 1889, is more commonly grown. Min. −15°C.

'Rival de Paestum' A dwarf Tea-China hybrid raised by Beluze in 1841. Buds sometimes tinged pink; flowers semi-double when open, slightly nodding. A charming delicate rose, up to 1.25m. Min. −15°C.

'Safrano' A strong-growing Tea rose raised by Beauregard in 1839, said to be a seedling of 'Parks' Yellow'. Flowers rich yellow with a hint of pink in the bud, opening apricot, fading to white in the heat of day. Height to 1.5m. Min. −15°C.

'Sophie's Perpetual' This striking rose has flowers that open pink before changing to red. Found by Humphrey Brooke in 1928 and named after his wife's grandmother Sophie, Countess Beckendorf, daughter of the last Czarist ambassador to London, who started the garden at Lime Kiln, Suffolk. Often classed as a Bourbon but the changing colour is a character inherited from wild *R. chinensis*, and a similar rose growing in a temple garden near Lijiang in NW Yunnan is shown here for comparison.

'Comtesse de Labarth' in Bermuda with coral cliffs behind

'Comtesse de Labarth'

'Mrs Fred Danks'

'Rosette Delizy' in Lorna Mercer's rose garden in Bermuda

'Comtesse de Labarth' syn. 'Duchesse de Brabant' A Tea rose raised by Bernède in 1857. Flowers pink, cup-shaped, well-scented. This variety does very well in Bermuda where it is generally known as 'Duchesse de Brabant'. Height to 1.5m, forming a strong shrub with nodding flowers. Min. −10°C.

'Dr Grill' A Tea rose raised by Bonnaire in 1886. Parentage: 'Ophirie' (a Noisette) × 'Souvenir de Victor Hugo' (a Tea). Flowers very double, all the petals scrolling when the flower is mature, varying from coppery-yellow to deep bright pink. Height usually less than 1m. Min. −15°C.

'Lorraine Lee' A *gigantea* hybrid raised by Alister Clark at Bulla, Victoria in 1924 from 'Jessica Clark' (a single pink *gigantea* seedling) × 'Capitaine Millet' (a Tea). Flowers large, formal, well-scented, produced throughout the year, in winter if pruned hard in late summer. A very popular rose in Australia. Height about 2m. There is also a climbing sport. Min. −10°C, perhaps.

'Mme. Antoine Mari' A Tea rose raised by M. Mari before 1895. Flowers rich pink shading to creamy white, the outer petals scrolling back. A most beautiful rose, highly regarded in its day and very free-flowering. Height less than 1m. Min. −15°C.

'Marie van Houtte' syn. 'The Gem' A Tea rose raised by Ducher in 1871. Parentage: 'Mme de Tartas' × 'Mme Falcot'. A large very double flower which does best in cool but dry weather, as the flowers ball in rain and fade in great heat. Makes a large bush in a warm climate. Min. −10°C.

'Monsieur Tillier' A Tea rose raised by Bernaix in 1891. Flowers fully double, deep carmine to deep red with purple shadings. Flowers particularly well in autumn and needs some shade from the hottest sun. Height around 1.25m. Min. −10°C.

'Mrs B. R. Cant' A Tea rose raised by Cant of Colchester in 1901. Flowers rose-red outside, pinkish and suffused with buff in the centre. This was a famous rose in the early years of the century, praised for its big globular flowers produced with great freedom; now it is probably extinct in Europe, though still grown in California. A climbing sport was introduced in 1960. Height to 1.2m. Min. −15°C.

'Mrs Fred Danks' A Hybrid Tea raised by Alister Clark in Australia in 1952. Flowers semi-double, well-scented, lilac-pink. Height to 2m. Min. −10°C, perhaps less.

'Rosette Delizy' A Tea rose raised by P. Nabonnand in 1922. Flowers rich yellow, suffused with apricot and deep red outside with a rich fruity scent. One of the larger Teas; leaves thick and dark green, not badly affected by mildew. Height to 2m. Min. −15°C.

'Squatter's Dream' A *gigantea* hybrid raised by Alister Clark in Australia in 1923. Flowers single, rich yellow, freely produced. Height to 2m. Min. −10°C, perhaps less.

'Sunny South' A Hybrid Tea raised by Alister Clark in Australia in 1918. Parentage: 'Gustav Grünerwald' × 'Betty Berkeley'. Flowers large, semi-double, produced throughout the year, pink with shades of yellow. Height to 3m or more. Min. −10°C .

'Lorraine Lee'

'Mrs B.R. Cant'

'Mme Antoine Mari'

'Marie van Houtte'

'Sunny South' in Orange, NSW

'Squatter's Dream'

'Dr Grill'

'Monsieur Tillier'

Prunus campanulata

Prunus campanulata in the garden at Chartwell, Beverley Hills

Peach 'Bonanza' at Read's Nursery

Rhaphiolepis indica at Kew

Nectarine 'Nectarella' in fruit

Rhaphiolepis umbellata

Rhaphiolepis × delacourii

Cowania plicata D. Don (*Rosaceae*)
An upright evergreen shrub with small
glandular leaves and purplish-pink rose-like
flowers, native of Mexico, especially in the
Sierra Madre Orientale, growing on bare
limestone hills at about 1800m, flowering in
June–November. Stems to 2m; leaves to 2.5cm
long with 5–9 deep teeth. Flowers 2.5–4cm
across. Styles feathery in fruit. An attractive
small shrub for a dry place, rare in cultivation.
Sadly we did not succeed in introducing it
from our 1991 C. D. & R. expedition.
Min. −10°C, perhaps. *C. mexicana* var.
stansburiana (Torr.) Jeps., from desert areas in
SE California, New Mexico and N Mexico has
pale yellow flowers 1.2–1.6cm across.

Crataegus species from Mexico (*Rosaceae*)
A small tree or large shrub with semi-
evergreen leaves and large yellow or red edible
fruit, native of Mexico in the limestone valleys
near Galeana at the foot of Mount Potosi, at
about 1500m. Tree to 8m; leaves small,
cuneate, double-toothed and with 2–3 shallow
lobes, sparsely hairy beneath, about 3cm long.
Fruits about 1cm across. Differs from
C.stipulacea in its smaller less pubescent leaves.

For well-drained soil. Min. −10°C. Introduced from Mexico by Yucca Do nursery, Texas.

Eriobotrya japonica (Thunb.) Lindl. (*Rosaceae*) Loquat   A handsome evergreen shrub or small tree with large leathery dark green leaves, small white flowers and yellow-orange edible fruit in spring, native of China where it was recorded by E. H. Wilson growing wild in valleys near Ichang at 300–1000m, and of Japan from W Honshu southwards, flowering in September–December. Tree to 10m in a warm climate; leaves oblanceolate, brown woolly beneath, to 30cm long and 12.5cm wide; flowers in a dense furry head; fruit pear-shaped, to 4cm long with 1–3 shining brown seeds. For any good soil. Min. −7°C and will survive against a wall in colder areas. When grown for fruit, plant a named variety such as 'Gold Nugget' with sweet orange flesh.

Heteromeles arbutifolia M. Roem. (*Rosaceae*) Toyon Christmas Berry   An evergreen shrub or small tree with small leathery dark green leaves, large panicles of small white flowers and red or yellow fruit in winter, native of California and Baja California, growing in chaparral, in dry valleys and canyons below 1200m, flowering in June–July. Tree to 10m with spreading branches; leaves elliptical to oblong, pale beneath, 5–10cm long; flowers in a flat loose panicle about 8mm across; fruit ovoid, to 5–6mm across with brown seeds. For any soil. Tolerant of drought and poor conditions. Min. −7°C.

Prunus campanulata Maxim. (*Rosaceae*) A lovely slender upright tree with bright carmine-pink bell-shaped flowers in early spring before the leaves, native of Taiwan and S China but widely cultivated in Japan, growing in hill forests below 600m. Tree to 10m; leaves ovate. Flowers in umbels, 2cm across. Fruit small, red. Suitable for areas too warm for most flowering cherries and does well in the hills around Los Angeles.
P. cerasiodes D.Don, syn. *P. puddum* Roxb., is the autumn-flowering pink cherry of the Himalayas. Var. *rubra* syn. *P. carmesina* Hara, from the E Himalayas and Manipur is a tall tree with carmine flowers in February–March, close to *P. campanulata*. All species need warm summers with a winter minimum of −5°C.

Prunus persica (L.) Batsch   Peach **'Bonanza'** and nectarine **'Nectarella'** are genetic dwarfs raised in California and particularly suitable for growing in pots indoors. They are sold budded as short standards; the shoots grow only 10–15cm each year but are crowded with leaves, flower buds and potential fruit. When grown or wintered indoors the leaves do not suffer from peach leaf curl, but they are susceptible to red spider mite in hot weather and care must be taken that the pots do not dry out while they are carrying fruit. Both are lovely in flower and the fruit have good flavour as well. Hand-pollination may be needed. Many other genetic dwarfs are available in California. Peaches may be grown in pots. Varieties such as 'Daily News Four Star' have been bred for the beauty of their flowers. Min. −15°C.

Rhaphiolepis × delacourii André (*Rosaceae*) A hybrid between *R. indica* and *R. umbellata* raised in Cannes in the late-19th century. It usually has pink flowers and named varieties are now popular in warm areas such as California, Texas and S France for flowering in

Cowania plicata near Saltillo, Mexico

Eriobotrya japonica with *Wisteria*

Cowania plicata flowers and fruit

Crataegus with *Tillandsia* in Mexico

Heteromeles arbutifolia

early spring or even autumn and winter. Height about 1.5m. 'Ballerina', a dwarf and 'Springtime' are good named varieties. 'Majestic Beauty' can reach 5m. Both drought- and irrigation-tolerant; for sun or part shade. Min. −10°C.

Rhaphiolepis indica (L.) Lindl. An evergreen shrub with lanceolate leaves and white flowers with a red centre and stamens, native of S China, including Hong Kong, growing on rocky hills, flowering in March–June. Shrub to 3m; leaves often red when young. Flowers about 1.5cm across. Fruits blue-black. For any good soil. Min. −7°C.

Rhaphiolepis umbellata (Thunb.) Mak. A small dense evergreen shrub with leathery rounded leaves and white scented flowers, native of Japan from Honshu southwards and to Korea, growing in scrub near the sea, flowering in April–June. Shrub to 3m. Leaves obovate, to 8cm long; petals 10–13mm long. Fruit pear-shaped, blue-black. For any soil and position in sun or part shade. Good near the sea, like *Pittosporum tobira* from the same area. Min. −10°C.

Glossary

* indicates a cross-reference

Acrid with an unpleasant sharp smell or taste

Acuminate gradually tapering to an elongated point

Acute sharply pointed, with an angle less than 90°

Amplexicaul with the base of the leaf encircling the stem

Anther the part of the *stamen which contains the pollen

Anthesis the time of opening of the flowers

Axil the angle between the leaf stalk and the stem

Basal at or near the base of the stem

Bract a modified leaf below a flower

Bracteole a small *bract

Bulbil a small bulb, sometimes produced by a plant instead of a seed

Calyx the outer parts of a flower, usually green

Canaliculate with the sides turned upwards, channelled

Capsule a dry fruit containing seeds

Carpel the part of the flower which produces the seeds

Ciliate with a fringe of hairs on the margin

Clavate shaped like a club, narrow at the base, swelling towards the apex

Clone the vegetatively propagated progeny of a single plant

Cordate heart-shaped, with rounded lobes at the base

Corolla the inner parts of the flower, comprising the petals, usually used when the petals are united into a tube

Corona crown-like arrangement of petals

Crenate with shallow, rounded teeth

Cultivar a cultivated variety, denoted by a fancy name in inverted commas, e.g. 'Hula Girl'

Deciduous usually of a tree or shrub that loses its leaves in the winter or dry season; as opposed to evergreen

Decumbent trailing loosely onto the ground

Dentate with sharp, regular teeth

Diploid containing twice the basic number of chromosomes (the usual complement)

Dissected sharpely cut into deep teeth

Elliptic shaped like an ellipse, a squashed circle

Ellipsoid of a solid shape, elliptic in section

Epiphyte a plant which grows on the bark of a tree, usually an orchid or bromeliad

Exserted sticking out, usually of the *style or *stamens from the flower

Filament that part of the *stamen which supports the *anther

Flexuous wavy, usually of a stem

Forma a minor variant, less different from the basic species than a *variety. Abbreviated to f. or ff. if plural

Fynbos a South African name for the scrub found on hillsides in the Cape region, a rich community of heathers, proteas, pelargoniums, bulbs etc., subject to renewal by fire

Genus a grouping of *species, such as *Hibiscus*, *Fuchsia* or *Pelargonium*

Glabrous without hairs or glands

Glandular with glands, which are usually stalked, like hairs with a sticky blob on the apex

Glaucous with a greyish bloom, especially on the leaves

Globose more or less spherical

Hastate with a broad but pointed apex, and two diverging lobes at the base

Hyaline transparent, often soft or papery

Hybrid the progeny of two different species

Incised with deep cuts in the margin

Inflorescence the flowers and flower stalks, especially when grouped

Keeled with a ridge along the lower side, like the keel of a boat

Laciniate deeply and irregularly toothed and divided into narrow lobes

Lanceolate shaped like a spearhead, widest below the middle, with a tapering point

Leaflets the parts of a compound leaf

Linear long and narrow, with parallel sides

Lyrate with a broad, but pointed apex and lobes becoming smaller towards the leaf base

Monocarpic usually dying after flowering and fruiting

Nectary the part of the flower which produces nectar

Oblanceolate shaped like a spearhead, but widest above the middle

Obtuse bluntly pointed, with an angle greater than 90°

Orbicular almost round

Ovate almost round, but with a pointed apex, broader than lanceolate

Palmate with lobes or leaflets, spreading like the fingers of a hand

Panicle a branched *raceme

Pedicel the stalk of a flower

Peduncle the stalk of an *inflorescence

Peltate shaped like a round shield, with the stalk in the centre

Petal generally the coloured part of the flower

Pinnae leaflets of a *pinnate leaf

Pinnate with leaflets on either side of a central axis

Pinnatifid with lobes on either side of a central axis

Pinnule a small *pinna

Puberulent with a fine but rather sparse covering of hairs

Pubescent with a fine coating of hairs, denser than *puberulent

Raceme an *inflorescence with the flowers on a central stem, oldest at the base

Rhizome an underground modified stem, often swollen and fleshy

Rootstock the part of the plant from which the roots and the stems arise

Rosette an encircling ring of leaves

Scarious dry and papery, usually also transparent

Sepal the outer, usually green parts of the flower vs. petal

Serrate sharply and finely toothed

Sessile without a stalk

Sinus a very deep notch between two lobes, towards the centre of a leaf

Spathulate with a broad, rounded apex and tapering into a narrow stalk

Species group of individuals, having common characteristics, distinct from other groups; the basic unit of plant classification. Abbreviated to sp. or spp. if plural

Stamen the pollen-bearing part of the flower, usually made up of *anther and *filament

Staminode a sterile *stamen, often a flattened *filament

Stigma the sticky part of the flower which receives the pollen

Stolon a creeping and rooting, usually underground stem which produces new plants

Stipule leafy lobes along or near the base of a leaf stalk, found especially in roses

Style that part of the flower which carries the *stigma

Subcordate weakly heart-shaped at the base

Suborbicular almost round, but usually slightly narrower

Subspecies a division of a species, with minor and not complete differences from other subspecies, usually distinct either ecologically or geographically. Abbreviated to subsp. or subspp. if plural

Succulent fleshy, storing water in the stems or leaves

Ternate in a group of three

Tetraploid with four times the basic number of chromosomes

Triploid with three times the basic number of chromosomes: these plants are usually sterile, but robust growers and good garden plants

Truncate ending abruptly, as if cut off at right angles

Tuber a swollen root

Tuberous swollen and fleshy, of roots

Umbel an *inflorescence in which the branches arise from a single point, usually forming a flat or gently rounded top

Undulate wavy, usually of the edges of a leaf

Variety a group of plants within a *species, usually differing in one or two minor characters. Generally referring to natural variations, the term *cultivar is used for man-made or chosen varieties. Adjective varietal, abbreviated to var. or vars. if plural

Index